Journal of Contemporary History: I

# INTERNATIONAL FASCISM
# 1920-1945

hARpER ⚜ τORChBOOKS

*A reference-list of Harper Torchbooks, classified
by subjects, is printed at the end of this volume.*

Edited by Walter Laqueur & George L. Mosse

# INTERNATIONAL FASCISM 1920-1945

**Gilbert D. Allardyce**
**Paul M. Hayes**
**Ludwig Jedlicka**
**Adrian Lyttelton**
**George L. Mosse**
**Erwin Oberländer**
**Hugh Seton-Watson**
**Robert J. Soucy**
**Hugh Thomas**
**Eugen Weber**
**Llewellyn Woodward**

**HARPER TORCHBOOKS ❧ The Academy Library**
**Harper & Row, Publishers, New York**

INTERNATIONAL FASCISM, 1920-1945

# Contents

# Editorial Note

Should the Journal of Contemporary History series open its first number with the publication of a credo? The great historical journals of the last century certainly felt such an obligation. The *Historical Review* noted in its preface that it had long been a matter of observation and regret that in England, alone among the great countries of Europe, there was no periodical organ dedicated to the study of history. The *Revue Historique* stressed that the study of history was becoming increasingly important and that it was more and more difficult even for the professional scholar to keep up to date with all the discoveries. In this respect the situation has not essentially changed since 1876 (or 1886, respectively), and a new journal of contemporary history, first published in 1966, need not really justify its existence. The idea that contemporary history could not and should not be written, prevalent between, roughly, the last third of the nineteenth century and the end of the second world war, no longer has many vigorous proponents. A more liberal view has prevailed; or is it perhaps only that the limitations of historiography have become more obvious? The main arguments against the writing of contemporary history were, broadly speaking, that the source material was usually not available to provide the necessary information about events and trends in the very recent past. Moreover, it was argued that, even if the facts were accessible and could be verified, the detachment required to deal with yesterday's events in an objective and balanced way would be lacking. Human passions, predilections, and prejudices would be too closely involved when dealing with events that happened in our own time and had a direct impact on our lives. These are weighty arguments, but they do not invalidate contemporary history. Historians in Britain still battle with the fifty (or forty) years rule, and the situation in most other countries is not very different. And yet there are few major secrets in modern democracies that can be kept for longer than a year or two; the time-lag in dictatorships is unfortunately considerably longer, but it seems doubtful whether anything really important can be kept secret for very long even there. In any case, more often than not the contemporary historian of Europe and America in the sixties is more likely to be confronted with a surfeit of source material rather than to suffer from lack of documentary evidence.

Will he have the necessary detachment to deal with his subject in an objective way? The ideal of the absolute objective truth in historical writing has been gradually abandoned in this century; few historians have ever written *sine ira et studio*, certainly not Tacitus himself, who accused Domitian of having killed Agricola on what modern historians would consider insufficient evidence. Few in our age are likely to follow Ranke's prescription to extinguish one's self (*sein Selbst ausloeschen*) in order to engage in historical research. Distance in time helps us to see historical events in wider perspective and thus adds an important dimension to our understanding; but distance in time also involves remoteness, lack of immediacy, difficulty in understanding the quality of life of a period that is hard to describe and define, but which may be as important as all the documents in the archives. 'If it is still too early to form a final judgment on the French revolution,' as Trevelyan said, 'how much more so with regard to more recent events'. But it is not the only, and perhaps not the main task of the historian to pass final judgments. Such judgments may be possible, if at all, only after the subject itself has ceased to make any direct impact on the present day, in other words when all but a few specialists will have lost interest in them. The historical journals of the nineteenth century excluded the 'discussion of unresolved problems of current politics' (*Historische Zeitschrift*), announced that they would 'avoid contemporary controversies' (*Revue Historique*), or even that they would refuse 'contributions arguing still burning questions with reference to present controversy' (*Historical Review*).

The Journal of Contemporary History, unlike its more distinguished predecessors, while not actively looking for controversy will certainly not eschew it; it will not shy away from the still unresolved questions of the recent past. 'Academic' is not, or at any rate should not be, a synonym for 'neutral', 'non-controversial', or 'irrelevant to today's world'. The field of study and discussion of the Journal will be Europe in the twentieth century. The editors realize that any such definition of their subject is bound to be to a certain extent arbitrary both in time and in space. They are for example aware that the first world war (not to mention more recent events) cannot really be discussed without reference to trends that go well back into the nineteenth century. But they will try to be sufficiently elastic in their editorial policy to accommodate contributions that at first sight seem to transcend the Journal's frame of reference. The editors are also aware that it is often difficult to view Europe in isolation from the rest of the world, that, to give but one example, a discussion of fascism that does not draw attention to fascist, proto- or semi-fascist movements outside Europe, would be incomplete. At the same time, it is their conviction that contemporary Europe is a legitimate subject of study and debate, requiring no special defence or explanation. After centuries of Eurocentrism the pendulum has swung to the other extreme, and current fashions have led to a neglect of contemporary Europe. There has been a void which the present series will try to fill.

The prospectus of the *Historische Zeitschrift* stated that it did not intend to become an antiquarian journal, and the *Historical Journal* announced in its first number that it addressed itself not only to professional students of history but also to the so-called general reader who (it was hoped) would read at least some of its articles with both pleasure and profit. These hopes were not fulfilled. Historical journals have become more and more academic in the narrow sense of the word. Precisely for that reason the same point has to be made with additional emphasis almost one hundred years later. The trend towards specialization and fragmentation has gathered momentum in history as in all other fields of academic study. To some extent this may have been inevitable; the polymath of the last century has become a very rare bird indeed. But unless an attempt is made to counteract this trend, the publications of historians will be read only by a diminishing number of fellow specialists, and that is hardly an encouraging prospect.

It is our belief that the gulf between the professional and the general student of history is not unbridgeable, and that where difficulties in communication exist, an effort should be made to overcome them. One other point should be made in this context. There are no doubt a great many subjects in contemporary history that are as yet insufficiently explored, and there are of course even more that could serve to demonstrate ability in research and competence in scholarship. There should be periodicals for publications of this character, but the Journal of Contemporary History series will not be one of them. Since resources are limited and the central problems of contemporary European history are still inadequately studied, the Journal will concentrate on the main issues of that continent in our time.

# The Study of Contemporary History

## Llewellyn Woodward

It cannot be said, with the illustrious example of Thucydides in mind, that the writing of contemporary[1] history is a modern development. No one, indeed, until the nineteenth and twentieth centuries thought of history as limited to the record of events which happened before the memory of living people. The modern change came with the elaboration of an apparatus of scholarship; the learned men who had acquired this particular and very remarkable skill in handling older material began to regard the history of their own time as outside the scope of exact scholarship; a candidate for an academic post before 1919 or even later would have had little chance of success if he had put forward contemporary history as his field of study. The *English Historical Review* from its first number in 1886 until after 1918 did not print a single article on English domestic history after 1852,[2] or on European history later than the Franco-Prussian war and the foundation of the German Empire. The syllabus of the Modern History School at Oxford in 1914

[1] It is necessary to begin a discussion of 'contemporary history' by defining the term. Obviously the subject-matter is not as wide as that of 'modern history'. Different historians have given different interpretations to the term 'contemporary'. Lavisse, when he began to publish under his editorship in 1922 a *Histoire de France contemporaine*, took the French Revolution of 1789 as the starting-point of his ten volumes, but no English historian would begin 'contemporary' history with the first administration of William Pitt or even with the battle of Waterloo. 'Recent' history is also too vague a term. To a historian of the Anglo-Saxon period the death of Queen Anne is recent. The 'history of our own time' is probably the best term, but unfortunately there is no appropriate adjective. One might notice that the term 'middle age' has also changed its meaning since it was first used over five hundred years ago. Freeman was right in disliking terms which seemed to ignore the unity of history, but for practical convenience some division is necessary, and a new agreed terminology becomes more desirable every year.

[2] Except for review-articles by Mr Gladstone on the last volumes of the Greville memoirs and by Adolphus Ward on the first three volumes of Queen Victoria's letters.

I

excluded English political history after 1837 and 'general history' after 1878. 'General history' in fact meant the history of Europe. The history of the United States after the treaty of Versailles in 1783 was read only cursorily and mainly in connection with the history of Europe. Indian history was almost entirely limited to the history of British rule in India; Chinese history meant only the trading activities of European merchants and the wars to which their activities led.

This neglect of nearly everything which happened in Great Britain after the Reform Act of 1832 and of the last fifty years of European history was general in British Universities. It would have been defended, if defence had been thought necessary, by two different lines of argument. The concentration on European civilization – and western Europe at that, since little attention was given to the internal history of Russia – was taken for granted, since European civilization was assumed to be morally as well as materially superior to the decaying or 'dead-end' civilizations of Asia and to the absence of any civilization over most of Africa. The exclusion of recent and contemporary British and European history would have been defended on the ground that recent events could not be seen in a proper perspective; it was necessary to know 'what happened next', and 'next' meant at least two or three generations.

I will come back to the question of perspective, but I should point out that the exclusion of contemporary history from the subjects of academic study had serious practical consequences. The English governing class, educated mainly at the public and grammar schools and the universities, went into politics or the civil service or the professions knowing less about the state of the contemporary world than they knew about ancient Greece and Rome. Ten or twelve newspaper correspondents in the late nineteenth or early twentieth centuries had a better understanding of the dangers which threatened the peace of Europe than most of the leading members of British Cabinets. Some of these foreign correspondents wrote books: Sir D. Mackenzie Wallace on Russia, Sir Valentine Chirol on India and the Middle and Far East, Wickham Steed on the Habsburg Empire.[3] These books were extremely

---

[3] Wallace, Chirol, and Steed were in turn directors of the Foreign Department of *The Times*.

good; they were rarely to be found on the shelves of academic libraries. Grey has admitted in his *Twenty-Five Years* that the British Government did not give sufficient consideration to the possible European consequences of a failure to solve the problem of nationalities within the Habsburg Empire. British public opinion – one might say, educated public opinion – as far as it concerned itself with foreign affairs, concentrated on Anglo-German relations and, in particular, on Anglo-German naval competition, and was almost totally surprised by the sinister development of an Austro-Serbian dispute into a war involving the British Empire.

The war of 1914–18 brought a change, though British academic historians were slow to recognize it. There was, however, a public demand for a better knowledge of recent events, especially in the field of international relations. The foundation of the Royal Institute of International Affairs in 1920 was one of the earliest attempts to meet this demand. The Institute was founded largely owing to the enterprise of a small group of people who had taken part in the Peace Conference in Paris. It is difficult now to recall that until the Institute was opened there was no centre in England for the furtherance of an impartial, non-party study of international affairs. The Royal Empire Society was concerned, as its title showed, primarily with the affairs of the British Empire; the Royal Historical Society did nothing at all, then or later, to develop an interest in the historical background of the problems with which British foreign policy had to deal.

All is different now, in Great Britain and other English-speaking countries, at the universities and among a wider public. The danger now, especially in the United States, is of going to the other extreme and concentrating too much on contemporary history and neglecting the development of western civilization for a superficial study of the past of Africa and Asia. The 'near distant' as well as the remoter European past is explored only by a minority with antiquarian interests sometimes described by the unfavourable term 'escapist'. The old scale of values – dependent ultimately upon a belief in the sovereign rule of reason – is overthrown. Timbuktu is assumed to be as significant as Athens in the history of human societies and a study of primitive tribal custom as valuable for the education of the young as Plato's *Republic*. The long perspective is not thought necessary for interpretation. History is a behavioural science and the scientist, by definition, occupies himself with counting, measurement, and prediction.

One may regard each of these views in its extreme form as mistaken. It is not the case that the writing of contemporary history is in itself unscholarly and indeed impossible except in the form of annals. It is also untrue that contemporary history alone has a claim to scientific validity, and that the old-fashioned, pre-computer methods of historical study were pieces of ingenious but haphazard guesswork or mere literary exercises. The old view of the perspective is not altogether wrong, though it may lead one easily into error. This so-called perspective really has nothing to do with the past as such, that is to say, with the past as a series of events now closed. The perspective is merely the standpoint from which the viewer and his own generation regard the past. One has only to read the historiography of any period to realize how quickly this standpoint changes, and changes not merely owing to the discovery of new evidence. Events in the past do not sort themselves out in the course of time by some automatic process; the present observer does the sorting, and contemporary reasons determine his order of arrangement. Reliance on the 'perspective' leads only to complete relativity. As far as history is an attempt to see the past as it appeared when it was present, the idea of a historical perspective is misleading. The real people in the real past knew as little as we know in our present what would 'happen next', and could not act with a foreknowledge which they did not possess. One of the most difficult tasks of the historian is to avoid singling out events which in the light of after-knowledge are seen to have had important consequences, but which could not have had any special significance to contemporaries. Thus in 1900, the compiler of a register of the most important events of the previous year would certainly not have included among them the expulsion of one J. V. Dzhugashvili, who had recently joined the Social-Democratic party, from the Orthodox theological seminary of Tiflis.

Nevertheless, some sort of after-knowledge is necessary if history is to be written at all. History demands intelligibility; it is more than a précis of events in different parts of the world linked together only by the fact that they happened simultaneously. Even if it involves a certain distortion of experience, a history of the past, whether this past is a week or a thousand years ago, requires knowledge of a sequence of happenings in time, a beginning and an end imposed upon the subject-matter. The contemporary historian therefore must know 'what happened next', to the extent that he must be dealing with a relatively 'closed' series of events. Thucydides began to collect material for his history of the Peloponnesian war while it was being fought, but did not write the work until the war was over. Tolstoi, who has described the confusion of battle better than any professional historian, knew the end of Napoleon's campaign in Russia before he wrote about the battle of Borodino. The length of time covered by the sequence of events must vary with the subject. The events of one day – 14 October 1066 – are enough for an account of the actual battle of Hastings; a longer time-span is necessary to explain why the battle was fought. In either case the sequence must be relatively complete – relatively, not absolutely, since all history hangs together, and the isolation of what I have called a closed series of events is only a matter of convenience.

Once the idea of sequence, and not simply that of simultaneity is accepted, the question whether contemporary history is feasible does not need elaborate philosophical discussion. The answer depends on the amount and quality of the source material for writing about a subject. The arrangements of modern society, the necessity, from a practical point of view, of getting, recording, and diffusing information, provide the historian with far more material than at any previous time. Consider the scope and quantity of the information printed in a single copy of *The Times*, and continued uninterruptedly day after day. How much would a historian of Periclean Athens gain from the equivalent of a couple of numbers of the Post Office London directory or the printed catalogue of a great department store? Not only does contemporary society leave, in the normal course of its operations, a more complete record of its manifold business, the historian examining this data within a limited period is also able to draw general conclusions which might not have been evident at the time (though, as I have said, he runs the risk of distorting the actual past as it appeared to those to whom it was not past but present). Many of these conclusions can be expressed statistically; hence the importance of the new methods of counting and measuring. For contemporary history there is also much more evidence than in earlier periods of what people actually said in conversation and argument; it is easier to notice new trends of opinion by the emergence of new terms – self-determination, collective security, colonialism, fascism, population explosion – or by different connotations given to familiar words; thus appeasement, a favourable and generally applauded political term in 1925, had taken on a sinister meaning thirteen years later.[4]

The mass of material left for him gives the contemporary historian another advantage. He can discover a great deal about events supposedly kept secret. The amount of secrecy in high politics and international relations is much less than is generally supposed. Delane, probably the greatest editor of *The Times*, always refused to be told anything 'under seal of secrecy' because he knew that, sooner or later, he would get the same information without any restriction on publishing it. The official publication of documents concerned with foreign policy is of great value to historians because such documents give precision and authority to knowledge already obtainable from other sources; they generally add significant detail not otherwise known, and are of special interest in revealing what may be called the personal side of a negotiation – the skill or otherwise shown by the parties in a discussion, the concessions offered in the course of bargaining, but, apart from these rectifications or clarifications, there is very little in the great official collections, at least in recent times, which a historian could not discover for himself from other published sources if he had sufficient skill and industry. As Sir Lewis Namier has pointed out, most secrets are in print if you know where to look for them.

The writer of contemporary history has another advantage over scholars investigating earlier periods. He can remember the impression left on him at the time by the events with which he is dealing. He can also consult other contemporaries and check their recollections with his own. Thus I can remember the days in London just before and after the outbreak of war with Germany in August 1914. I find that my recollections differ from a good many accounts written about half a century later by people who were not there at the time – accounts of excited crowds, bellicose enthusiasm and demonstrations around the central areas of Westminster. Some such demonstrations did take place and some demonstrators were

---

[4] One can of course go a long way even before the age of print in following the history of political and legal terms, but there is now much more material, and changes in usage can be observed in much closer detail and among more sections of society.

excited, but the vast majority of Londoners did not stand or move around Buckingham Palace, Downing Street, or the precincts of Parliament. They went back to their homes in the suburbs at the usual times, by their usual trains, trams, or buses; they were neither elated nor frightened, only bewildered by news of which they could not guess the consequences. There had been many more signs of hysterical excitement over a single and comparatively simple event such as the news of the relief of Mafeking more than a dozen years earlier.

One's own recollections, however, as well as those of one's contemporaries, may become blurred and unreliable with the passing of time. None of us can escape from the distorting influence of after-knowledge. The memories of persons who have held positions of power tend, with some notable exceptions, to be unreliable. Few politicians who have written autobiographies or memoirs have had as their sole or principal motive the historian's aim of giving an impartial view of an age. They are concerned as much or more with staking out their own place in it. They nearly always exaggerate and antedate their own importance, forget the number of their mistakes, overrate their own foresight. During the 1920s and early 1930s, a good many historians, especially from the United States, took the trouble to interview leading figures in different countries on the question of responsibility for the outbreak of the war of 1914. These interviews added very little to the previous store of information; many of the persons interviewed gave answers deliberately intended to mislead their interviewers, but, oddly enough, the conscious deceivers give the historian least trouble. Liars, even clever liars, are fairly soon found out.[5] The memories of people in less exalted positions, in other words, persons less positively 'committed', are generally of greater historical value. Thus accounts of 'top-level' conferences written by subordinates are nearly always more revealing and accurate than accounts composed by the principals at the meetings. A note by the American Admiral Leahy of the first meeting of Churchill, Roosevelt, and Stalin at the Teheran Conference of 1943 shows in a curious way what may not unfairly be called the naiveté of the Americans with regard to Stalin: 'The talk among ourselves . . . was about Stalin. Most of us, before we met him, thought he was a bandit leader who

[5] The analysis of Talleyrand's memoirs in Sorel's *Lectures Historiques* shows how unsafe it is for even the cleverest politicians to try to trick posterity.

had pushed himself up to the top of his government. That impression was wrong. We knew ... that we were dealing with a highly intelligent man who spoke well and was determined to get what he wanted for Russia.'[6]

However great the advantages of possessing an immense quantity of source-material, of knowing from personal experience the atmosphere of events, and of cross-examining those who took part in them, contemporary history is not exempt from some of the limitations of all historical writing. Precision and certainty are obtained most easily in impersonal matters. We can be sure of averages; when we come to ask questions about individuals our authorities often fail us. Consider one of the most important events in our own time, the refusal of the British Government, led by Churchill and supported by the great majority of the nation, to make overtures for peace to Germany after the collapse of France. Future historians are likely to ask whether Churchill and his colleagues thought that Great Britain, after the French defeat, had any real chance of repelling a seemingly inevitable German attempt at invasion and ultimately of defeating Germany. Or was the resolution to continue fighting an act of defiance with very little hope of victory (though defeat in war is never certain until it has happened), but upheld by the belief that death and destruction were less terrible than the consequences of submission? It is not possible to give an answer to this question, or rather, to the first part of it, since most people who lived through the decisive weeks and months would have chosen destruction rather than surrender. The evidence of any belief in the likelihood of victory must be contemporary; one cannot accept recollections written down years or even months after the critical period was over. On the other hand, it is most improbable that anyone near the centre of authority would have written down, even for his own melancholy satisfaction, that he thought further resistance hopeless; it is almost certain that in the heavy stress of work the most responsible people had no time to

6 W.D. Leahy, *I was there*, p. 205. General Deane, US Secretary to the Combined Chiefs of Staff, also noted that the Americans were 'all considerably and favourably impressed with Stalin, probably because he advocated the American point of view in our differences with the British. Regardless of this, one could not help but recognize qualities of greatness in the man.' General Deane commented that Churchill's oratory lost effect when it was translated into Russian by an interpreter. J.R. Deane, *The Strange Alliance*, pp. 42–3.

put any general thoughts on paper. There is contemporary evidence in the form of reports to the War Cabinet from the Chiefs of Staff, and especially a report considered by the War Cabinet on 27 May 1940,[7] the first day of the Dunkirk evacuation, and before it could be known how many troops could be brought back. The report was in answer to a direct question from the Prime Minister about our chances of being able to continue the war alone. The Chiefs of Staff thought that the crux of the matter was air superiority; they believed that the morale of the British fighting personnel and of the civil population would counterbalance the numerical and material advantages held by Germany. One cannot read this estimate without feeling that while it upheld continued resistance, it did not express a strong conviction of certain victory.

There is another important piece of contemporary evidence. On Sunday, 26 May, M. Reynaud, the French Prime Minister, came to London to get British support for an approach to Mussolini not only to try to stop him (by the offer of territorial concessions) from entering the war, but also with the idea that he (Mussolini) might not want a complete German domination of Europe, and might therefore be willing to suggest to Hitler an offer of terms to Great Britain and France which these Powers would feel able to accept. Lord Halifax did not altogether rule out an approach of this kind; he had already spoken in a guarded way to the Italian Ambassador in London about such a possibility. Churchill strongly opposed the French plan as useless, since Mussolini would not accept it, and dangerous because the approach would become known and would have a disastrous effect upon British morale.[8] Within a few days, although the position was still extremely grave, and the French moved on to surrender, the success of the Dunkirk evacuation gave Great Britain a respite, and the later course of events showed how right Churchill had been to refuse the French plan. Nevertheless, this evidence of Churchill's firm resolution not to surrender does not tell us whether on 26–8 May he really expected that Great Britain would be able to avoid defeat. It may well be that he thought that, if the country were prepared to set no limit to the

---

[7] See Sir James Butler, *Grand Strategy* (Official History of the Second World War), Vol. II, chapters VIII and IX.

[8] The War Cabinet, at Churchill's suggestion, did not give the French an immediate refusal. They sent a definite rejection on the night of 28–9 May. The French (against M. Reynaud's judgment) persisted in approaching Mussolini, only to be told that Italy had decided to enter the war on the German side.

sacrifices which would be necessary, the chances of survival and victory were not unfavourable, since, at the last, the interest of the United States would bring about their participation in the war on the British side. Beyond this point, this 'balance of conjecture', if one may so call it, the historian cannot go.

If, however, there are questions of the greatest importance which the contemporary historian cannot answer, one must remember how many more of such insoluble problems are found in earlier periods. Most students of contemporary history have become so much accustomed to an abundance of source-material that, if they had to content themselves with the evidence available for most problems in the first thousand years of English history, they would hardly venture to write at all.

On the other hand, the abundance of material brings its own difficulties. There is a real risk of contemporary history being smothered under the wealth and diversity of its available sources. I have mentioned one type of authority in one branch of study – the collections of official documents on foreign policy published by the Great Powers since 1919.[9] The British collection, now in course of publication, on foreign policy between 1919 and 1939, gives nine large volumes to the period between March 1938 and the outbreak of war on 3 September 1939. The American publication *Foreign Relations of the United States* has five volumes for each of the years 1936, 1937, and 1938. These collections cover only a fraction of the correspondence preserved in the archives. Moreover, with the increase in the number of independent states, in the spheres of activity controlled by governments, and in the number of international bodies, the deposit of reading material for the future historian is continually increasing in size. It could be argued that this rising mass of paper is also submerging politicians and administrators; one may leave open the question whether those who direct policy now spend too much time in reading and too little time in thinking. The historian, who has not the advantage of a body of officials trained to sift the wheat from the chaff, must find some way for himself out of the difficulty; otherwise history will be splintered into innumerable monographs. Inevitably, the writer who aims at some kind of synthesis will have to take on trust

9 For this increase in the amount of business, and some of its consequences, see an excellent account in Lord Strang, *The Foreign Office*, especially chapters II and XII.

to a greater extent than in the past the work of colleagues and pre-decessors. He must, like the Minister who relies upon the sifting done by his officials, take advantage of the summarizing and dis-carding work done by others. Obviously he will want to test this work; no amount of objectivity on the part of other people can be a substitute for examining a document oneself, since, as every historian knows, the important sentences in a document may not be those for which one has actually been looking. The good, one might say the born, historian, develops an expertise (Michelet called it a kind of divination) in this matter of knowing when he should do again for himself the minute examination already done by his colleagues, but in contemporary history he cannot possibly re-examine everything.[10]

Must one then revive the somewhat futile controversy whether history is a science or an art? Clearly, in the collection of statistical evidence on subjects which admit of mathematical treatment, the scientific element predominates; but historical writing is and must remain primarily an art if it is to be read by others than experts. The Belgian peasant who acted as guide to Napoleon in his flight after the French army had been broken at Waterloo was not mak-ing a scientific statement when he said (if he did say it) that Napoleon's face was like a clock gathering itself to strike, yet it would be hard to find a more vivid analogy. A good many popular misconceptions of what writers of contemporary history can and cannot do would be avoided if the distinction between the scientific and artistic sides of the historian's work were kept in mind. Too many readers of contemporary history go to it not out of historical interest in the immediate past but out of a belief (which, indeed, has itself a venerable history) that historians are in a better position than other people to forecast the future and to find 'solutions' for present problems. Such readers know that, nationally and inter-nationally, the community to which they belong is today in an extremely difficult predicament. They expect the historian to tell them how and why they got into this predicament and what is the

[10] Schwertfeger's *Wegweiser* for the fifty volumes of the pre-1914 documents in the German collection *Die Grosse Politik* is a good example of this kind of sifting. The *Wegweiser* is not less useful because it follows the tendentious character of the collection which it summarizes. There is little difficulty in deal-ing with what one might call a steady bias or a declared apology.

best way out of it. The historian himself is well aware of the terrible dilemmas of modern society, and may have his own view of a possible way of escape. Nevertheless, he must resist the temptation to prophesy and to use his historical knowledge to present his solution in what seems to be a compulsory or inevitable form. A knowledge of contemporary history may prevent a statesman or a society from making the same mistake twice over, though in fact such an elementary blunder is all too common; this knowledge should prevent people from being taken by surprise, as I have said the British people were taken by surprise when war suddenly broke out in 1914. It may suggest certain lines of approach to the solution of a problem, but the so-called lessons of history do not help overmuch because in the variety and flux of human affairs no two situations are exactly similar; the recurrences of history are real, but they are not like those of Halley's comet. It is safer to say that history has no lessons than to claim to have discovered one of them.

Moreover, the plain man, seeking guidance from history, would do well to remember that the historical – not to mention physical or psychical – reasons why we are now at a crisis in western civilization cannot be learned merely from a study of the last two or three generations, though this study is indispensable. Much of our present malaise has its origin in the first seven centuries of the Christian era; some of the most striking parallels with our own time can be found in the history of the Roman Empire between the accession of Marcus Aurelius and the pontificate of Gregory the Great. Furthermore, a good prophylactic against making forecasts even about the immediate future is to read those put forward in the past by eminent historians. Overconfidence in the future was one of the faults of most historians in the nineteenth century. Those few who forecast catastrophe did not expect it to be total; some, like Marx, expected the consequences to be beneficial. If one examines the lives and careers of those historians who took part in politics the result is not encouraging; that is to say, their historical knowledge did not save them from wrong forecasts. Niebuhr, who was not an optimist about his age, thought that the French Revolution of 1830 marked the beginning of a period of anarchy like that of the Roman world in the third century; Ranke was persuaded by the Prussian Government after this same revolution to edit a review in the interests of political conservatism. The historians of the Prussian school believed in the permanence of the work of Bismarck. The most remarkable case is that of Guizot. Guizot was the ablest historian to take a prominent part in public affairs in any European country during the nineteenth century. He acted on his own political theory, deduced from the past few centuries of European history culminating in the French Revolution of 1789 (which to him was contemporary history; his own father had been guillotined). Nevertheless, Guizot was driven from power by another revolution, and in all the political changes in France since the fall of the monarchy of July there has been no return either to Guizot's 'system' or to the political and historical ideas upon which it was based.

On the other hand, although the historian cannot or should not forget the essentially tragic nature of his subject – the nearness of death and oblivion – the study of contemporary history does not justify a descent into total pessimism about human affairs. Gibbon, in a somewhat superior mood, described history as a record of the crimes, follies, and misfortunes of mankind. Our own age has added more than a normal share to this grim catalogue, but the age has also been marked by heroic action on an unusually wide scale and by a most remarkable development of intellectual power in many fields. If the future, inevitably, seems dark, at least our own studies should keep before our minds the extraordinary and not altogether unrewarded tenacity of the political animal man in an environment which has nearly always been hostile to him.

# Introduction: The Genesis of Fascism

## George L. Mosse

In our century two revolutionary movements have made their mark upon Europe: that originally springing from Marxism, and fascist revolution. The various Marxisms have occupied historians and political scientists for many decades, but fascism has been a neglected movement. The reason for this seems plain: the war and the pre-eminent position of Germany within this revolution have obscured its European-wide importance. That is why, in this special number on fascism, we have not concentrated on Germany but have, for once, given space to the rest of the story. For by the 1930s there was no nation without a native fascist party, and by 1936 a fascist Europe seemed within the realms of possibility – this even before Germany came to exercise its dominance over the movement. To be sure, Italy provided an important model and even tried (if unsuccessfully) to form a fascist international, but the national fascist parties had their own élan and their own problems to deal with. Yet if we want to get closer to the essence of the fascist revolution we must analyse it on a European-wide scale, taking into account important variations, but first trying to establish what these movements had in common. Fascism lacked a common founder, but all over Europe it sprang out of a common set of problems and proposed a common solution to them.

Fascism (although of course the word was not used at the time) originated in the attack on positivism and liberalism at the end of the nineteenth century. This was a general European phenomenon, and examples readily spring to mind. In Italy, for example, D'Annunzio praised man's instincts: 'never had the world been so ferocious'.

The writings of these men reflect the same basic paradox of industrial society: man seems on the one hand robbed of his individuality but on the other it is precisely this individuality which he wants to assert once more. The phenomena of mass man were accompanied by a feeling that the bourgeois age had culminated in conformity while those personal relationships upon which bourgeois morality and security were built had dissolved into nothingness. The tone among many intellectuals and among the young was one of revolt, of a desire to break out of the fetters of a system which had led to such an impasse. Much has been written about the aspect of this revolt which found its clearest reflection in expressionism; it is not often realized that fascism had *revolt* its origins in the same spirit of rebellion.

Indeed, the idea of both fascism and expressionism share the urge to recapture the 'whole man' who seemed atomized and alienated by society, and both attempt to reassert individuality by looking inwards, towards instinct or the soul, rather than outwards to a solution in those positivist, pragmatic terms which bourgeois society prized. There is nothing surprising in the fact that fascism felt an affinity with expressionist art and literature, and that even a not wholly unimportant segment of national-socialism tried to embrace them.

The key to fascism is not only the revolt but also its taming. For the problem before the fascist leaders was how to make this attitude towards society effective, and to counter the chaos which it might produce. How could the 'constant feeding of one's own exaltation' which D'Annunzio advocated, or the instinctualism of Nietzsche be captured and redirected into politically effective channels ? That fascism could find an answer to this dilemma, play the cowboy to this widespread *fin de siècle* mood, explains much of its later success.

Both George Sorel and Gustave Le Bon had suggested answers, for they had shown concern for precisely this problem in the 1890s. A political movement must be based upon the instincts of men and these instincts harnessed to a dedicated leadership. Sorel's myth was the overt rationalization of the deepest feeling of the group. For Le Bon politics had to be based upon the fact of mass man and his irrationality. These two Frenchmen accepted as 'given' the view of human nature which the revolt of the *fin de siècle* had posited and proceeded from there. Fascism shared the ground Sorel and Le Bon had prepared not only by accepting their view of human nature, but also by following out the content they gave to it and the prescription they made for it. Gustave Le Bon believed in the conservatism of crowds clinging tenaciously to traditional ideas.

15

The appeal must be made to this irrational conservatism and it must be combined with the 'magic' influence of mass suggestion through a leader. In this way mass man can be harnessed to a political mass movement, his tendency towards chaos can be curbed, and he can be redirected into positive action.

Le Bon describes admirably how to tame the revolt. The conservatism of crowds was reborn in fascism itself as the instinct for national traditions and for the restoration of personal bonds, like the family, which seemed fragmented in modern society. This conservatism was closely connected with the longing for an end to alienation, for belonging to a definite group. But the group had to be a traditional one, and it had to represent the restoration of the traditional morality. Hitler, for example, believed mass movements necessary because they enabled man to step out of his workshop, where he feels small, and to be surrounded by 'thousands and thousands of people with like convictions'.[1] Alienation was to be exorcized, but on the basis of accepting a view of man as both irrational and conservative. Similarly in Italy an historically centred nationalism was to provide the 'national consensus'.

But the taming was always combined with activism, and this kind of conservatism inevitably went hand in hand with revolution. Both Hitler and Mussolini disliked drawing up party programmes, for this smacked of 'dogmatism'. Fascism stressed 'movement' – Hitler called his party a 'Bewegung', and Mussolini for a time favoured Marinetti's futurism as an artistic and literary form which stressed both movement and struggle. All European fascisms gave the impression that the movement was open-ended, a continuous Nietzschean ecstasy. But in reality definite limits were provided to this activism by the emphasis upon nationalism, racism, and the longing for a restoration of traditional morality. The only variety of fascism of which this is not wholly true we find in France. There a man like Drieu La Rochelle exalted the 'provisional', the idea that all existing reality can be destroyed in one moment.[2] But elsewhere that reality was 'eternal', and the activism was directed into destroying the existing order so that the eternal verity of *Volk* or nation could triumph, and with it the restoration of traditional morality.

The impact of the first world war shows this rhythm of fascism,

---

[1] Adolf Hitler, *Mein Kampf*, p. 536.
[2] Drieu La Rochelle, *Socialisme Fasciste* (Paris, 1943), p. 72.

just as it gave the movement a mass base. The *élan* of the battle-field was transformed into activism at home. The *fasci*, the German storm troopers, and the Iron Guard in Rumania all regarded their post-war world as an enemy which as shock troops they must destroy. Indeed, the leaders of these formations were in large part former front-line officers: Roehm, the head of the SA; Codreanu, founder of the Iron Guard; De Bono in Italy and Szalasi in Hungary – to give only a few examples. But this activism was tamed by the 'magic' of the leadership of which Le Bon had written so much earlier. Among the returned veterans it was tamed all the more easily, for they sought comradeship and leadership with some desperation. Not only because of the war experience, but also because of their sense of isolation within a nation which had not lived up to their expectations. [3]

The 'cult element' was central to the taming process; it focused attention upon the eternal verities which must never be forgotten. The setting was a vital part: the balcony of the Palazzo Venezia, the Casa Rossa, the window of Hitler's new Chancellery. Activism there must be, enthusiasm is essential, but it must focus upon the leader who will direct it into the proper 'eternal' channels.

The liturgical element must be mentioned here, for the 'eternal verities' were purveyed and reinforced through the endless repetition of slogans, choruses, and symbols. These are the techniques which went into the taming of the revolution and which made fascism, even that which leaned on a Christian tradition, a new religion with rites long familiar in traditional religious observance. Fascist mass meetings seemed something new, but in reality contained predominantly traditional elements in technique as well as in the ideology.

To be sure, this taming did not always work. The youthful enthusiasm which presided at the beginning of the movement was apt to be disappointed with its course. Italy, where fascism lasted longest, provides the best example, for the danger point came with the second fascist generation. There the young men of the 'class of 35' wanted to return to the beginnings of the movement, to its activism and its war on alienation – in short, to construct the fascist utopia. By 1936 such youths had formed a resistance movement within Italian fascism which stressed that 'open-endedness' the

[3] Raoul Girardet, 'Notes sur l'Esprit d'un Fascisme Français 1934–39', *Revue Française de Sciences Politiques* (September 1955), p. 543.

17

revolution had seemed to promise: to go to 'the limits of fascism where all possibilities are open'.[4] They would have felt at home in the French fascism of Drieu La Rochelle and Robert Brasillach, but they were not pleased with the fascism in power. We can discern similar signs as Nazism developed, but here the SS managed to capture the activist spirit. Had it not been for the war, Hitler might well have had difficulty with the SS, which prized ideology less than power of the will as expressed in naked and brutal action. But then fascism never had a chance to grow old, except in Italy: given the ingredients which went into the revolution, old age might have presented the movement with a severe crisis.

Fascism was a movement of youth, not only in the sense that it covered a short span of time, but also in its membership. The revolt of the *fin de siècle* had been a revolt of the young against society, but also against parents and school. They longed for a new sense of community, not for a 'chaos of the soul'. They were of bourgeois background, and their dominant concern for several generations had been with national unity and not with social and economic change – something for which they felt little need. Thus they were quite prepared to have their urge to revolt directed into national channels, on behalf of a community which seemed to them one of the 'soul' and not an artificial creation. Such were the young who streamed not only into the German youth movement, but also into the *fasci* and the SA, and made up the cadres of the Iron Guard as well as the Belgian Rexists. Returned from the war, they wanted to prolong the camaraderie they had experienced in the trenches. Fascism offered it to them. It is well to note in this connection that fascists were a new grouping, not yet bureaucratized, and the supposed open-endedness made them more dynamic than the other and rival political parties. The fascist leaders too were young: Mussolini was 39 when he became Prime Minister, Hitler 44 on attaining the Chancellorship, Léon Degrelle was in his early thirties, and Primo de Rivera as well as Codreanu were in their late twenties.

Youth symbolized vigour and action: ideology was joined to fact. Fascist heroes and martyrs died at an early age in order to enter the pantheon, and symbolic representations of youth expressed the ideal type in artistic form. Hitler liked speed and was a motorcar and airplane enthusiast; Mussolini loved his motor bicycle, but when it came to directing their movements, both stressed the rootedness of the true community. Indeed, when they inveighed against the bourgeoisie they meant merely the older generation which could never understand a movement of youth.

The traditionalism of the fascist movement coincided with the most basic of bourgeois prejudices. When Hans Naumann spoke at the Nazi book-burning in 1933 he praised action; the more books burned the better. But he ended his speech by exalting the traditional bonds of family and *Volk*. Such a traditionalism was in the mind of Giuseppe Bottai when he called for a 'spiritual renewal', or when the leading Rexist, Jean Denis, held that without a moral revolution there can be no revolution at all.[5] Some fascisms defined the moral revolution within the context of a traditional Christianity: this is true of the Belgian Rexist movement, for example, as well as of the Rumanian Iron Guard. The Nazis substituted racism for religion, but, once more, the morality was that shared with the rest of the bourgeoisie.

The revolution of youth, of a virile activism, ends up as a revolution of the 'spirit', asserting the primacy of ideology. It is the shared world-view which binds the Nation together and it is this which must be realized. The world-view restores the dignity of the individual because it unites him with those of his fellow men whose souls function in a similar manner, and they do so because all are part of the *Volk*, the race, or the nation.

This is an organic view of the world. It is supposed to take in the whole man and thus end his alienation. A fundamental redefinition of politics is involved in such a view of man and his place in the world. 'Politics', the Italian fascist Bottai wrote, 'is an attitude towards life itself',[6] and this phrase can be repeated word for word from national-socialist literature. The leader of the Iron Guard, Horia Sima, summed it up: ' We must cease to separate the spiritual man from the political man. All history is a commentary upon the life of the spirit.'[7] Such an emphasis meant that cultural

[5] For Hans Naumann's speech, see Hildegard Brenner, *Die Kunstpolitik des Nationalsozialismus* (Hamburg, 1963), p. 188; Giuseppe Bottai, *Il Fascismo e l'Italia Nuova* (Rome, 1923 ?), pp. 18 ff.; Jean Denis, *Principes Rexistes* (Brussels, 1936), p. 17.

[6] Bottai, *op. cit.*, p. 19.

[7] Horia Sima, *Destinée du Nationalisme* (Paris, n.d.), p. 19.

expressions of the true community moved to the forefront as symbols of the new society. The national-socialist emphasis upon art and literature did not stand alone; for the leader of Flemish fascism, Joris van Severen, culture was the principle of unity and coordination. He added, typically enough, that culture presupposes a tradition.[8]

The emphasis upon the organic, the creative national community, was supposed to overcome not only political but also class divisions. Georges Valois, the founder of French fascism, made the point when, before the first world war, he described the differences between his beliefs and Marxism. Marxism stressed one class, but he wanted to harness the energy even of the bourgeoisie to the new society.[9] Valois' statement was prophetic, for fascism not only harnessed the energy of the bourgeois class but indeed became a movement whose spiritual revolution, the quest for organic, rooted man, coincided with bourgeois longings, at least in most of the West. It is significant that the classless society was always supposed to be a hierarchical one as well.

Fascism believed in hierarchy, not in terms of class but in terms of service to the *Volk* or nation as exemplified by the leader. In Western, but not German, fascism, the ideal of a corporate state was adopted; a state operating not through parliamentary representation (with its divisive political parties) but through workers and managers sitting together. However they did not sit together as equals; the manager was the 'leader'. Though there exists a considerable fascist literature about such a shaping of the state, in the last resort it was secondary. For if all members of *Volk* and nation shared a common myth, a common soul, then their participation in government need only be symbolized by the leader who has activated their shared human natures through his own activism, his 'heroic will'.

Fascism did stress the aim of social justice, but it would bring this about through the nation, the *Volk*, and not through the imposition of equality. The political and social hierarchies were to be open to all who served. This meant opposition to the old ruling circles, whether bourgeois or noble, and the substitution of new men for

---

[8] Joris van Severen, *La Constitution des Pays Bas* (St. Nicholas-Waes, 1938), pp. 23, 24.

[9] Georges Valois, *L'Homme qui Vient* (Paris, 1906), *passim*, and 'La Bourgeoisie Capitaliste', *Histoire et Philosophie Sociales* (Paris, 1924), pp. 404–5.

the old. Economic hierarchy was also preserved but within this framework a note of social justice was struck: Mussolini had his Charter of Labour and other fascisms drew up similar documents. Once again, fascism offered the best of all possible worlds: order and hierarchy would be maintained, private property would not be expropriated, but social justice would be done nevertheless. Once more this meant the primacy of ideology, ending spiritual alienation as a prerequisite for improving economic conditions.

Lest we brush this aside as inconsequential and lacking in appeal for the workers, it should be remembered that some fascisms did attempt, and successfully, to base themselves on the workers and peasants rather than the bourgeoisie. This was true in those countries where the working classes or the peasants had not been preempted by Marxist movements. Spain and Argentina provide examples in the West, and it is true of the Iron Guard as well as of the Hungarian fascist movement. To be sure, in those countries the bourgeoisie was not as strong as elsewhere, but another factor is of greater importance in explaining the fascist appeal to the labouring classes. Here, for the first time, was a movement which tried to bring these segments of society into political participation. In under-developed countries, the stress upon the end to alienation, the belief in the organic community, brought dividends – for the exclusion of workers and peasants from society had been so total that purely economic considerations could take second place.

Economics was indeed one of the least important fascist considerations. Jose Primo di Rivera, the founder of the Spanish Falange (which attracted much lower-class support), believed that 'people have never been moved by anyone save the poets', while the Belgian fascist Léon Degrelle called Hitler, Mussolini, and Codreanu 'poets of revolution'. The mystical side of the ideology dominated, the 'magic'; a fascist revolution must recognize the 'primacy of the spiritual'.[10] Not control over the means of production was important, but the 'new man' about whom all fascists talked. He was man made whole once more, aware of his archetype and of those with whom he shared it, an activist in that he was not afraid to join in a revolution which would make society correspond to the longings of his soul. These longings were for unity with the

[10] Stanley G. Payne, *Falange* (Stanford, 1961), p. 40; Robert Brasillach, *Léon Degrelle* (Paris, 1936), p. 78; Degrelle in *Je Suis Partout*, 24 October 1936.

21

group, for the recapturing of those virtues which were being submerged in the modern world. As Hitler stated clearly throughout his career: a man rooted in the world-view to which he belonged was not afraid to make it come true. Once he had joined he released his creative instincts, his power of will, in the common cause. Triumph meant that the whole nation would now share this creativity and renew itself. Economic well-being was subordinate to the stress upon art, literature, indeed the total cultural endeavour. Fascism was a revolution, but one which thought of itself in cultural, not economic terms.

In spite of the working-class support which it attracted in the more backward countries, in the West this was primarily a bourgeois revolution. The bourgeoisie could have a revolution as an outlet for their frustrations, and at the same time rest assured that order and property would be preserved. But for all that we must sharply distinguish fascism from the reactionary regimes in Europe. To be sure, the Rexists supported the Belgian monarchy and the Flemish fascists did likewise, but the differences are nevertheless far-reaching. Reaction rejected all revolution, opted for the *status quo*, and looked back to the *ancien régime* for its models. It stressed hierarchy, but this was the traditional hierarchy of entrenched privilege. It needs no demonstration that such regimes discouraged activism and mass movements. Moreover, they thought in strictly territorial terms and the 'shared soul' of all nationals or of the *Volk* would have had little meaning for them. For such regimes were not interested in bringing the disfranchised into politics or in ending man's alienation from his society. Their efforts were directed towards keeping men away from politics in order to maintain the monopoly of the traditional ruling class. Culture was not important here, and reactionary regimes gave wide latitude to all sorts of artistic expression so long as it did not encroach upon the monopoly of political power. The description of the Horthy regime by a modern historian is significant in this regard: Horthy did not intend to allow opposition to challenge his own will, but he did not think it any part of the duty of government to pry into and regiment each detail of his subjects' conduct, much less their thoughts.[11]

Just so the French fascists split from the Action Française

[11] C. A. Macartney, *October Fifteenth, A History of Modern Hungary*, Vol. I (Edinburgh, 1961), pp. 55–9.

because it was not revolutionary enough, as shown by its inaction in February 1934. Francisco Franco destroyed his fascist movement, the Falange, in favour of a Horthy-like dictatorship. Fascism and reaction had different visions, and the two must not be confused.

But what of the differences between the diverse fascisms from nation to nation? These are best exemplified in the problem of racism and anti-semitism. Neither of these was a necessary component of fascism, and certainly not of those sections of the movement which looked to Italy for a model. There, until 1936, racism did not exist. In Belgium and the Netherlands the fascist situation was, in this respect, similar to that of Italy. Léon Degrelle explicitly repudiated racism – hardly surprising in a multi-national nation. What, he asked, is the 'true race' – the Belgian, the Flamand, or the Walloon? From the Flemish side, the newspaper De Daad inveighed against race hatred and called on 'upright Jews' to repudiate the Marxists in their midst.[12]

Even Dutch national-socialism under Anton Adrian Mussert at first did not write racism on its banner, and kept silent about the Jews, a silence that the German Nazis were later to find incomprehensible. The French fascist group around the newspaper Je Suis Partout did go in for anti-semitism, but even here the Germans were accused of exaggerating the racial issue, for one could have good relations with a foreign people like the Jews.[13] It is not astonishing that the early Falange was free from such ideas, for there were hardly any Jews in Spain. Yet the actual existence of Jewish groups cannot be linked too closely to fascist anti-semitism – for example both Belgium and the Netherlands had a relatively sizeable Jewish population. To be sure, in those countries a single-minded concentration on Marxism as the enemy tended to exclude all other considerations. But even this does not provide a satisfactory explanation, for the Marxist-Jewish equation could easily have been drawn there as it was in Germany.

This state of affairs did not last. By 1936 Mussolini had turned racist, and not merely because of German influence. Through racism he tried to reinvigorate his ageing fascism, to give a new cause to a youth becoming disillusioned with his revolution. The Italian reversal of attitude on this question seems to have affected the Falange as well, in spite of the absence of a native Jewish

12 Rex, 23 September 1938; De Daad, 2 September 1933.
13 Je Suis Partout, 18 April 1938.

population. But here also a need coincided with this change of attitude – namely to make a more powerful appeal to the lower classes. As in Italy, so in Spain, anti-semitism helped to give the movement a greater and renewed dynamic. However, the Falange always rejected secular racism and based itself on the militant Catholic faith of Spain's crusading tradition. Similarly Oswald Mosley's fascists adopted anti-semitism when they found that this could give them a greater dynamic, a true feeling of struggle (and much free publicity) as they paraded through London's predominantly Jewish East End.

It was only in central and eastern Europe that racism was from the beginning an integral part of fascist ideology. Here were to be found the masses of Jewry, and still under quasi-ghetto conditions. They were a wholly distinct part of the population and vulnerable to attack. Moreover, in countries like Rumania or Hungary, the Jews had become *the* middle class, forming a distinct entity within the nation as that class which seemed to exploit the rest of the population through its commercial activities. No wonder the Iron Guard, in appealing to the nationalism of the peasants, became violently anti-semitic and even racist despite their Christian orientation – for they had begun as the legion of the 'Archangel Michael'.

After the First World War, the masses of east European Jewry began to emigrate into the neighbouring countries, predominantly Germany and Austria. The account in *Mein Kampf* of how Hitler reacted to the sight of such strangers in Vienna, may well have been typical. However that may be, the facts of the situation in that part of Europe gave fascism an enemy who could be singled out as symbolizing the forces which must be overcome. Moreover, in eastern Europe the struggle for national liberation had become associated with romanticism and racism long before fascism made its appearance on the scene. Hitler captured this tradition, and built upon the 'Jewish question'. This led to a further differentiation of national-socialism from Western fascism. For Hitler the enemy was not a vague Marxism; it was physically embodied by the Jews. Building on the Central-European tradition of a racist-orientated nationalism, he could give to the enemy of his world-view a concrete and human shape. Thus mass terror, and eventually mass extermination, could be built into German fascism as it was not built into other western fascisms. Both in Germany, and during the short-lived dominance of the Iron Guard, mass terror and pogroms became the manifestation of an activism which identified a distinct human group as the enemy.

Mass terror cannot, therefore, be a part of the definition of fascism as a European-wide movement. Hannah Arendt's *Origins of Totalitarianism* is wrong in this regard, and forced to concentrate solely on the German example. There is a difference between fascist violence and street fighting on the one hand, and mass terror on the other, which is explained partly by the predominance of the racial and anti-Jewish direction of the movement in central and eastern Europe.

Mass terror and violence were restrained by another factor within several of the fascist movements. A certain moderation was forced upon the fascisms which identified the nation with the existing state as over against those which sought to liquidate all existing political institutions for the sake of the *Volk*. Thus in Italy Mussolini never attempted to depose the monarchy, and in England, Belgium, and Holland fascism proclaimed its loyalty to the symbol of the state. This was not the case in central and eastern Europe, and as a consequence the activism there could have greater play and a more consistent goal, since *all* existing political institutions were to be abolished and founded anew.

The fascist revolution cannot be understood if we see it merely in negative terms or judge it entirely by the dominance which national-socialism achieved over it by the late 1930s. For millions it did satisfy a deeply-felt need for activism combined with identification, it seemed to embody their vision of a classless society. The acceptance of the irrational seemed to give man roots within his inner self, while at the same time making him a member of a spontaneous not artificial community. Bourgeois youth streamed into its ranks because to them it seemed to offer a positive solution to the problems of industrial and urban society.

The negative side of fascism triumphed in the end. How can the activist dynamic be tamed once the 'eternal verities' have triumphed? Can the emphasis on liturgy overcome the emptiness of a programme fulfilled? The answer was war upon the internal enemy, the adoption of racism; but another general solution lay in the realm of foreign policy. The activism must now be tamed by being directed towards the outside world. Hitler dreamed of his new Europe, Mussolini of the *Mare Nostrum*, Péron of an

Argentine-dominated South America, and in Eastern Europe there were enough irridentas to fulfil this function.

The 'new man' of whom fascism had dreamed went down to defeat, the victim of a dynamic which had, after all, not been satisfactorily curbed. The dream turned out to be a nightmare.

# The Nature of Fascism in France

## Robert J. Soucy

In 1961 Maurice Bardèche, a French writer who had been a fascist before the war, published a provocative new work entitled *Qu'est-ce que le Fascisme ?*. Bardèche boldly reaffirmed his commitment to fascism and argued that it is an ideology, especially in its French version, that has been badly misunderstood, unfairly maligned, and wrongly given up for dead. True fascism, he contended, is no more brutal than the democratic or Marxist philosophies that condemn it; German atrocities committed against Frenchmen during the Occupation derived largely from wartime conditions and the need to deal with guerrilla warfare, atrocities duplicated in any case by Allied soldiers against German civilians. Nor should true fascism be confused with Nazi racist and extermination policies – aspects of German national-socialism which were 'deviations' from the basic creed. Because of confusion in the public mind as to what fascism really is, said Bardèche, there has been a failure to acknowledge that fascism is rapidly being reborn today in many parts of the world, including France, although, because the word itself has fallen under a cloud, the phenomenon itself now exists under new labels. Consequently, neo-fascists like Nasser in Egypt and young technocrats in France, men working to fuse nationalism and socialism together once again, are seldom associated with an ideology that is discredited in theory if not in practice. Thus, there are thousands of young men in the world today who are fascists without knowing it.

Whatever the shortcomings or insights in Bardèche's analysis, it once again raises a basic problem faced by historians of modern France: what exactly was the nature of French fascism both before and during the Second World War; what exactly were its fundamental or predominant characteristics ? Bardèche himself points out one of the very real difficulties in dealing with the subject: the

27

very diversity and complexity of the movement. This is perhaps much more the case with fascism in France than in other countries, because it never had a single, unified, centralized party. Instead of one fascist party, there were several, running all the way from Georges Valois' *Faisceau* founded in 1925 to Jacques Doriot's *Parti Populaire Français* established in 1936. Even if the historian limits himself to discussing the two largest French fascist movements of the 1930s, Doriot's PPF and Marcel Déat's *Rassemblement Nationale Populaire* (RNP), or to the ideas advanced by one of France's leading fascist newspapers, *Je suis partout*, or by prominent French fascist intellectuals like Robert Brasillach and Pierre Drieu La Rochelle, a great deal of variety, contradiction, and sheer ideological confusion remains. Nevertheless, patterns and common denominators do exist which permit generalizations about even a phenomenon as protean as French fascism.

The few historical studies to date that have attempted to characterize fascism in France before the war[1] have raised a series of important questions in approaching the matter. Was French fascism rooted in native French political traditions or was it simply an ideology imported from abroad? Why was it a relatively weak force on the French political scene before, and even during, the Second World War – because it was not an indigenous philosophy? Was it closely related to traditional French conservatism (or, as some prefer, conservatisms), or was it an altogether separate entity? Were its goals primarily nationalistic or European? Did it differ markedly from German national-socialism, and if it did, why did many French fascists collaborate with the Germans during the war? And finally, did French fascism even possess an ideology, a clearly defined set of political, social, and economic goals, or was it, as some have said, a sort of fever, an emotional indulgence lacking doctrinal respectability? Several scholars have suggested, in this regard, that it was essentially a kind of romanticism, one which relied upon a vague 'aesthetic' approach to politics, an approach wanting in both reason and realism, and that consequently French fascism can hardly be viewed as a serious ideology at all.

---

[1] René Rémond, *La Droite en France de 1815 à nos jours* (Paris, 1954); Eugen Weber, *Varieties of Fascism* (New York, 1964); Jean Plumyène and Raymond Lasierra, *Les Fascismes français 1923–63* (Paris, 1963); Paul Sérant, *Le Romantisme fasciste* (Fasquelle, 1959); Peter Viereck, *Conservatism from John Adams to Churchill* (New York, 1956); Michele Cotta, *La Collaboration, 1940–1944* (Paris, 1964).

Certainly, of all these questions, the problem of the origins of French fascism is one of the most difficult. According to René Rémond's *La Droite en France*, fascism was a phenomenon quite alien to French political traditions. Most of the so-called fascist leagues of the 1920s and 30s were not really fascist at all but Bonapartist and Boulangist in character and inspiration, connected with past nationalistic movements rather than with 'contemporary foreign experiences'. The riots of 6 February 1934, which led many at the time to talk of a fascist peril, actually resembled more a 'Boulangist agitation than the March on Rome'. There were, Rémond concedes, a few organizations which did copy – in a dull and unimaginative way – Italian or German fascism, movements like *Francisme*, the *Solidarité Française*, and the *Parti Populaire Français*, but by their very failure, by their inability to win any mass public support, they demonstrated just how foreign was fascism to French political thinking. Only Doriot's *Parti Populaire Français*, founded in 1936, was able to win any significant political following and even it remained relatively feeble. 'Thus, before 1936, nothing justifies the legend of French fascism,' concludes Rémond.[2]

This kind of analysis has several drawbacks. First of all, it totally discounts various statements made by leading French fascist writers acknowledging their ideological debt to thinkers like Sorel, Péguy, Barrès, Proudhon, La Tour du Pin, and Maurras. As one French national-socialist declared: 'Our doctrine has its roots in the soil of France.' On the other hand, French fascists like Marcel Déat freely admitted that there was a 'European' side to their fascism, that it was part of a general revolution which crossed

---

[2] Rémond, *La Droite en France de 1815 à nos jours*, p. 207. In general agreement with Professor Rémond's interpretation is the recent book by Jean Plumyène and Raymond Lasierra, *Les Fascismes français 1923–63*. The authors of this work argue that fascism in France was at first, that is, in the 1920s and 30s, largely a myth manufactured by propagandists of the Left for their own partisan purposes, a means of discrediting the Right in its entirety and of uniting their own camp by presenting it with a stereotyped, villainous opponent, a technique which it used again during the Liberation. Eventually, genuine fascist organizations were established in France, say Plumyène and Lasierra, but these organizations received their doctrines 'at first' from abroad, through newspaper reports and journalistic commentary on fascist teachings in other countries. 'Fascism in its origins is a phenomenon foreign to France' (p. 15). Yet earlier the same authors remark that French fascism 'indeed seems to have formed itself from something other than itself, from political formations of the [French] Right as well as of the [French] Left' (p. 10).

frontiers, and that some imitation did occur. True as this may be, it by no means rules out the many intellectual antecedents which fascism had in French thought well before the 1920s. As Eugen Weber has pointed out, national-socialist and fascist ideas in France have a lengthy history; they can be found in the political campaigns of Maurice Barrès at the turn of the century and even in the Jacobinism of the French Revolution.[3] Certainly, in terms of intellectual history, there was little that was un-French about a great many of the ideas associated with fascism. Anti-Semitism, surely, was nothing new to a nation that had lived through the Dreyfus Affair, nor were such things as anti-parliamentarianism, anti-intellectualism, authoritarianism, hero-worship, and justifications of political violence. Simply because these ideas were rooted in Bonapartism or Boulangism or some other political heritage makes them no less proto-fascist, for not only were these movements events unto themselves but they sowed the seeds for later movements, and some of these were fascist. If French fascism was influenced by other fascisms, it also had a national past of its own; consequently, in many instances developments abroad merely served to fortify a set of pre-existing attitudes at home. Moreover the fact that fascism failed to achieve mass public backing in France hardly demonstrates that it was an ideology non-indigenous to that country. A political party need not win popular support to be rooted in several of its country's political traditions. Were this not so it might be said that Hitler's Nazi party was 'un-German' because it lacked mass public support before the onset of the depression.

If it was not because of the lack of a native intellectual ancestry, why then did fascism fail to capture a wide public following in France? Why was it that even France's largest fascist party, the PPF, never attracted more than 250,000 adherents? Economic and social factors were undoubtedly important. France not only escaped the economic consequences of the devastating inflation which plagued Germany in the early 1920s, but she was spared the political and social consequences as well; the threat that the lower middle classes might be proletarianized was never as serious in France as it was in Germany, and thus the pressure on this segment of French society to support the cause of fascism was considerably less.

[3] Eugen Weber, *Varieties of Fascism*, pp. 12, 19.

Moreover, the depression itself never hit France as catastrophically as it did her neighbour across the Rhine; partly because of the balance, partly because of the relative stagnation, of her economy. Less industrially developed than Germany and more agricultural, France, although far from untroubled during this period, never suffered the same degree of widespread economic hardship and mass discontent which gave such a boost to the Nazi Revolution. Bardèche makes the point, for example, and quite cogently, that fascism is a doctrine which lacks a natural clientele among the electorate; only during times of crisis does it find one among the petty bourgeoisie, a class which, feeling threatened from above and below, responds emotionally to 'heroic' leadership. Consequently, 'when there are no occasions for heroism', fascism declines.

Another major weakness of French fascism was its failure to coalesce behind a single individual or a single party. Fascism in France was a movement of sects which never overcame their differences, often largely personality differences. Even during the Nazi Occupation, Doriot's PPF and Déat's RNP failed to merge; the reasons are still vague, but the personal animosity and distrust between the leaders of the two formations was at times almost comic.[4] There were also bitter conflicts, both personal and political, within the PPF, conflicts which eventually tore the party apart. Sometimes feelings were rooted in old literary feuds, as was primarily the case with Brasillach and Drieu La Rochelle.[5] But the most devastating division of all involved important matters of policy. In October 1938, just after the Munich settlement, several leading members of the PPF resigned in protest over Doriot's position on foreign policy; they now denounced the policy of pacifism and

[4] There was, for example, the episode during the last weeks of the war, Doriot and Déat having fled to Germany, when first Ribbentrop then Hitler recognized Doriot as the most qualified representative of French interests in Germany – at which point Déat and Darnand formed their own counter organization to speak in the name of France. Not until the very last moment did Doriot and Déat arrange a personal meeting, at a village half-way between their two residences, to settle their differences. It was on his way to that meeting that Doriot's car was strafed by an Allied aircraft and he was killed; Déat disappeared into Italy during the last days of the war 'sans laisser de traces'.

[5] Although not a member of the PPF as was Drieu, Brasillach expressed great sympathy for the movement in his articles in Je suis partout; but Drieu could never forget a brutally critical review of his work written by Brasillach in 1935, in which Drieu was described as a raté who wrote 'the most empty and the most stupid stories', notable for their 'bad taste, bombast, and confusion' and for their 'clumsiness, digressions, tedious passages, and emotional falseness'.

appeasement towards Germany they had accepted until then, and called for a rapid build-up of France's military strength and for a firm stand against Hitler. Among those who defected were important party ideologues like Drieu La Rochelle, Bertrand de Jouvenel, and Paul Marion. The issue of foreign policy was not their only reason for leaving. Doriot's quest for financial support from French business interests helped disillusion individuals like Drieu who took the party's avowed 'socialism' somewhat more seriously. As he later complained, Doriot was no different from the Radical politicians he had so long despised: both in domestic and foreign policy, Doriot had behaved 'like a vulgar La Rocque'.

In effect, both Doriot and Déat failed to build a lasting political bridge to either the Right or the Left. According to Brasillach, French businessmen eventually concluded that it suited their interests more to subsidize the Radical Party than the fascists, while, at the same time, the PPF and the RNP were unable to overcome the image the working classes had of them, that they were simply agents of capitalism, an image abetted by newspaper accounts of fascists killing workers in the Spanish Civil War. 'Fascism, Hitlerism, [and] totalitarianism for twenty years have succeeded each other in the naïve abomination of the mob,' Déat wrote bitterly in 1942. 'Simply because, very astutely, they have been made synonyms for social and political reaction.' After the fall of France in 1940, of course, fascism for most Frenchmen also became associated with the hated invader, but it had begun to decline as a domestic political force as early as 1938, having failed miserably in its attempt to become a mass movement.

In this regard, it is necessary to make a distinction between fascism and conservatism in France before and during the Second World War; millions of Frenchmen were conservatives, but only a small minority were ever fascists. The Vichy regime was chiefly a regime of conservatives, not fascists, at least until the very last months of the war when French fascists, with the help of the Germans, were finally given several key governmental positions. The differences between conservatism and fascism in France have been underlined repeatedly by students of the French Right since the war, by René Rémond, Eugen Weber, Peter Viereck, and others. Not only were French fascists often critics of 'social-reactionaries' and 'bourgeois' values during the 1920s and 30s, but their editorials attacked Vichy policies time and time again during the war years. In 1942, for example, Doriot accused the men of Vichy of having led France down the road to decadence and defeat before 1940 by opposing social change at home and war against bolshevism abroad, adding that France would suffer further setbacks if Vichy insisted upon continuing a policy of conservative *attentisme*. Weber has shown how French fascists were often at loggerheads even with the *Action Française*, how Maurras broke with Georges Valois, for instance, in 1925, when Valois founded the *Faisceau*, and later with Brasillach, another former disciple, when Brasillach took the leap to fascism and then to complete collaborationism.

Understandably, perhaps, post-war scholarship has tended to emphasize the various areas of disagreement between men like Maurras and Brasillach. Conservative historians especially have concentrated their efforts on showing the doctrinal incompatibility between the fascist Right and the conservative Right (denying at times that fascism even belongs to the 'Right'). Scholars have argued that Maurras and his followers, as well as most French conservatives, were fundamentally different from fascists in several respects: they were enemies of 'Jacobin' centralization, *étatisme*, and the authoritarian state; they were devoted to the restoration of decentralized government and local freedoms; they were hostile to theories of popular sovereignty (which submerged the *pays réel* beneath the *pays légal*); and they were believers in social stability and a rational approach to politics rather than in revolutionary turmoil and fascist romanticism. 'Fascism dreams only of upheaval,' says Rémond. 'The Right wants to be reassured and aspires after stability.' Above all, it has been emphasized, conservatism in France was a philosophy of the bourgeoisie, of the socially-reactionary bourgeoisie, and as such it was clearly at odds with the 'social' programme put forward by French fascists, men who failed to view social justice with the same 'horror' as conservatives.[6] Finally, some scholars have held that fascism and conservatism in France also differed radically in their respective loyalties to nationalism. Whereas conservatism was a highly nationalistic faith in the 1930s,

[6] Eugen Weber, *Varieties of Fascism*, pp. 134, 141; René Rémond, *La Droite en France*, p. 204; René Rémond, 'Y a-t-il un fascisme français ?', *Terre Humaine*, No. 7–8, 1952; Stanley Hoffman, 'Aspects du Régime du Vichy,' *Revue française de science politique*, January–March 1956, pp. 45, 50; Paul Sérant, *Le Romantisme fasciste*, pp. 12, 265; Jean Plumyène and Raymond Lasierra, *Les Fascismes français*, p. 8; Peter Viereck, *Conservatism from John Adams to Churchill*, p. 62.

grounded as it was in the thought of anti-German patriots like Barrès and Maurras, it was the European, non-nationalistic orientation of French fascism which led many of its adherents to collaborate with the Nazis during the Occupation. Because of all these differences then, it is a mistake to regard fascism and conservatism as one: 'The two notions are, in fact, irreducible.' Indeed, Paul Sérant has even gone so far as to declare: 'to pretend to establish a kinship between fascism and traditional [conservative] doctrines would be in vain. . . .'

The difficulty with this view of the relationship or lack of relationship between fascism and conservatism in France is that many of the lines that have been drawn dividing the two were never as distinct and tidy as has been suggested, and furthermore, that the two philosophies shared many common denominators which were often far more important in determining their political behaviour than the elements which separated them. Ideologically, certainly, there were many ties. Respected conservative thinkers like Barrès and Maurras had long preached many of the doctrines which fascists like Brasillach and Drieu adhered to, from a glorification of power, 'realism', and authoritarian leadership to a hatred of parliamentarianism, politicians, and humanitarian liberalism. Moreover, those who emphasize Maurras' commitment to decentralized government and local freedoms fail to mention, at least in this regard, his willingness to condone and even praise authoritarian and *étatiste* measures when they were taken by the Vichy regime. There was nothing surprising about this, however, for, as Professor Rémond himself once observed, the principles of the *Action Française* had long been, in effect, a 'melange of authority and indiscipline, tradition and insubordination'. Hence, while condemning 'Jacobin' centralization, Maurras acknowledged that when a monarchist state came to power again it might have to institute a temporary dictatorship in order to impose a proper state of affairs. In this, Rémond notes, Maurras was not unlike totalitarian Marxists.[7] Nor, one might add, was he unlike totalitarian fascists.

As for the contention that conservatives differed from fascists in their coolness towards theories of popular sovereignty (although Barrès, for one, advocated during his lifetime a kind of authoritarian democracy based on his notion of *la terre et les morts*), this

[7] René Rémond, *La Droite en France*, p. 107.

coolness, in fact, was much more of a common trait with French fascism than an uncommon one, for French fascism generally was more elitist in doctrine than German national-socialism. More true is the observation that French fascists tended to glorify revolutionary, direct-action tactics far more than conservatives, although even here one can cite the violent activities of the *Camelots du Roi*, the activist wing of the *Action Française*, to show that resort to force was not foreign to 'conservatives'. Nevertheless, on balance, fascists did *talk* revolution more than conservatives, especially more than the sort of conservative who dominated the Radical Party throughout most of the 1920s and 30s. Still, the lines between fascism and conservatism in France were often blurred.

What the two camps had most in common, of course, was their anti-communism. It was this above all which made them political bedfellows on so many occasions, uncomfortable ones no doubt but still bedfellows. Indeed, French fascist writings sometimes leave the impression that all else was secondary to one primary goal: to mobilize France against communism at home and abroad. 'Our policy is simple; we seek the union of Frenchmen against Marxism,' declared Doriot in 1938. 'We want to clear France of agents of Moscow.' Or, as Bardèche said of fascism after the war: 'Its mission of defending the West remains in one's memory, and it is still the principal meaning of the fascist idea.' It was this fixation, among others, which led many French fascists to favour Germany during the Munich crisis of 1938 and to collaborate with the Nazis after 1940: Germany presented a check against Soviet penetration into Europe. This notion, too, contributed mightily to the often remarkable, or perhaps not so remarkable, editorial agreement between the conservative press and the fascist press in France during the late 1930s, this and the growing disenchantment with a Third Republic which among other things could allow Léon Blum's Popular Front to come to power. Consequently, as Professor Rémond puts it, the conservative press in France after 1936 displayed 'a more and more marked inclination for fascism' as it happened that 'a part of the classical Rights let themselves be won over by the vocabulary and circumvented by the propaganda of fascism' (pp. 220, 218). Actually, it is probably more correct to say that instead of being 'won over' and 'circumvented' by fascist notions, French conservatives simply found that many of these notions coincided with their own. A conservative traditionalist, for example, would not have had to change thinking caps to have accepted Brasillach's contention that one's identity is rooted in the soil and heritage of one's country (an idea that Brasillach himself received from Barrès and Maurras), or to have approved Doriot's statement that 'a nationalism understands itself only if it looks for its sources in the old traditions of the French provinces'.

Too often historians of the French Right have made the mistake of rigidly divorcing conservatism from fascism in theory when in practice, that is historically, these movements interpenetrated one another in a very disconcerting way – disconcerting at least if one expects intellectual and political phenomena to be nicely compartmentalized and self-contained. Scholars like Sérant, Plumyène, and Lasierra, it is true, have acknowledged that fascism in France did take some of its elements from the conservative Right, but then they contend that, once formed, fascism acted *against* the Right. As has been shown, this simply was not always the case. The beliefs which fascism and conservatism had in common drew them together on more than one occasion, especially when communism or Soviet Russia was at issue. That they disagreed on some questions does not mean that they did not agree on others. The most that can be said is that while French conservatives, to be sure, were *not* fascists, they often behaved as if they were, and while fascists were not conservatives they often shared many conservative positions.

Perhaps the best way to see how blurred and untidy were the lines which separated them is to examine their respective positions on the question of socialism. It is this measurement which many historians of the French Right have selected as the primary criterion for dividing the two camps, despite the fact that socialism was only one of many elements in fascist ideology – and not necessarily the most important element at that. Eugen Weber, for example, has argued in his study of the *Action Française* that Maurras cannot be called a fascist because he was opposed to socialism and in any case always regarded economic questions as secondary. '*Politique d'abord*', not economic reform, was Maurras' principal concern. Weber's definition of fascism at this point becomes quite important. By focussing on the economic issue, his definition *excludes* the conservative Right; yet had he concentrated on other Maurrasian and conservative doctrines, he might just as well have *included* it. Moreover, if one assigns so much weight to the matter of socialism in defining fascism, one might wonder whether Hitler was a fascist or a conservative; after all, in purging the socialist wing of the Nazi party in 1934, Hitler, too, followed a policy of *politique d'abord*. The same can be said of Mussolini's much publicized corporatism, a 'social' programme which, once in operation, benefited Italian employers more than Italian workers. Finally, if one closely examines the economic programmes advocated by France's two largest fascist parties in the 1930s, one can question whether these movements, too, were not less concerned with a fundamental economic transformation of society than with other matters.

To be sure, French fascist speeches and tracts were filled with attacks upon 'plutocratic' capitalism and expressions of devotion to 'fascist socialism'. Typical was Drieu's proud comment in *Socialisme fasciste* (1934): 'Fascism is a reformist socialism, but a reformist socialism which has, it seems, more fire in its belly than the old classical parties.' Yet when one examines the exact content of the socialism which was espoused, the gap between their social-economic programme and that of many conservatives is not nearly as wide as expected. This is particularly striking in regard to the position which Doriot and the PPF took vis-à-vis the middle classes. In *Refaire la France* (1938), for example, Doriot lamented the 'ruin' of the middle classes and the 'frightful' crisis they faced as a result of the devaluation of the franc and the fiscal burdens they had to bear. He noted sympathetically that not only did their situation differ from that of the proletariat but that they represented 'a state of soul quite distinct from the proletarian state of soul'. The real enemy, he emphasized, was not the bourgeoisie as a whole but rather big business, monopolies, the great financial trusts. In fact, one of the major sins of the Popular Front was that it favoured these large institutions at the expense of small and middle-sized businesses. The solution was not to nationalize industry (which was to confuse socialism with 'the bureaucratization of production' and 'super-protected industry'), but to suppress the protected sector of the economy, the web of monopolies, and to strengthen the free sector, the sector of small private enterprise. Under fascism, political representation would be based upon new criteria, upon professional rather than geographical lines, but economic life would operate according to traditional capitalist principles, especially according to the principle that 'Individual profit remains the motor of production'. There would be a ceiling, however, on the profits of big business (the surplus falling into a social welfare fund), and corporations which used their capital without social responsibility would be challenged; but the principal economic task of government would be to protect the free sector from the protected sector by taking measures to decentralize industry and democratize capital.

The economic programme which Déat presented in his book *Le Parti Unique* (1942) was much the same. Like Doriot, Déat paid his respects to the petty and middle bourgeoisie as 'guardians of precious traditions' and declared that their position in French society had to be safeguarded if they were not to be wiped out by the larger industrial and commercial enterprises. A corporate state would help small businessmen band together in employer organizations which would enable them to overcome their weakness vis-à-vis big business. Fascist socialism, consequently, was far from hostile to the great bulk of the middle classes; in fact it would be their saviour:

> The necessary rescue of our middle classes will be one of the happiest effects, one of the most essential objectives of the National Revolution. And that is what socialism should mean to them. At this point, we are a long way from any Marxist nonsense about the automatic concentration of our large enterprises and about the inevitable elimination of our small producers, people whom Marxists would discard, throwing them into the wage-earning class.

Déat made it quite clear also that fascist socialism was not an enemy of private property. 'All property is legitimate to the degree that it is not harmful to the common interest, even more so if it serves it.' Industry, he insisted, should be controlled and regulated but not nationalized. Nationalization indicated distrust of industry on the part of the State and failed to make wage-earners any less wage-earners. A fascist economy would be a planned economy to the extent that no factory would be allowed to manufacture 'no matter what at no matter what price and pay no matter what salaries', but private management, which had the competence and the staff, would look after the 'details'. Fascist socialism would excommunicate no one; services rendered would alone count. The industrialist who was intelligent and efficient would prosper, although he would no longer be driven solely by the profit motive, for he would be a leader in the full sense of the word, one who would continue to know the 'joys of command' but who would also know the joys of responsibility towards his workers. Finally, unlike Marxism, fascist socialism would not be abstract, doctrinaire, and monolithic, a system run by a centralized bureaucracy; instead it would be 'realistic and concrete', empirical and dynamic, leaving each employer to take his chances, with a great deal of freedom to operate his business as he saw fit.

Both Déat and Doriot agreed, therefore, that a 'brutal transfer of property' was unnecessary and unwise and that there was no need for the workers to become 'co-proprietors' of the factories. Once the power of big business was broken, small businessmen could be counted upon to meet their social responsibilities. 'Our personal working-class experience has taught us', said ex-worker Doriot, 'that small employers easily come to agreement with their workers against the Marxists in order to insure social justice and to protect themselves against the enemies of production and prosperity.' Fascism, therefore, would end class struggle and inaugurate class cooperation. Indeed, wrote Déat, this was the very meaning of totalitarianism: 'Totalitarianism is conciliation, a reconciliation.'

Stripped of its rhetoric, what Doriot and Déat's socialism amounted to was a programme designed more to suit the small and middle bourgeoisie than the proletariat. Highly significant in this regard was Déat's statement in 1942 that the socialism he advocated was not simply a programme for the working class but a programme for all classes, for, he said (and here his candour was exceeded only by his opportunism), France was not a country of large industrial enterprises nor was it even primarily an industrial country, and thus if fascism addressed itself to only one part of the nation it would lack 'élan'.

No doubt this was one reason why French fascist party programmes were as attentive to the grievances of the peasantry as they were to those of the lower bourgeoisie. Doriot and Déat both expressed their regret at falling agricultural prices and the growing exodus from the farms. Déat called for a rigorously equal exchange of products and services between the countryside and the cities, and condemned what he said was a situation in which the city-dwellers 'duped' the peasantry. Doriot emphasized that fascism, unlike Marxism, had no intention of making the peasant a 'diminished citizen'; it wanted to put an end to the migration from the farms because it abhorred 'the frightful concentration of large cities generating misery, unemployment, and social troubles'. Instead of liquidating or collectivizing the peasantry, fascism would work to preserve the small private farm by creating new credit facilities, by helping the peasants to specialize in products of quality, and by expanding the domestic market for their products by diverting the agricultural output of France's colonies elsewhere. Such measures had to be taken because 'the peasant is the essential support of a society such as ours', and 'represents the best virtues of our people'. Déat agreed. He, too, insisted that France must maintain a strong peasantry, 'physically robust and healthy, morally solid and balanced'. Indeed, so much did he agree with Doriot's glorification of the peasantry and its virtues that he announced that the cultivation of these virtues was a major goal of fascist socialism. 'Peasant socialism has no other aim and no other meaning,' he said. 'And it is indeed socialism since here again it is a question of integrating the mass of the peasantry, in accordance with its proper rank and place, into the community.'

As a matter of fact, fascist socialism seemed to have something for everybody. At the same time, for example, that the PPF called for less *étatisme* and fewer bureaucrats, it stated that 'dignity commanded' that lower functionaries be paid better salaries and that higher functionaries be treated in a manner 'worthy of their functions' – especially in regard to pensions. The dignity and rights of women were also identified as special concerns of the PPF; subsidies should be granted to mothers with many children and jobs easy for women to fill should be made available to them. The 1936 platform of the PPF also made provision for the material needs of the liberal professions, the intelligentsia, and the artisan class. 'In short,' it said, '[the PPF] will defend the interests of all those whose activity constitutes a traditional element of social equilibrium in France.'

If this was socialism, it was hardly a socialism far removed from a great deal of traditional French conservatism. In the middle-class and peasant orientation of its party platforms, at least, it was certainly much closer to French conservative thought than to Marxian socialism. If French fascism offered a 'third way' between communism and liberalism, as its proponents argued, it was a third way which nudged the Right far more than the Left. To point to the socialism advocated by French fascists as the major factor distinguishing their ideology from conservatism before and during the Second World War is to misjudge the character of that socialism. This is not to discount entirely, of course, the French fascist criticism of the evils of capitalism, especially big capitalism, nor its commitment to a certain amount of government economic regulation and planning. This kind of socialism *was* part of their creed, but it was simply not as revolutionary nor as divorced from conservatism as many scholars have suggested.[8]

Some French fascists, it is true, did take the avowed socialism and anti-capitalism of fascist ideology more seriously than others, especially literary intellectuals like Drieu, Brasillach, and Bardèche, men who were violently opposed – emotionally, intellectually and morally – to bourgeois society and bourgeois values. Indeed, one must always keep in mind the temperamental differences between *literati* like these and party organizers like Doriot and Déat; the latter, constantly faced with the practical problem of trying to enrol large sections of the public, often a bourgeois public, behind their banners, were more apt to dilute the movement's socialism than were some of their followers (a phenomenon likewise present in German national-socialism). One reason which Drieu later gave for his break with Doriot in 1938, it will be recalled, was his disenchantment with Doriot's dealings with conservative financial backers.

Yet even in the fascism of someone like Drieu, a concern for socialism or economic reform was not the primary motive force. Like many French fascists, Drieu was more concerned with advancing a 'spiritual' revolution than a material one. As a result, his conception of socialism was almost ascetic at times, equating as

---

[8] This is one reason, perhaps, for the curious phenomenon which Professor Weber describes, the phenomenon of wealthy business interests pouring money into the campaign coffers of fascist and proto-fascist organizations at various times during the 1920s and 30s despite the 'anti-capitalist' programmes which these organizations advanced. (Eugen Weber, 'Nationalism, Socialism and National-Socialism', *French Historical Studies*, Spring 1962, p. 302.) Weber sees this mainly as a technique which men of wealth used to channel the activist energies of these groups away from the Left and into a useless sound and fury. This may have been true, but also, surely, the 'anti-capitalist' programmes of these movements could not have been particularly frightening to such backers, while the anti-communism which French fascists espoused was a definite attraction.

he did materialism and creature comforts with moral decadence and physical weakness, and rejecting Marxian socialism because of what he felt was its too great emphasis on material and scientific goals. Moreover his contempt for those who hungered after the goods of this world was not restricted to the bourgeoisie, for, as he once scornfully remarked, the workers in this regard 'were more bourgeois than the bourgeois'. Yet his brand of socialism was sufficiently different from Hitler's to cause him, on several occasions during the 1930s, to condemn Hitler's professions of socialism as sheer hypocrisy. After visiting Germany in 1934, for instance, he expressed his disappointment at the fact that Nazi economic policies remained quite conservative and that German capitalists continued to profit handsomely; in 1936 he dismissed Hitler and Mussolini as nothing more than 'armed guards of capitalists'; and in 1939 he agreed with Hermann Rauschning that the Nazi Revolution was, for this reason, essentially a revolution of nihilism. Consequently, it is highly questionable that Drieu decided to collaborate with the Germans in 1940 primarily out of a commitment to socialism. Nor did men like Doriot and Déat have any more reason than Drieu to believe that the Nazis would bring economic reforms in their wake. Before Hitler came to power in Germany this might have been the case, but by 1940 his economic record was there for all to see.

Why then did many French fascists become collaborators? If the 'socialism' of the Nazis was not the major reason, then what was? Was it because they shared with their German counterparts a belief in racism, a mystical faith in the masses, a devotion to the *Führerprinzip*, because they were Nazi sympathizers in all things? Or was it because they were Europeans first and nationalists second? Or finally, was their anti-communism the most important factor? Of all these possible reasons, only the last seems to have played a major role, and even it was not the most important motive for some French fascists.

Paul Sérant indicates in his *Le Romantisme fasciste* (p. 78) that anti-semitism and racism were not central to French fascism until rather late in the day. He gives 1936 as the turning point, the year Blum's Popular Front came to power in France. It was only then that the fascist press in France made anti-Semitism a cardinal issue, for at least two reasons, neither of which had much to do at first with racial theory: Blum's Popular Front government, the major threat to French fascism at that time, was particularly vulnerable to such a campaign (Blum himself and several of the members of his government were Jews); and the charge could also be made that it was the Jews in France who, because of their hatred of Hitler, were trying to drag France into a war with Germany. That this campaign was more a matter of expediency than conviction is seen from the fact that even after 1936 most spokesmen for French fascism equivocated agonizingly on the question of race, not becoming full-fledged racists until the German Occupation.

Drieu La Rochelle is a good example of this development. In 1931 he heaped scorn upon the Nazi idea of a biologically distinct German race, ridiculing it as a delusion held by 'nostalgic petty bourgeois' who ignored the migrations of history. In 1934, after his visit to Germany, he took issue with the 'eugenic conservatism' of the Nazis and what he called their tendency to divide humanity into castes on the basis of blood. After 1936, however, his writings reflected a definite turn towards anti-semitism, yet of a sort which still condemned Hitler's brand as excessive and which was notably ambiguous as to whether Jewishness was 'an irreducible biological fact' or a matter of cultural conditioning. At one point in 1938, for example, he was tortuously on both sides of the question when he concluded that there *was* a biological difference which '*en gros*' differentiated Europeans from Jews, but at the same time refused to dismiss the possibility that *certain* Jews could be modified by education and assimilated into French society. (Even as late as 1942, Marcel Déat distinguished between the Jew who was harmful to the French community and who should be deported, and the Jew who fought and shed his blood for France and who should be accepted as 'an honourable and honoured ally'.) It was not until after the fall of France that Drieu began to talk about 'the very simple laws by which the life of peoples is based upon the fecundity of soil and blood', and even then he felt it necessary to justify his new position by equating racism with Aryanism and Aryanism with Europeanism. 'From this point of view, Germanism is simply the advanced guard of Europeanism,' he wrote.

Does this suggest then that French fascism was more European in orientation than nationalist ? Not necessarily. Here again the gap between conservatism and fascism in France was not so wide as might be expected. It is true that after 1940 Drieu and many of his colleagues tended to emphasize the European aspect of fascism, presenting Hitlerism as a means of creating a third force between communist Russia and the democratic capitalist powers. In Drieu's case, Europeanism had been a major tenet of faith as far back as 1931, when he wrote a tract entitled *Europe contre les patries*. However, by the late 1930s, after his conversion to fascism, he was like most French fascists a nationalist first and a European second. Indeed, so prominent was his nationalism during these years that he presented French fascism as an important means of strengthening France *against* Nazi Germany and fascist Italy, believing as he did that it was 'the only method capable of barring and turning aside the expansion of [other] fascist countries'. French national security came first, he said, and it counted far more than ideology when it came to making alliances. Thus he urged France to bolster its diplomatic ties with liberal-democratic England against national-socialist Germany. 'Systems change, but countries remain,' he declared. He vehemently condemned the idea of allowing France to be invaded by foreign troops, even fascist troops. In retrospect, a passage he wrote in 1937 is both ironic and tragic:

> It is all very nice to shout: 'Long live the Soviets' or 'Bravo Hitler' when one is tranquilly at home, among Frenchmen, comfortably settled. It might not be so pretty when there are thousands of Stalinist or Hitlerian mercenaries tramping their boots across our soil, singing their own songs, swearing in their own languages and looking at our women. ... Why do you expect Russians or Germans trained by dictatorships to conduct themselves better than French soldiers during the Revolution, men thought to have been made tender by utopian speeches? Foreign troops can be nothing but humiliating.

This kind of nationalism, however, did not prevent Drieu and other spokesmen for French fascism favouring the appeasement of Hitler during the Munich crisis of 1938, although not without misgivings. They did this not so much because they were pro-German as because they were anti-Russian, and also, even more important, because they felt that France had no chance of winning a war against Germany in 1938 – a position, it should not be forgotten, that was generally shared by the French conservative press – a nationalistic press – at that time. Nor should it be forgotten that shortly after Munich, Drieu and several others quit the PPF

in protest against Doriot's continued pacifism towards Germany –
and that, not long afterward, Doriot himself adopted an ultra-
nationalist, anti-German posture. Indeed, the reasons for this
split within the PPF are still obscure. It may well have resulted
more from a dispute over tactics than from any fundamental differences over ideological issues like nationalism. After all, Doriot
himself had left the PCF in 1936 in order to establish a party
of *national* socialism, free from Russian dictation. The doctrine
of the PPF was one of 'intransigent nationalism', Doriot said;
'Our credo is *la patrie*'. Later, in less happy circumstances, he
collaborated with the invader – for the same reason many conservatives did: to serve the interests of France (as he conceived them).
In 1942 he insisted that French fascism must retain a certain
identity and autonomy of its own within the New Order – the
pathetic plea of a hard-pressed nationalist.

Finally, the notion that French fascists before the war were
sympathetic to Germany in all things and therefore collaboration
was temperamentally a natural path for them to take after the fall
of France is one that can easily be disputed. Not only were most
French fascists quite nationalistic before 1940 and committed to a
distinctively *French* brand of fascism, but most of the leading intellectuals of the movement looked more to Latin fascisms for inspiration – to Italy, Spain, and Portugal – than to German nazism.
Drieu's disenchantment with many aspects of Hitler's Germany
from the mid-1930s onward has already been mentioned. When
Drieu wrote what was perhaps the most popular French fascist
novel of the pre-war period, *Gilles* (1939), it was among the fascists
of Spain not those of Germany that his hero sought fulfilment.
Brasillach, also, was much more an admirer of Spanish fascism
than German. The ideas of its founder, José Antonio de Rivera,
were a major source of his early attraction to fascism, while Spain
itself was for Brasillach the place of 'all audacities, all grandeurs,
all hopes'. On the other hand, when he crossed the Rhine and
attended the Nuremberg rallies in 1937, he failed to respond with
equal enthusiasm. Although some recent commentators on Brasillach's career have made a great deal of his descriptions of these
rallies, suggesting that they were wholly sympathetic accounts,
what Brasillach actually emphasized a great deal of the time was the
*strangeness* with which these rites struck him. To him, he said,
Germany was 'prodigiously and profoundly and eternally a *foreign*

country'. He did admire the emotion and vitality which these rallies generated in their German audiences, and he admired their emphasis on youth, but many of the ideas and symbols which characterized them, and which he found peculiarly German, struck him at times as almost ridiculous. When he wrote in his death cell in 1945 that throughout most of his life he had not been intellectually in touch with Germany, he was being perfectly honest.

The differences between French and German fascism, certainly, were many and great. Not only was racism much less important in the French version, but (perhaps as a consequence of this difference) neither was there such an emphasis on *Massendemokratie*, on totalitarian democracy, on the *Volk* as the ultimate source of political sovereignty and national greatness. Despite the provisions in its party programmes aimed at winning a broad mass following, French fascism was generally a much more elitist ideology than its German counterpart. In part, it may have been forced to exaggerate its elitist side because of its failure to become a mass movement. But there was also a genuine ideological distaste on the part of many of the intellectuals of the movement for any doctrine which glorified the masses rather than small groups of exceptional men. After all, the major criticism which French fascists made of their country was that it was decadent – and by implication that most of their countrymen were decadent too. Men like Drieu and Brasillach were especially critical of what they felt was the lack of vitality and will displayed by the French people in comparison with other peoples, and consequently they called for an authoritarian elite to pull the nation out of its slothful habits. Even the politicians of French fascism, men like Doriot and Déat, sensitive as they were to public opinion, made it clear that, in the last analysis, the government they had in mind would be a government much more for the people than by the people. Despite their talk of political representation through syndicalist corporations, ultimate political power, under fascism, was to reside in the hands of a single party and a single elite. The membership of this elite, it is true, was to be recruited from all classes of the population and from all regions of France. This was an important difference between fascist thought and a great deal of conservative thought, for fascist theoreticians insisted that those who governed should not be drawn from *just* the traditional hierarchies and authorities but from the lower classes as well, from wherever exceptional ability manifested itself. Thus, while both camps shared a common distaste for notions of popular sovereignty, they disagreed, although only in part, as to who would compose the ruling elite. Fascists, in this respect at least, were more democratic than many conservatives. However, their attitude towards the broad body of the masses remained quite as undemocratic.

Indeed, one of the major differences between French and German fascism was that Nazi ideology conceived of the Leader as a figure who derived his powers from the *Volk* and whose will was therefore law even unto the ruling elite, whereas French fascism with its far less exalted notion of the masses never subscribed to the *Führerprinzip* with the same degree of zeal. Drieu, for example, insisted that members of a true elite were partners not servants of their leader, and that their voices carried great weight in the decisions that were made. In fact, in *Socialisme fasciste*, he denounced all dictators, contemptuously remarking that they arose only when men were at their weakest. He concluded that while the masses, being 'a little female', were prone to abandon themselves to these 'living gods', a truly virile elite would always resist this kind of subservience. As he had declared a year earlier in his play *Le Chef*: 'There is an appalling weakness in men who give themselves to another man. When there is a dictator, there is no longer an elite; it means that the elite is no longer doing its duty.'

This elitist side of French fascism cannot be emphasized too much. It was one of the major attractions which fascism held for sensitive, intelligent *literati* like Drieu, Brasillach, Bardèche, and others. They were especially seduced by the notion of being part of a tightly-knit group of young, loyal, virile comrades – of being part of a *team*. Fascism was first of all a spirit, Brasillach once said, and 'it is the spirit of the team above all else'. At times the fascism of these men seemed little more than a schoolboy dream, a cult of masculine friendship, a notion of camaraderie – but there was more than this involved: there was the sense of enhanced personal power which comes from being part of a dynamic company of men, and, perhaps most of all, there was an end to the feeling of isolation and alienation which plagued people like Drieu. No longer, said Drieu shortly after his conversion to fascism, did one have to be like thousands of individuals in the modern world who tremble with cold in their little rooms in the great cities and who feel the need to rush together to keep warm. By joining the PPF, the 'paralysis' of individualism is overcome and men relearn *'la vie de groupe'*. 'There, one no longer lives alone, one lives together,' Drieu wrote in *Avec Doriot* (1936). 'There, one does not die each in his corner, . . . there one lives.' Freedom becomes no longer a matter of individual autonomy but of personal force, and the greatest personal force comes from being in and living through a group. Hence Drieu defined liberty as 'the power a man receives from being bound to other men'. Much the same sensation was described by Brasillach in his *Notre Avant-Guerre* (1941) when he told how he and many of his fascist comrades were exhilarated by 'living together' in mass meetings 'in which the rhythmic movements of armies and crowds seemed like the pulsations of a vast heart'.

Drieu underlined, however, that not just *any* group would do; it had to be a truly elite group, its members young, militant and courageous. It was these qualities, he argued, which particularly distinguished fascists from their political opponents, especially from the great bulk of communists and socialists, and herein, he said, lay one of fascism's greatest appeals and sources of strength. In fact there were moments when Drieu put so much emphasis on personal qualities, activist qualities – aggressiveness, courage, vitality, force – that his fascism seemed little more than a mystique of action for action's sake – as when he declared in 1937, for example, that it was not the programme of the PPF which counted so much as its spirit, its spirit of combat and action. Perhaps the most striking example of this aspect of his fascism occurs in his novel *Gilles*, during the episode in which the hero, after witnessing the February 1934 riots in Paris, proposes a remarkable plan of action to the leader of one political organization:

> Open an office immediately to recruit combat sections. No manifestos, no programme, no new party. Only combat sections, which will be called combat sections. With the first section that is formed, do no matter what. Attack Daladier or defend him, but with acts that are completely concrete. Invade, one after another, a newspaper of the Right and a newspaper of the Left. Have this person or that person beaten up at his home. At all costs, break with the routine of the old parties, of manifestos, of meetings, of articles and speeches.

A revolution of nihilism? Not necessarily. The fact that Drieu was inclined to downgrade certain ideological questions at certain moments does not mean that he lacked an ideology or that he was unconcerned with doctrine. His cult of action and force was itself a doctrine and the source in turn of other doctrines. It was precisely because fascists like Drieu glorified power and energy and vitality, and condemned French society for its decadence, for its lack of these qualities, that they demanded a radical transformation and a spiritual regeneration of that society. Not only was this critique the inspiration for a variety of doctrines and programmes, but more than anything else, perhaps, it separated fascists in France from conservatives and traditionalists.

For what preoccupied one French fascist writer after another – and what was one of the most distinctive features of their ideology – was their overwhelming sense of national decadence, their feeling that France was debilitated and weak, that it was sunk in torpor and somnolence. The underlying premise of so much of their thought was that France had declined drastically since her former days of glory and that this was largely due to the moral and physical degeneration of her people. Part of the blame was placed on 'plutocratic capitalism', and thus a brand of national 'socialism' was advocated to enhance the economic power of France vis-à-vis other nations, but on the whole French fascists viewed French decadence as primarily a moral problem (which is one reason, perhaps, why the economic programmes they devised seem mild by Marxian standards). Like Drieu, most French fascists conceived their revolution to be essentially a spiritual revolution. They argued that France suffered from a declining birthrate, from egoism and individualism and materialism, from a lack of vitality and force, not so much because of economic conditions (French fascist thinkers unanimously rejected a strictly economic or materialistic explanation of history and society), but because of certain philosophical conceptions, especially democratic and liberal philosophical conceptions, which had misled the French people. Once these conceptions were replaced by superior conceptions, French society would be regenerated.

For someone like Brasillach fascism was also, in no small measure, a revolt of youth against its elders, a revolt of a young, healthy, idealistic generation against an old, sick, rotten one. It was not a point of view likely to endear itself to middle-aged conservatives.

No doubt, too, most Frenchmen were less interested in being regenerated than in eating well, less concerned with youthful asceticism than with the material comforts of life. Here again there was a distinct difference between fascists and many conservatives, especially well-established, comfortable conservatives. Like Drieu, Brasillach and his friends at *Je suis partout* despised the materialistic values of the bourgeoisie and their debilitating attachment to creature comforts, and, like him, they dreamed of a new generation of Frenchmen, strong in body, comradely in spirit, and 'scornful of the thick possessions of this world'. One result was that there was often a good deal of primitivism involved in their revolt. 'In truth,' Bardèche tells us, 'man, such as he is conceived of by fascists, is a young savage who believes only in those qualities which one needs in the bush or in the arctic; he denounces civilization, for he sees in it only hypocrisy and imposture.'

But there was a great deal more to the fascist concept of man than that. Indeed to a large extent the central vision of French fascism was its vision of ideal manhood, its concept of the *homo fascista*, its notion of the 'new man' that a fascist society would produce. The aim of fascism, said Déat, was to create the 'total man', or, as Bardèche later said, 'to form men according to a certain model'. And they were sure that the model was there before them. Brasillach declared proudly in 1941:

... during the last twenty years we have seen the birth of a new human type – as distinct and as surprising as the Cartesian hero, as the sensitive encyclopedist of the eighteenth century, as the Jacobin 'patriot' – we have seen the birth of fascist man. In fact, as science distinguishes the *homo faber* from the *homo sapiens*, we should perhaps present to classifiers and to amateurs at this sort of thing this *homo fascista*.

Again and again, spokesmen for French fascism emphasized that it was 'this new image of man' that was the most essential part of their movement and which more than anything else set them apart from their rivals.[9]

What is the portrait of the *homo fascista* which emerges from their writings ? He is a man of energy, virility, and force – above all

---

[9] One of the shortcomings of Paul Sérant's work is that he deliberately ignores the fictional writings of French fascist authors. Yet it is precisely in such writings that the fascist image of the ideal man is often best found.

of force. He views life in Darwinian terms, as a struggle for survival in which the strong triumph over the weak. He believes that the only justice there is in this world, as Brasillach expressed it, is 'that which reigns by force'. Hence he does not avoid fighting and bloodshed but welcomes it, for only in combat does he fully become a man. His physical courage is fortified by a strong body. In times of peace he is an athlete hardened by sport. He is no egocentric individualist, however, because he realizes that he finds personal fulfilment only through the group, and consequently he respects cohesion, discipline, and authority. He is a man of action, will, and character; he is, in short, a *hero*, one who determines history rather than being determined by it.

Thus, said the defenders of Fascist man, he contrasts sharply with Marxist man or Democratic man. Men are born neither naturally good nor naturally equal. There is no inevitable progress in history nor is history determined solely by economic conditions. The fundamental error of Marxism is to believe that mankind is simply the product of material forces and that man himself is nothing more than 'a certain number of kilos of organic materials'. Unlike Marxism, fascism does not ignore the 'human factor' in history and the role of dynamic individuals. 'Fascism,' said Drieu, '. . . surpasses socialism by its sense of man.' Or as Bardèche puts it:

Fascism does not furnish as does communism an explanation of the history of the world; it does not propose a key with which anyone can decipher reality. It does not believe in fate; on the contrary it denies fate, opposing it instead with the will of men and believing that man forges his own destiny. . . . Fascism judges events and men in relation to a certain idea of man which is its own.

This certain idea of man, it was emphasized, has little in common with what democracies try to make of man. Democratic theory produces human beings who can read but have no morality, who seek comfort and security rather than the heroic life, who are petty individualists concerned solely with their own self-interest rather than members of a community devoted to something greater than themselves. Fascism wants to break the 'shell of [this] egoism', wrote Paul Marion in his *Programme du Parti Populaire Français* (1938), and revive 'the taste for risk, the confidence in self, the sense of the group, the taste for collective *élans* and the memory of those unanimous faiths which made possible the cathedrals and the miracles of France'. Democracies lack this *beau idéal*, and consequently they fail to produce the heroes fascist societies do. Nor do most conservatives, even those of the royalist *Action Française*, often approach this ideal, bogged down as they are in material self-interest and bourgeois decadence, lacking dynamism and – according to Drieu La Rochelle at least – a certain necessary brutality: 'A monarchist is never a true fascist, because a monarchist is never a modern: he has not the brutality, the barbaric simplicity of the modern.'

It was this striking vision of man, perhaps more than anything else, which attracted figures like Drieu and Brasillach to fascism in the 1930s and was responsible for their eventual conversion. Certainly it was one of their most powerful motives for collaborating with the Germans after 1940. It was something which they did have in common with the Nazis, something which weighed more heavily in the scales of decision than the differences which separated them. Sickened by France's easy defeat, convinced that their countrymen had proven their decadence in that defeat, they looked to the Germans to provide Frenchmen with a new ideal to pattern themselves after, and they felt that the Germans presented such an ideal in what Drieu called the 'Hitlerian man', the new kind of conquering German forged by the Third Reich. As Bardèche said later, not only did nazism appear to him and his friends as the best agency available at the time for combatting communism and liberalism in Europe, but if the Germans lost the war there would be no chance at all of implementing 'the new idea of man' which the Nazis embodied. Men like Bardèche collaborated not so much because they agreed with each and every doctrine the Germans espoused, but because they were enamoured of many of the personal qualities of the invader, their vitality, their force, their capacity for struggle. Indeed, even at the end, in 1945, when all was lost and nazism lay under a cloud of war crimes, Brasillach, writing in prison while awaiting execution, would, partly to justify the cause which had been his undoing, call attention to the last-ditch stand the Germans had made against the Allies:

In these years when she had been hard on others, Germany showed that she accepted, with the same hardness, the blows she received from others. She proved, superabundantly, her vitality, her genius for adaptation, her courage, her heroism. Throughout her cities burned by phosphorous bombs, a whole people stiffened, and in the conquered countries from which American and Russian power finally expelled him, the German soldier, besieged as he was, fought with the energy of the outlaw that some used to admire when their souls were loyal. . . . It is impossible that all these virtues will be lost forever. They are part of the common treasure of our civilization.

A final question remains. Was French fascism an ideology at all? Was it, as some scholars have concluded, primarily a 'fever', a movement lacking clear-cut goals and doctrinal seriousness, a movement, to quote Professor Weber, in which 'the ends of action count less than action itself', a movement lacking 'an anterior plan or series of plans inspired by the original doctrine'? Was it, as these scholars suggest, essentially a romantic adventure, a kind of sentimental, emotional fling whose participants were 'more interested in gestures than in doctrine', more concerned with style than substance, more apt to be irrational, subjective, and aesthetic in their approach to politics than realistic, objective, and tough-minded?[10] The trouble with descriptive adjectives of this kind, of course, is that they have a way of rebounding. In the first place, all ideologies no doubt have a certain emotional content that affects their doctrines if it does not inspire them. There is nothing very remarkable about French fascism in this respect. 'To treat [political] ideas as the offspring of pure reason would be to assign them a parentage about as mythological as that of Pallas Athene,' Sir Lewis Namier once said. 'What matters most is the underlying emotions, the music, to which ideas are a mere libretto, often of a very inferior quality.' Secondly, most ideologies have what could be called a subjective vision of the good society (all value-systems, surely, are subjective in this sense), and most ideologies, certainly, are accompanied by a definite aesthetic of their own. To be sure, a man like Brasillach did speak of fascism as a 'poetry' and was fascinated by 'poetic' images, images of young men camping around fires at night, of mass meetings, of heroic exploits of the past – but then Marxism, too, has its conception of life in the classless society, and conservatives their idylls of the hallowed past. An image-laden

[10] Eugen Weber, *Varieties of Fascism*, pp. 138–42; 'Nationalism, Socialism and National-Socialism in France', *loc. cit.*; Paul Sérant, *Le Romantisme fasciste*, pp. 10, 31; William R. Tucker, 'Politics and Aesthetics: the Fascism of Robert Brasillach', *The Western Political Quarterly*, December 1962; Jean Turlais, 'Introduction à l'histoire de la littérature "fasciste"', *Les Cahiers français*; May 1943, quoted in Sérant, *op. cit.*, p. 11.

vision of the good society – which few ideologies equate with the present society, with present objective reality – is hardly unique to French fascism and cannot be dismissed as mere 'subjectivism' or 'aestheticism'. Finally, French fascism was certainly as notable for its glorification of realism and pragmatism as for its expressions of 'romanticism'. Its belief that the strong triumph over the weak and that might makes right, its scorn for ivory-tower intellectuals divorced from concrete reality, its emphasis upon confronting the harsh 'facts' of life, its equation of violence with virility, its contempt for 'Romantics' who refuse to dirty their hands in political action – were all fundamental aspects of fascist 'realism'.

As to whether French fascists, realists or romantics, were seriously committed to a definite ideology or not, the evidence is mixed. Literary intellectuals like Drieu and Brasillach did often emphasize the spirit of fascism more than its programmes, and even Doriot, on one occasion at least, admitted that the doctrines of the PPF were 'insufficient and flabby' compared to the energy and force of its members. (Indeed, this emphasis upon spirit instead of doctrine made it that much easier for French fascism to penetrate the conservative Right during the 1920s and 30s, and for conservative attitudes to penetrate it.) Still, it would be wrong to conclude that French fascism was only a 'fever'. Its party programmes took quite explicit positions on the major issues of domestic and foreign policy, and even if some of its doctrines may be labelled romantic they were still doctrines. As suggested earlier, French fascism's disgust with all that was decadent and its cult of energy and force had important doctrinal consequences. Not only did France, the nation-state, have to be made strong again, but a new society had to be created to produce a new kind of man. In this, French fascists were just as doctrinaire as Lycurgus when he set out to legislate a new Spartan man into existence. Besides corporatism and an authoritarian state, French fascist writers called for 'a revolution of the body', a multiplication of athletic teams, scouting groups, hiking associations, youth hostels, sport stadiums, and above all, the eventual replacement of France's largest cities by colonies scattered through the countryside connected by ultra-rapid means of communication. Only when the bodies of Frenchmen were freed from the dehumanizing effects of a purely urban existence, wrote Drieu La Rochelle, would they overcome the spiritual decadence that engulfed them. 'Thanks to us,' said Paul

Marion of the PPF, 'the France of camping, of sports, of dances, of voyages, of collective hiking will sweep away the France of aperitifs, of tobacco dens, of party congresses and of long digestions.' According to Drieu, all the other reforms of fascism should be subordinated to the reform of the body, to what he called physical reform:

... the physical reform of man must be our immediate enterprise, inasmuch as it is the most urgent task before us, and it must be instituted concurrently with the reform of the economy; in fact, the reform of the economy must take its lead from the necessities of physical reform (which is the essential programme of the fascist revolution).

Not only did French fascism have a definite ideology, as should be clear by now, but it was a highly moralistic, highly serious-minded one. Indeed, despite its glorification of realism and force, perhaps the most striking thing about this ideology was its *moralism*, its righteous indignation at all it deemed decadent and its zealous determination to root out sinfulness (e.g. weakness) wherever it was found. Bardèche remarks in *Qu'est-ce que le Fascisme?*, for instance, that no regime is more concerned with the 'moral health' of a society than a fascist regime, and this is why fascism devotes itself to 'the systematic elimination of all that discourages, dirties, or disgusts'. Democracies, on the other hand, are known for their moral laxity:

[Democracies] allow all aspects of life to be open to all sorts of inundations, to all sorts of miasma, to all sorts of fetid winds, building as they do no dikes against decadence, expropriation, and especially mediocrity. They have us live on a steppe where anyone can invade us. There is only one purely negative password: to defend liberty. . . . The monsters who make their nest on this steppe, the rats, the toads, the snakes, they transform it into a cesspool. . . . As for mediocrity, it takes over like an insidious poison in peoples whom democracies cram with education without ever giving them a goal and an ideal; it is the leper of the souls of our time.

It was this kind of moralism which led many French fascists to risk public animosity and even death in behalf of their cause – and which also led them to condone some of the most authoritarian and ugly political acts of their times.

# The Political Transition of Jacques Doriot

## Gilbert D. Allardyce

'If I could triumph over my natural repugnance and write a bio-graphy of Jacques Doriot,' Ignazio Silone wrote in *The God That Failed*, 'my theme would be: militant Communist into Fascist.' What follows is an attempt to develop Silone's theme, concentrat-ing mainly on the final stages of Doriot's political transition, the period between his exclusion from the French Communist Party (PCF) on 27 June 1934, and the formation of his own *Parti populaire français* (PPF). It required two years to the very day.

In his study on the sociology of communism, Jules Monnerot identified a new breed of men that emerged out of the bolsheviza-tion process in the European communist parties, men of little formal education, of proletarian background, men who had achieved their rank in the party through discipline and submission, who owed everything to the party and who were nothing without it. Doriot was certainly one of them, and in the middle 1920s he appeared to be the most promising one. Impressively tall, ascetic in his personal habits, marked with the indelible sign of Moscow's tutelage, he became as leader of the Communist Youth a kind of *beau idéal* among the young proletarians who were advancing through the party. In a movement which at the time left the rank and file little to admire beyond intransigence towards the class enemy, Doriot put together a reputation for political extravagance and parliamentary outrage that made him, by the end of the party's first decade, the most popular militant in the organization, 'the living incarnation in France', as one journalist later recalled, 'of the man with a dagger clenched between his teeth'.[1]

But Doriot's emotional moods and the course of party develop-ment were soon pulling in different directions. Personally disposed

[1] Jean Maze, *La Flèche*, 21 March 1936.

towards action and the deed, he was always convinced that the party's success would be commensurate with its will to act. First in the campaign against the Ruhr occupation, then in the opposition to the Moroccan war, he had associated his interests and prestige with the efforts to concentrate the organization's energies outward on to the struggle against war and imperialism. The ultimate effect of the bolshevization process, however, and the 'class against class' tactic that followed in 1928, was to turn the party back upon itself, to give priority to internal concerns, and to favour leaders of a more administrative bent.

Sensing the failure of his projects, Doriot turned his dissatisfaction on those in the leadership who, in exercising their bureaucratic functions, were turning the party inward. Most prominent among them was the young Maurice Thorez, probably the most capable of the rising proletarians, but a man who had been buried in the provincial apparatus of the Pas-de-Calais at a time when Doriot was already active in the political bureau, and one whom Doriot, as he later admitted, always considered an *arriviste*.[2] Tireless and thorough in his work habits, implacable towards enemies and subservient to superiors, Thorez was the very model of the armed bureaucrat that Moscow was trying to fashion in France. It was perhaps inevitable that Doriot's opposition to the increasing bureaucratism of the party would be conducted as a personal rivalry between the two men.

Historians have recognized that it was the 'class against class' tactic that first brought Doriot's dissidence into the open, but they have not sufficiently acknowledged the extent to which his opposition preoccupied the attention of the Latin Secretariat at the Communist International Executive and its confidants in the French leadership. Conscious that opposition was rife throughout the party, the supporters of the new line no doubt sensed that Doriot, the most popular and volatile of the dissenters, was the most likely candidate to set off a stampede of the membership against them. The manner in which he was disarmed and subdued will not be recounted here. It suffices to say that he was badly treated, and this may well have embittered him forever against many of his comrades in the leadership. It was a brutish affair. As early as January

2 See Doriot's comments on Thorez in the PPF organ *Emancipation nationale*, 28 July 1939.

1928, when the internal dispute had scarcely started, the International's own representative in Paris had urged the Latin Secretariat to restrain the 'pogrom spirit' in which the new tactic was being imposed, to assure the French comrades that Moscow was 'supporting the party line and not certain people', and to try to patch up the personal feud with Doriot.[3] But matters only grew worse. Henri Barbé later recalled that in 1929 Doriot had become a man transformed, the fanatic revolutionary turned cynical politician, disabused, sceptical, 'mocking and ridiculing everything that he had venerated some years earlier'.[4]

At the sixth party congress in April of that year, Doriot, to the surprise of the leadership who had feared open rebellion, delivered a critique of his own errors, and in the following year plunged into the affairs of his home municipality of Saint Denis. Isolated in the ruling party organs, cut loose from his old base of power in the Communist Youth, his personal following decimated by resignations and purges, he had apparently decided to lie low until the new tactic had run itself out, and to concentrate on organizing a political fief in the old city of the kings. As far as the party was concerned, he prospered too well. Elected mayor of the city in 1930, he was to become so popular in Saint Denis that a local communist recently attributed his success to a manifestation of the 'cult of personality' in France.[5]

Between the congress of 1929 and his open rupture with the party in the 'February days' of 1934, Doriot increasingly became an alien element within the leadership. Undisciplined, absentee, masking his opposition to the party line behind intermittent proposals that were hostile to its spirit, he had only the saving grace of an

---

[3] See Manuilsky's letter of 25 January 1928, in the *Archives Jules Humbert Droz* (microfilm, Hoover Institution, Stanford, California).

[4] *Souvenirs de militant et de dirigeant communiste* (manuscript, Hoover Institution, n.d.), p. 234. Barbé had been Doriot's protégé in the Communist Youth, and succeeded to its leadership upon the latter's promotion in 1926. When Doriot opposed the 'class against class' tactic, Barbé led the organization away from its former master, and was himself pressed into service by the Comintern at the head of an extra-constitutional assemblage of subordinates (known in party parlance as 'the Group') charged with directing the application of the new line. After the Group was disavowed by Moscow in 1931, Barbé withdrew into inactivity; he linked up with Doriot again in 1934 and became in 1936 the major administrative official in the PPF.

[5] See the article of the present mayor of Saint Denis, Auguste Gillot, in the local newspaper, *Saint Denis Républicain*, 24 July 1964.

unshakeable popularity with the membership and the voters that none of his colleagues could match. It was no secret to anyone that the 'class against class' tactic had crippled the party, but the new leaders had been raised on commitment and loyalty, and they were willing to make the best of Moscow's worst directives. Doriot had to be tolerated, but he must indeed have seemed to them, as Marcel Cachin later put it, 'the spoiled brat of the PCF'.

From Doriot's side, things no doubt appeared otherwise. The new leaders, organized around Thorez, seemed more concerned with controlling the ruins of the party than with mitigating its sectarian policies. And '*le grand* Jacques' must surely have suspected the machinations that were keeping him isolated within the ruling committees. They were not all imaginary: the later revelations of Albert Vassart, for example, clearly demonstrate the pressures brought to bear upon those among the leaders who appeared sympathetic to Doriot's arguments.[6] Perhaps Doriot had his own experience in mind when he later asserted that the communists had squandered more sincere devotion than any other party in France, and had treated their best militants with a 'revolting indifference and a lack of moral respect that is scarcely believable'.[7]

At the Riom trials in 1942, Léon Blum identified Doriot as one of the godfathers of the Popular Front. This appears too generous towards Doriot's original intentions, for the proposals he made, and which earned him the label of 'right opportunist', envisaged no more than greater flexibility in the party's traditional sectarian policies. Some flexibility certainly seemed to be in order. Not even the Left's obsession with working-class unity could blind its advocates to the fact that the communist appeal for a 'united front at the base' with the socialist workers was merely an attempt to 'pluck the chicken' (as the former party leader Albert Treint put it), a trap to lure the socialist workers away from their chieftains. The disastrous failure of that strategy, as applied by the communists in Germany, had apparently convinced Doriot that history had at last adjudicated things in his favour; but the party line held firm in France.

It was Doriot's contention that although the tactic was correct

---

6 See Branko Lazic, *Informations fournies par Albert Vassart sur la politique du PCF entre 1934 et 1938* (manuscript, Hoover Institution, n.d.).

7 *Toutes les preuves. C'est Moscou qui paie* (Paris, 1937), p. 84.

in intent, it was too transparently deceitful to have success. With his customary faith in the salutary powers of direct action, he proposed that revolutionary sincerity would work where sectarian duplicity had failed. The important thing was to get at the socialist workers, to draw them into united action with the communist militants, even if that meant doing some honest business with their leaders. On 24 January 1934, in the heat of the Stavisky crisis, he urged the party to 'complete' its strategy for a 'united front at the base' by direct negotiations at the summit, thus cornering the socialist leaders between the enthusiasm for genuine unity on the part of their followers, which he felt they could not ultimately resist, and their own reactionary character, which he was sure they could not ultimately conceal. As he later explained to the International, the prospects for genuine unity would bring the requisite action that could set things right:

> It will create a strong urge towards action in the masses and open up to them the prospects of achieving power. Social-democracy being what it is, it is obvious that it could not remain in this movement up to the logical end: proletarian power. What is important today is to move the masses, to maintain and develop the existing movement, and to carry it along to revolutionary victory. This is the correct role of our party. Our party and the revolutionary movement could only benefit from the proposals made for the realization of this great movement, a movement which they alone are capable of conducting to final victory.[8]

Thus presented, his scheme seemed no more than chicken-plucking on a higher level. Indeed, such negotiations were within the letter of the existing tactical line, but, as everyone recognized, they were foreign to the spirit in which it was currently being applied. For the moment the socialist leaders were 'social-fascists'. It was another of Doriot's deviations, and a very dangerous one. With the leadership irrevocably committed to executing Moscow's sectarian policies, and with the French Left emotionally susceptible to any initiatives towards a loyal proletarian unity, the proposal could too easily turn the existing strategy into reverse, isolating not the socialist but the communist leaders. The leadership had been running from such an eventuality since the very inception of the new tactical line, and resolutions condemning Doriot's latest descent into the 'social-democratic vomit', as Thorez was soon to describe

[8] *Les Communistes de Saint Denis et les événements du 6 au 12 février: Lettre ouverte à l'Internationale communiste* (Paris, 1934), p. 22.

it, were dispatched down through the party even before the events of February.

'The population of Paris and its suburbs is living in a state of tension and fever unknown since the great demonstrations and strikes of 1919–20,' Doriot wrote in the aftermath of the 6 February rioting. 'Those who lived through the demonstrations of Tuesday and Wednesday will long remember the extraordinary dynamism of that crowd, its hunger for action. What a lesson for revolutionary organizations.'[9] The immediate lesson, for him, was that it could be used to force Moscow's hand in his favour, to compel the Kremlin to choose between Thorez and himself. On 11 February, before a meeting of all the political organizations in Saint Denis that were cooperating in the *journées* of 9 and 12 February, Doriot proposed the formation of an anti-fascist vigilance committee. Undertaken without the authorization of his party, and in violation of its tactical line, it was inevitable that the enemy would be as much the communist leaders as the fascists. Doriot had apparently determined to make his stand on the issue of *unité d'action*, to organize a 'united front at the base' directed more against Thorez than against Blum, and to carry on the struggle against the party line from his barony in Saint Denis. 'If I meet anyone in our organizations who isn't totally committed to united action,' he told the supporters of the Vigilance Committee, 'I will be the first to fight him and to call upon the working class of our locality to crush him.'[10]

Doriot appeared to have chosen his ground well, for the movement towards unity was to prove irresistible; but even before the Comintern intervened on 23 April to summon him and Thorez to Moscow, the probability of his ultimate defeat was already

[9] *Emancipation* (communist paper for the Saint Denis district), 10 February 1934. The district of Saint Denis encompassed a number of neighbouring localities as well as the city of Saint Denis itself, and was the strongest of the dozen odd districts that made up the party's North Paris region. Surprisingly enough, it numbered in early 1934 only 870 members (*Humanité*, 15 April 1934).

[10] *Emancipation*, 13 February 1934. The Vigilance Committee assessed its support in Saint Denis at between 15 and 20,000 workers. It was always to remain a basically *doriotiste* enterprise. The Comintern admitted that he began his opposition with a 'crushing majority' behind him in the local party organization. *Humanité*, 31 May 1934. At a conference in early March, the district delegates voted 110–61 on a resolution supporting Doriot against the party's central committee. *Emancipation*, 24 March 1934. (Unless otherwise indicated, all quotations in the remainder of this essay were drawn from this source.

becoming apparent. Confronted with the enticements of Doriot, the majority of communist members remained loyal to their leaders in much the same way as the socialist workers had when communists had wooed them in the past. Nor did the socialist chieftains themselves volunteer much help, preferring to play a waiting game. After an imposed silence on all events in Saint Denis throughout February and March, the communist leaders were ready to count heads in the area. At the conference of the party's North Paris region on 1–2 April, the delegates supported the resolution of the Central Committee against Doriot by a vote of 84–54. Afterwards Doriot insisted that the vote had been determined by discipline rather than conviction, and that it revealed his strength as much as his weakness, for the great majority of his votes had come *en bloc* from the representatives of his own district. But this permits another conclusion as well – that he had been successfully isolated in Saint Denis.

It has been argued that Doriot would have won his case had he made the trip to Moscow. But although the Comintern was about to change its line, it is difficult to believe, considering Doriot's long history of indiscipline and dissent, that the Kremlin would install him at the head of the French party. Moscow wanted to adopt his tactics and to salvage his followers for the PCF. But Doriot demanded some sign of capitulation in advance, and the trip became impossible. 'I want to go to discuss things with the directors of the Communist International as equal to equal,' he was quoted in *Emancipation* on 19 May. 'I will go to Moscow when the leaders of the Communist International have disavowed and rectified the slander and lies that have been spread about me for the last three months by the party press and the Central Committee.' In a word, he wanted to be 'right' against the party, and that of course was intolerable.

In his absence, the Comintern decided to appropriate his tactics and to use them against him. It was clear, Moscow announced, 'that Doriot speaks and writes on the united front not in the interest of its effective realization, but simply to be able, under cover of some phrases on the united front, to prepare a split in the party. The Communist International does not believe that Doriot, who breaks the united front of the party, can be honestly and sincerely for the united front of the working class.'[11] Doriot had thus be-

---

[11] *Humanité*, 19 May 1934.

come a schismatic; the advocate of the new policy had become its enemy.

Ignoring party discipline, Doriot had resigned as mayor of Saint Denis on 9 April, and invited the party leaders to submit their ideological differences with him to the arbitration of the electorate. 'My friends and I', he wrote on 24 April, 'like to keep the situation clear.' Unwilling as yet to face a test of strength in the city, the Central Committee kept silent, and on 6 May Doriot presented himself unopposed at the polls, drawing a total of 12,000 votes (76%) in what was no more than a plebiscite run against his own party. But when the PCF shortly thereafter set out on its new course, it became difficult to perceive where the policies of one side stopped and the other began. 'What was criminal and opportunist in January,' Doriot remarked on 9 June, 'becomes indispensable and revolutionary in June.' At the party conference at Ivry on 23–6 June, the affair at last had its illogical conclusion, with the leadership proposing the expulsion of Doriot and the official endorsement of his tactical line at one and the same time. Thorez added the final ironic touch: '. . . as Doriot intended it,' he observed, 'it was not a question of achieving a united front, it was a question, as with Treint, of a mere manoeuvre, of "plucking the chicken".' That, he said, was why the Central Committee had opposed Doriot from the beginning.[12]

The socialists had followed all this with some bewilderment, but with the prospects of unity at last in the offing they seemed willing not to pursue their questions too far. 'The Socialist Party speaks of a non-aggression pact and of a loyal united front,' Thorez had remarked at Ivry, 'but is *Le Populaire* demonstrating its loyalty by reproducing the slanders against our party made by the schismatic Doriot?' The socialists got the message, and henceforth Doriot was an embarrassment to both sides, the socialists finding it convenient to forget him, the communists unwilling to be reminded.

Now adrift between the two parties, Doriot suddenly stood in danger of being submerged under the very wave of enthusiasm for proletarian unity with which he had hoped to swamp the communist leadership. Within Saint Denis he seemed well entrenched,

---

[12] *Ibid.*, 29 June 1934.

controlling the municipal government, the party newspaper, the bulk of the old membership, and the leading personnel almost to a man. All this, however, was merely the debris of a communist district, now politically isolated and deprived of its ideological justification for existence. Later, Doriot recalled that in the heat of his struggle with the party, an envoy of the Comintern had warned him: 'If you want to become a government minister we will not interfere. But, if you want to mix in our affairs, then so much the worse for you – it will be war to the knife.' The continuation of the struggle seemed inherent in the logic of things, for Doriot had either to recapture the initiative or, eventually, to go under in Saint Denis as well. The feud had left too much bad blood. Doriot had none of that awe of the party which so often reduced its intellectual excommunicates to paralysis; he was too much the proletarian, had been too badly abused, and had too much contempt for the quality of its leaders. They had routed him with his own programme, but he still had designs to go them one better. 'It is easier to cut the head off someone who has one, than to put one on someone who does not,' he wrote on 30 June. 'Those who have excluded me would perhaps do well to meditate on this advice.'

Convinced that the communists had stolen his strategy only as a temporary expedient in order to outflank him, he was determined to trap them, just as he had earlier proposed to take the socialist leaders, in the snare of their own duplicity. 'In matters of united action,' he declared on the same date, 'we fear no initiative, no boldness, no manoeuvre. We consider working-class unity indispensable in the struggle against capitalism, and we will go as far and as fast as it's possible to go in order to achieve it.' Beginning on 5 July, Doriot expounded his proposals for a united proletarian party, a higher synthesis of revolutionary bolshevism and socialist parliamentarianism, internally democratic and externally militant; it was to be based on the Unity Charter of 1905 and the experiences of the 1914 war. There was nothing original in this, but it offered the chance of stealing a march on the PCF leadership, of confronting its hypocrisy with the sincere desire of the masses for the political unity of the Left. Unity in action, he now observed, had been designed for a defensive alliance against fascism; unity in organization would carry the proletariat on to the offensive.

By late August, Doriot and his comrades at the *mairie* were actively organizing what sympathizers they could find in Paris and the provinces into groups calling themselves the *Amis de l'unité*. These groups, he insisted, were intended neither as a weapon against any existing political party nor as the nucleus of a new one; they were rather being recruited in the no man's land between the two great working-class parties, and were designed to bring them together. But Doriot can have had no illusions about the communists consenting to such a scheme. Despite his disclaimers, the project could be put through only by turning the weight of the PCF's membership against its leaders and, ultimately, against Moscow itself. Again, it was the strategy of *plumer la volaille*.

At first Doriot apparently imagined himself to be again riding the wave of working-class opinion. 'Unity already exists in the spirit of the masses', he wrote on 11 August, 'even if not in the minds of all the leaders.' In October *Emancipation* first appeared in a weekly national edition, bearing the motto 'Central organ of the total unity of the workers', and throughout the winter months Doriot was stumping the provinces, accompanied by a bodyguard of Saint Denis toughs to counter the persistent communist assaults upon his meetings. It was all an exercise in futility. The cause of united action had been driven on by the Left's sense of urgency and frustration; the cause of organizational unity seemed only desirable and opportune. While most of the leaders on the Left acknowledged the need for organic unity with the communists, not all were in a hurry to get there. In any case, the communists were moving on towards greater things and were soon to take the socialists in tow, thus again stealing Doriot's initiative and reducing organizational unity to a secondary consideration. Although it was not immediately obvious, Doriot had begun a pursuit of lost causes, each of them ending in a frustration that would drive him on more desperately to the next, and each proving itself more compromising than the last.

Meanwhile the slow erosion of his power in Saint Denis was under way. Starting almost from scratch, even to the extent of importing leaders from outside the city, the PCF officially constituted a new district there on 4 November 1934, and the struggle for Saint Denis settled down over the winter to a dogged war of attrition, with the local socialists in the Vigilance Committee becoming progressively alienated from Doriot by the bitterness of the hostilities, and by the urgings of their parent organization to reach an accord with the local communist organization.

But something new appeared to be breaking in Doriot's favour. From the beginning, he had sought to broaden the appeals of both the Vigilance Committee and the *Amis de l'unité* by tempering the traditional communist pledge of 'unconditional support' for the Soviet Union. Although this had initially created difficulties for him, since the communists accused him of disloyalty to the Russian revolution, it seemed during the fall and winter of 1934–5 to be working to his advantage. With the obvious evolution of Soviet diplomacy towards a rapprochement with France, the communists were set adrift between their two historic traditions of revolutionary defeatism and unconditional support for the Soviet Union. Should an alliance be concluded between the two powers, the defence of Soviet Russia would logically imply the defence of imperialist France. This, observed Doriot, snared the workers between their obligations to the Soviet Union and their hatred of war, it pressed them into the service of one imperialist camp confronted with the ambitions of another, it threw them into the defence of Versailles, and it deprived them of their most effective weapon for both preventing war and defending Russia: revolutionary defeatism. 'For the imperialists', he repeated on 13 October, 'the fear of revolution is the beginning of wisdom.'

What began in September 1934 with some rather muted queries about communist intentions in the event of war became an open wrangle over the winter, with the cause of revolutionary defeatism becoming an ideological partner of Doriot's campaign for organizational unity. With a rather sarcastic sanctimoniousness, he now drew upon all the old Leninist strictures against national defence. 'Who is the renegade in this affair?', he asked the PCF on the following 20 April, 'You or we?'

At the time, the communists were rather badly exposed. Since negotiations between the governments in Paris and Moscow remained indecisive during the winter, the Comintern had no choice but to let the French party continue clumsily and precariously on its way between the contradictions in policy. The formulas of revolutionary defeatism had been ingrained into the consciousness of the Left, and with the communists unable to dissociate themselves from the need for national defence, Doriot drew the conclusion that had probably been in his mind from the beginning. The workers being ideologically united on revolutionary defeatism, they could never be organizationally united with those who opposed it. It was now clear, he wrote on 16 March 1935, that revolutionary unity could be achieved only in opposition to the Communist party.

With his customary extravagance, Doriot pressed his advantage to the point of an irrevocable commitment to the struggle against war. At the municipal elections of 5 May 1935, he made the question of national defence a basic issue between himself and the candidate dispatched to Saint Denis by the communists, thus once again calling upon the voters to adjudicate his ideological dispute with the party. Urged on by both communist indecision and the general malevolence of the election campaign, he left nothing ambiguous: 'We will not march', he insisted in public debate with his opponent, 'on any pretext.' No doubt his decisive victory at the polls encouraged his belief that, once more, he was 'right' against the party.[13]

But within little more than a month things had changed. After the famous communiqué from Moscow on 16 May, containing Stalin's public approval of French national defence, the communist theoretical line was settled, and the task of reorienting proletarian opinion could be undertaken openly. It was undertaken in a political climate that was already turning favourable. The communists had done well at the May elections, and the parties of the Right were growing concerned about the possible effect of the alliance with Moscow on domestic politics; this naturally set opinion on the Left flowing in the opposite direction. By the end of June, the socialists were unmistakably falling in behind the communists on the question of the pact – the decisive transformation of values in French political life of the 1930s was beginning. But if the socialist leaders could acknowledge their errors on national defence, Doriot could not. Isolated on the issue of revolutionary defeatism, and with his designs for organic unity having thus lost their logic, he had little choice but to go to the end with his commitment on the war question. 'Faced with these desertions', he remarked on 22 June, referring to the socialist conversion to national defence, 'it is essential to regroup the forces opposed to war.'

[13] Running first on his organization's list for the municipal council, Doriot got 9,796 (56%) of the 17,375 valid ballots cast, and the PCF candidate 3,959 (23%). While his hold on the city thus remained secure, the communists had nonetheless re-established an electoral base of support.

Doriot's ideological position had from the beginning been fraught with contradictory implications. 'The struggle against fascism,' he wrote on 16 March 1935, 'cannot be separated from the struggle against war.' But it would appear that things were rather the other way around: the struggle against war was incompatible with the struggle against fascism. The strategy of combating the fascist threat at home by means of proletarian unity in action and organization seemed to involve the obligation, should the situation dictate, to combat its threat from abroad as well. A strategy that proposed a working-class offensive against fascism in France could not be reconciled with a refusal to take up the defence against fascism threatening from across the Rhine. Alone among the major communist leaders, Doriot had insisted that the rise of fascism made a decisive turning in tactics mandatory, but he himself apparently failed to comprehend the full implications of the turn. While the Left pursued the logic of the new tactical direction to the end, Doriot maintained the old anti-militarist attitudes, thus remaining stranded in the wake of the Left's ideological transition. It was there that the parties of the Right found him when they came to take up the fight against the Soviet pact. Compared to the ideological migrations of these great political blocs, Doriot's transition from Left to Right was to require relatively little ground.

On the question of containing the fascist regimes abroad, regimes within which the premises of revolutionary defeatism were obviously invalid, Doriot's commitment to peace left him only the alternatives of negotiation and diplomacy. The rise of Hitler was consistent with everything that his communist experience had taught him to expect of the Versailles settlement – it was inevitable, he declared, that an imperialist peace would yield such a 'monstrous product'. It was the treaty which had made revision in Europe necessary, and it was only realistic to take the side of necessity. 'Germany is what it is', he wrote in April 1935. 'It is not our fault if it is not socialist or communist. But above all we must maintain the peace, and to do that we must speak with Hitler just as we speak with all the other governments, whatever the regime they represent.' Hitler's word, he contended, falling back on what seemed his eternal strategy, should be put to the test of its own sincerity. Having reached this point, Doriot was later to oppose all moves which threatened the prospect of negotiations, and from there the standard maxims of appeasement followed.

'It is not paradoxical to say', an observer of Doriot's struggle with the party had remarked in April 1934, 'that the break is a manifestation of Gallicanism against the papacy.'[14] Indeed it would appear that a progressively nationalist orientation had been a silent partner in his ideological attitudes even before his struggle with the PCF came into the open. Party doctrine had always insisted that the fight against war and fascism was to be waged at home, against the French bourgeoisie; Doriot's own convictions in the matter were no doubt reinforced by his personal advocacy of a more activist line in France, and by his long opposition to men and policies imposed on the organization from Moscow. Even in his personal feud with Thorez, Doriot was the man whose strength rested on his popularity in France, and Thorez the one whose strength rested on Moscow's confidence. Doriot was the one who insisted upon exploiting opportunities at home, Thorez the one who insisted upon obedience to the International. Doriot's solutions were always inherently French solutions. 'It is not in Moscow', he told his followers shortly after his expulsion from the party, 'that the problem of the French revolution can be solved.'

The formation of the Popular Front in July 1935 seemingly reduced his programme for organic unity to a mere sectarian concern; by its association with the Soviet pact, it ran counter to the tenets of his campaign for peace. Unwilling to yield on the war question, he could now carry on the struggle only by attempting to turn opinion within the Popular Front against the Soviet Union and its communist partisans in France, or, this failing, to turn a broader mass of French opinion against the Popular Front itself. 'For the communists', he had written on 13 July, 'the Popular Front is not simply a French anti-fascist *rassemblement*; it is also the method of leading the masses into support of the foreign policy, so dangerously modified, of the Soviet Union. It is a method of systematically supporting the USSR against Germany, and of checking the peaceful *rapprochement* of France and Germany desired by the French masses.' Here, for the first time, Doriot spoke not simply for proletarian opinion, but for national opinion,

14 See the article of Ludovic Barthélemy, extracted from an unidentified Saint Denis newspaper, in the notebook entitled *Histoire d'un crime en 1934*, compiled by the local resident Marien Lesbre (Bibliothèque de Saint Denis), p. 122.

for a mass consensus in favour of peace against a foreign influence intent upon war.

Through the remaining months of 1935, the logical implications were worked towards their conclusion. What had begun as a programme of unity against fascism became by September a programme of unity for peace. The struggle against war, originally the prerequisite to the struggle for unity, had now become its object. It would take Doriot some time to complete the identification of the French masses with France, but already his vocabulary was in transition, allusions to 'the proletariat' and 'the workers' giving way to a broader concern with *le pays* and the *masse populaire*. But he was never to come around fully to the traditional phraseology of nationalism until after the formation of the PPF. He appeared in 1935 to be becoming a nationalist more by opposition to foreign influences than by his commitment to French ones.

By the fall, Doriot's position seemed hung up in its own contradictions. He was at once against fascism at home and for rapprochement with Germany abroad; for the cause of the Ethiopian people but against any participation in the imperialist struggle between England and Italy; against Moscow's leaning towards war and for the defeatism of Lenin. Gaining favour in the Faubourg Saint-Germain for his denunciations of the communists, especially after revealing their financial secrets, he was also holding on in Saint Denis. Barbé may well be right in asserting that Doriot was already thinking of opportunities elsewhere on the political spectrum,[15] for nothing remained for him on the Left except capitulation to the Popular Front, and the tightening communist siege of Saint Denis was no doubt pressing him on to other paths.

At the senatorial elections on 20 October, Doriot cut the remaining bridges with the Left. Maintaining the incompatibility of desiring peace and voting for the communists, he withheld the votes of the Saint Denis delegates from the communist candidates, thus breaking the electoral discipline demanded by the Popular Front. Repercussions followed; first his dismissal from the unification committee set up to consider the amalgamation of the working-class parties, then his exclusion from the Amsterdam-Pleyel movement, and finally the breakup of the Vigilance Committee in Saint Denis. Faced with the irreconcilable hostility between Doriot and

---

[15] *Souvenirs*, p. 362.

the communists, the organizations of the French Left had no choice but to go with the communists, for there was little to be gained from going with Doriot. Proletarian unity without the communists was inconceivable, and although the others suspected that the worst of what Doriot was saying of the PCF was probably true, it was Doriot, the original advocate of proletarian unity, that had to be sacrificed as the schismatic.[16] The other organizations could make accommodation with the communists, but that alternative did not exist for Doriot. The Left had now passed him by, and on 1 December 1935 he gave his comrades in Saint Denis the first outlines of an entirely new design to prepare 'a revolution in France with French materials':

We have still to try to construct a great programme for the working class, for the middle class, and for the peasantry; a programme that will rally a popular front of action and of mass, that will enable us to rally forces that we are not accustomed to seeing, forces that want to understand . . . They are the young forces that are in the habit of considering themselves in two different camps but that, in reality, think the same; forces that are disgusted with the old parties that have betrayed them. What will be our programme, comrades? I have already explained it tonight: our programme is peace.

It was the first hint of the PPF, of a kind of 'peace fascism' that seemed to take its inspiration as much from the struggle against the communists as from the models in Rome and Berlin. But anything further would have to wait until after the elections scheduled for the following Spring; things had become difficult in Saint Denis, and Doriot preferred to renew his mandate in the Chamber before embarking upon a political experiment of this nature in the Red belt.[17]

Thus, from the beginning, there was a kind of desperate logic

[16] Cf. Jean Gaudeaux, *L'Unité politique de la classe ouvrière: les travaux de la Commission d'Unification* (Paris, n.d.), p. 2.

[17] Doriot's speech of 1 December is reproduced in *Emancipation*, 16 January 1936. In the second round of the elections, on 3 May 1936, Doriot was hard pressed to retain his seat, getting 11,587 votes (50%) to 10,887 (47%) for the communist candidate. Within the municipality of Saint Denis alone, where 18,904 voters turned out, Doriot received 9,830 votes (52%) to his opponent's 8,665 (46%). Although his count within the city was holding reasonably stable, it seems fair to assume that its social and political character was changing, and that the communists were winning over those working-class and leftist elements alienated by Doriot's new orientation.

in Doriot's progression through the tactical manoeuvres that took him over to the Right, carried along by the very propensities for involvement and intransigence in the execution of strategy that were the products of his education on the Left. More important, perhaps, was his obsession with getting even with the communists, with satisfying a grudge that was above all else deeply personal. But the roots of the change would appear to go deeper.

Doriot had always had an inclination towards action and movement that seemed innate rather than acquired, an inclination that the enforced discipline of party life had at times frustrated but never tamed. He had long observed that fascism had taken the initiative in Europe. 'It was fascism', he wrote on 23 February 1935, 'with its pseudo-socialist and nationalist ideology, that had known how to profit from the depression in order to take power, and not the parties of Marxist origin.' Perhaps he was attracted as much by the prospects it offered for action, and for a more vigorous anti-communism, as by any intellectual or moral affinity. Certainly he should not be understood merely as one 'dehumanized' by communism. In matters of demagoguery and calculated violence he had nothing to learn from the fascist dictators abroad, and the stormy scenes he had made as a communist in the Chamber had even then moved many of the young intellectuals of the Right to a kind of admiring wonder. He seemed a man of moods that communism could never completely contain, or that the fascism of the PPF could never wholly exhaust. 'He had within him an accumulation of energies that could never be fully consumed', one of his close disciples in the PPF wrote recently. 'He was too much opposed to his times. Impelled alternately into incomprehensible behaviour, into apathy, or into unchained hatred, he could never find fulfilment in the PPF. He remains a unique phenomenon in the political history of our land.'[18]

Certainly the opportunities for a fascist experiment in France would seem to beckon such a man. The political fortunes of the Right had been on the wane since February 1934, and with the Popular Front looming progressively larger on the Left, the more volatile elements were off in search of a new man and a different

---

[18] Maurice-Yvan Sicard (J. Saint-Paulien, pseud.), *Histoire de la Collaboration* (Paris, 1964), p. 512. On the admiration of right-wing intellectuals, see Robert Brasillach, *Notre avant-guerre* (Paris, 1941), p. 280, and Georges Suarez, *Nos seigneurs et maîtres* (Paris, 1937), p. 72.

direction. Thus while Doriot had supposedly made his call to the disillusioned of all parties, it was inevitable, given the monopoly of the Popular Front over the Left, that the PPF should become enveloped by the Right, and that it should be inherently anti-communist. 'We counted on him', recalls Alfred Fabre-Luce, 'to form, in opposition to the communists, another party of iron.'[19]

Although Doriot may be said to be 'fascist' in mood and manner in the Spring of 1936, he had few of the ideological accoutrements conventionally associated with that term. Nationalist only by default, without trace of racism, never much attracted to the themes of elitism, intuition, and 'blood wisdom', he brought with him only a rather un-fascist devotion to peace and an intractable anti-communism. In his brand of fascism, communists took the place of the Jews.

Ideologically, the PPF was not the creation of Doriot, but of the disparate elements around him: men from the disbanded paramilitary leagues that were to give the party an increasingly nationalist orientation; social authoritarians whose concern with the technical problems of corporatism and industrial planning had evolved into a kind of Utopian fascism; young intellectuals from the right-wing newspapers and cafés who provided, especially in the case of Pierre Drieu La Rochelle, the classic statements that historians would later extract to document the movement's fascist character. To all these groups, theoretical, abstract, poetic, and often either apolitical or anti-political, Doriot brought the smell of the streets and the sagacity of an experienced politician. Most of all he brought the ideal personage of the *chef*, the living incarnation of 'the miracle of Saint Denis', of the workers reconciled with the nation, the Left reconciled with the Right, the men of 9 February with those of 6 February. In one way, he did indeed bring Left and Right together, for while the PPF was an ideological creation of the Right, it was an organizational creation of the Left, constructed on the Bolshevik model, run largely by ex-communists, and directed

[19] *Journal de la France*, vol. I (Paris, 1940), p. 221. On 17 April 1937, *Emancipation nationale* claimed that sixty-five per cent of the PPF members were 'workers', but this term was always used rather loosely. There does seem to have been a fairly large contingent of ex-communists, estimated at 35,000. Total membership reached its pre-war peak in the first half of 1938, although the figure 250,000, given in the party newspaper *La Liberté* on 10 March, is probably exaggerated.

73

by a leader convinced that the struggle against communism could be won by turning its own organizational methods against it. 'In France', Doriot predicted, 'final victory will go to the side that is best organized.' The PPF itself, throughout its pre-war history, denied either that it was fascist or that fascism could ever be French. Certainly there was no single element in its ideology or structure that could not be found elsewhere in the nation's political life. What was unique about the movement was the way that the elements were put together, and the spirit that their fusion generated among the membership. In this sense, the *doriotistes* were perhaps justified in taking for themselves on the Right the same slogan that the communists were so proud of on the Left: 'We are not a party like the others.'

For the PPF, as for Doriot, the struggle against war and communism were one and the same. But faced with political realities, this wishful identification of the war danger with the communist danger could not long endure. When the real dimensions of the fascist threat abroad could no longer be denied, and when the disintegration of the Popular Front reduced the communist menace, the emotionalism within the party inevitably wore through the patience demanded by the policies of appeasement. Under the pressure of diplomatic events in 1938, the ideological elements within the movement started heading off in different directions. Doriot could now only hold on to what remained of the organization, and await the coming of something more promising. It arrived with the German occupation and the opportunities of the collaboration. With his characteristic disposition for political involvement, Doriot gave the same total commitment to this last futile cause that he had given to the earlier ones. It was perhaps to be expected that he would complete his political transition in the uniform of the Waffen SS.

# Fascism in Italy: The Second Wave

## Adrian Lyttelton

*[handwritten annotation: Compare with Nazi movement (a) Radical fringe (b) way of dealing with them]*

The fascist seizure of power was a lengthy process. Beginning in the autumn of 1921 with the piecemeal destruction or absorption of the machinery of local administration, it was finally completed only with the reform of the Chamber of Deputies in 1928. But in this slow process two dramatic 'leaps' have always been recognized as decisive. The first, obviously, is the March on Rome; the second is the end of the Matteotti crisis in January 1925. Mussolini's speech on 3 January was taken by the Italian Republic to mark the break between the constitutional regime and the dictatorship. There is an important difference between the two leaps; the March on Rome was the culmination of a steady process of encroachment on the powers of the State, whereas the action of Mussolini in January 1925 was the reversal of what seemed like the fatal disintegration of his power and of the whole fascist movement, and the initiation of a new phase, the 'second wave' of fascism.

How was it possible that eighteen months after the March on Rome the murder of an opposition deputy could threaten the very foundation of Mussolini's power? This harsh question needs to be asked; without the existence of a parliamentary opposition, a partially free press, and a partially free magistracy, the whole Matteotti crisis would have been unthinkable. Moreover, the murder itself was in a sense characteristic of a regime which lacked legal sanctions against its opponents. The fascist leaders continued to find terrorism necessary, but they were not prepared to assume full responsibility for it. The significance of Mussolini's 3 January speech was that he took this decisive step; 'I declare . . . that I, and I alone, assume the political, moral, and historical responsibility for all that has happened . . . If fascism has been a criminal association, if all the acts of violence have been the result of a certain historical, political, and moral climate, the responsibility for this is mine.'[1]

Fascism claimed to be a revolutionary movement. But the content of this revolution remained obscure. In his celebration of the anniversary of the March on Rome, Mussolini had boasted that 'the fascist revolution had not fallen short of its goal'; but when he came to list its merits, they consisted principally in the things it had *not* done: it had not destroyed the authority of the monarchy, the church, or even parliament: and it had not introduced special emergency legislation.[2]

If the extremists within fascism regretted the absence of repressive legislation, even the moderates, or 'revisionists', were concerned at its failure to create an institutional foundation for its exercise of power. At the party's National Council in August 1924 a delegate asked, 'What has fascism brought that is new? What is there on which one could base the formula that there shall be no turning back? Nothing!'[3] Before the Matteotti crisis removed the veneer of official optimism such frankness was less encouraged and rarer, but not unknown. Fascism had created one new institution, the Militia; but even that had a somewhat uncertain status and future, continually disputed between those who wished to reduce it to the innocuous role of an auxiliary reserve and training corps for the regular army, and those who wished to accentuate its political character.

The successful elections of 6 April 1924 might seem, however, to have finally legitimized the dominant position of fascism in the State, and, by ending its previously insecure constitutional position, to have made possible that normalization, or return to legal methods, which was the central theme of political discussion. But the end of the provisional period of fascist government had its disadvantages; it became harder to postpone the basic choices. The question of the character that the fascist State was finally to assume became an inescapable and actual political problem. Would the new legislature signify, as the liberals hoped, the definitive re-entry of fascism into the constitution and into legality? Or would it, instead, be the constituent assembly for the new fascist State? In the second case, it was not easy to define the plan of the project.

The difficulty of giving fascism a definite shape, its refractoriness to discipline or stabilization, cannot be explained simply by the practical difficulties of implementing this or that reform. Not even the repressive legislation demanded by the extremists would have been capable of immediately satisfying the 'revolutionary' demands of the movement; this was made clear by the events of 1925-6. There was a fundamental contradiction between such a rational and conservative notion as the restoration of the authority of the State, and the irrationalist activism which had inspired the fascist movement. Ideas of constitutional reform, of any kind of definitive organization, were regarded by this mentality as anti-pathetic or at least irrelevant. Camillo Pellizzi, a writer who in retrospect has criticized, with intelligence, the failure of fascism to take a technocratic or managerial turning, expressed this attitude with eloquence: 'Fascism fought for a principle of authority . . . Authority: but not that of a written law or a constitutional system.' and again: 'The genuine fascism has a divine repugnance for being crystallized into a State . . . The fascist State is, more than a State, a dynamo.'[4]

Nor was this merely the pose of a few intellectuals; the leader of a group of dissidents who revolted against the *fascio* of Pistoia, under the name of the 'old guard', explained that 'We fascists must never abandon that dynamism which is one of our most marked characteristics; to remain in the static position which has recently been reached was for us the negation of the fascist idea'.[5] One could speak, in fact, of an ideology of *squadrismo*; in effect, this ideology served to cover and confuse, to mystify, realities which were more simple.

For a real restoration of the authority of the State the first necessity was to reduce the power of the local fascist bosses, or '*ras*'. But this was not easy. Mussolini himself desired, in principle, to bring the *ras* under control; he had convinced himself by October 1923, if not before, that it was in his own interest, as head of the State machine, to re-establish its supremacy over the party. This might not appear obvious: for was not Mussolini also the head of the party? However, the party had not yet shown itself capable of controlling the local leaders. The frequency of crises in the central organizations of the party, which were continually formed, dissolved, expanded, contracted, re-named, given greater or lesser powers, is a proof of the difficulty of making the Fascist party into a unity. Indeed, the March on Rome had in a sense aggravated the problem. Previously, a certain unity of action had been imposed on the movement by the necessities of combat; now this centripetal force was removed, and on the other hand the competition for office aroused new rivalries. This was well seen by G. Bottai, the most acute analyst of fascism's internal difficulties: 'While homo-geneity is more or less possible in parties formed around a rigid and precise programme, it is almost impossible in a party whose re-cruitment stemmed from an atmosphere of passion. While strong feelings are active, it is possible to unite different types of men; calm revives their disagreements.'[6]

1923 therefore had seen an intense struggle for power within the fascist movement, at both the national and local levels. The central leadership sought to make or break the provincial chiefs; this meant that in turn the more powerful of the *ras* increased their efforts to gain influence at the centre. The result was a general increase in confusion and instability. Contemporaries spoke of the crisis of fascism.[7]

The Matteotti crisis began, in a sense, not with the murder of the socialist deputy, but with his speech to the Chamber on 30 May 1924. The idea of the secession of the opposition from Parliament, of the 'Aventine', and the answering project, on the fascist side, of a 'second wave' of illegal violence or repressive legislation, both date from then. A circular from Cesare Rossi[8] to the fascist press on the day of the speech ordered the editors to unmask the 'concerted plan' of the opposition to prepare for a secession: 'These plans are destined to compromise seriously the long hoped for and now achieved normalization of national life, because of the inevitable and legitimate reaction that the fascist regime will at the right moment unleash.'[9] However, the effect of the murder was to make such a reaction impossible. According to his own story, Rossi proposed to Mussolini that he should at once assume responsibility for the crime, as he was to do on 3 January 1925.[10] But Mussolini felt himself, with reason, too weak for such action. The opposition had won a great moral victory; the question was whether they could translate it into political terms. Their failure to do so is notorious; but in order to understand the position of Mussolini and the fascist movement it is necessary to ask what chances they might seem to have had of success.

The use of force was not wholly excluded. During the moments of greatest political confusion there were possibilities of success for a blow at the centre, carried out by a small and determined group, although this solution presented difficulties sometimes too easily ignored. But the most serious danger to Mussolini came from the legal opposition. In retrospect, this appeared doomed by the attitude of the King, but at the time this could not be taken for granted. Mussolini had three dangers to fear. The first was the hostility of the elder statesmen; only the event was to prove the lack of effect on the Crown of an alliance between Giolitti, Orlando, and Salandra against fascism. Second, a disintegration of Mussolini's parliamentary majority was not out of the question. When the Liberals, Combatants, and others were subtracted, the Fascists were only a bare majority; and among the fascist deputies there were a number whose nerve might fail, or conscience revolt, faced with the necessity of extreme measures. Finally, there was danger from the Cabinet itself. The broadening of the Ministry, with the inclusion of two Liberals, was imposed upon Mussolini by the threatened resignation of four of his ministers, Oviglio, de Stefani, Federzoni, and Gentile.[11] The *Giornale d'Italia* (5 July) claimed that 'the dominant elements of the situation are legalitarian; there is a Cabinet, that would never approve a revolutionary policy'; later it appealed to the 'eight legalitarian ministers'.[12] There was a large element of illusion in these hopes. But it is true that Mussolini could count on the absolutely wholehearted support of only one other member of the Cabinet, Ciano.

Only these dangers can explain the hesitancy of Mussolini's political strategy. At first the extremists had his favour. It was imperative for him to conserve all the strength he had left, and this implied dependence upon the enthusiasm of the provincial masses and the armed forces of the Militia. The high-water mark of the extremists' success was the Consiglio Nazionale of the party in August. Its resolutions marked the decisive formal break of fascism with the liberal State. However, Mussolini, having achieved his object by uniting the party behind a programme of constitutional reform which had little relevance to the actual political situation, turned to try to regain the lost or wavering support of the Liberals. But the elementary, if often effective, technique of the stick and the carrot was inadequate in the new political situation. The tensions were too great; distrust could no longer be disarmed by promises, and the support alienated by the encouragement given to the extremists in the first phase could be won back, if at all, only by very tangible concessions. Commenting on Mussolini's message to the Fascist party on 30 November, the *Giornale d'Italia* (2 December 1924) explained why its opposition was now irrevocable;

between June and the present 'there is a whole series of actions and speeches by the rt. hon. Mussolini himself which are in absolute contrast with the spirit which animated his speech to the Senate in June, or the present letter . . . the Prime Minister in yesterday's document as in his recent speech to the Chamber, appears not as a man of decided conviction, but rather as a man constrained to change tactics in order not to lose power'.

There was another important sense in which Mussolini's early line increased the tensions. The fascists themselves were wrought to a dangerous pitch; this was, of course, necessary, and provided the element of intimidation on which Mussolini counted. However, the new insecurity in the position of fascism made it more difficult than in the past for him to prevent the enthusiasm from boiling over. The first, extremist, phase had also had tangible consequences. The provinces had regained the dominant role in the direction of the party, and Farinacci in particular had become its virtual leader.

For these reasons, by the end of November Mussolini's policy was in ruins; on the one hand, fascism was isolated; on the other, this conspicuous failure to prevent the continued hemorrhage of supporters was sapping the confidence of the fascists in his leadership, and in consequence the movement was threatening to escape from his control altogether. His only way out of the dilemma was to take advantage of the heightening of tension to proclaim his indispensability as the only man capable of dominating the crisis. A judgment of Massimo Rocca's is relevant here, even though it refers to the situation before the murder of Matteotti; in a conversation with Carlo Bazzi, 'we agreed that Mussolini's real guarantee in respect of the monarchy consisted in a latent menace of civil war'.[13] It was this menace which Mussolini brought out into the open on 30 December 1924 when he replied to the suggestion of his resignation: 'I am ready to resign – but only in order to descend into the piazza.'[14] Legal repression was justified on the pretext that it was the only means of averting the 'second wave' of illegal violence. In his speech on 3 January Mussolini claimed that 'If I had put the hundredth part of the energy that I spent in compressing fascism into releasing it, ah then . . . But there will be no need of that, as the Government is strong enough to cut short the sedition of the Aventine absolutely and definitively.' As a pretext the argument deceived no one; but as a threat it had its effect.[15]

If the menace of the 'second wave' was finally incorporated into

Mussolini's strategy, it does not follow that it was always merely an element in his plans, a carefully solicited orchestration of his main theme. The objection to the threat was not that it was unreal, but that its fulfilment, if it preceded the legal, police reaction, might have fatal political consequences; ministers would resign, and the Crown and the Army might feel compelled to intervene to restore order. Consequently it was essential for Mussolini that the Government should act first and forestall any general, undisciplined terror action carried out by the provincial fascists or the Militia. Such an action would probably have caused the downfall of fascism, and in any case would have seriously damaged the Duce's prestige in his own movement. To this extent one can say that the threat of the extremists to take the law into their own hands was really a decisive factor in precipitating Mussolini's decision.

Towards the end of November he was still on the normalizing tack. His intentions were serious enough to arouse stubborn opposition within the party. The communiqué of the Grand Council meeting of 20 November noted that the discussion of Mussolini's new policy directives had been particularly long and animated. Some days later a curious *ballon d'essai* was launched by a member of the party *Direttorio*, Ciarlantini. In an interview with the *Giornale d'Italia* (27 November) he declared, 'Fascism is not a phenomenon which can be exhausted by the fortunes of a party . . . The present formation of fascism may last for one year or five.' This cannot have reassured those who believed that Mussolini was preparing to salvage his own fortunes at the expense of his party.[16] The fascist revolution was declared at an end, and the energies of the movement were concentrated in the appeal for a new amnesty.[17] A general pessimism prevailed, shared even by the Duce's brother Arnaldo. Thanking Michele Bianchi for a present, he wrote that the gift was specially welcome 'in these days in which we see the disintegration of a great part of the men and the programme on which we had worked and pledged ourselves. I won't hide from you that for months and months I have been living in the gravest distress, condemned to a particularly difficult situation . . . But the battle is not yet over.'[18]

The situation was worsened by an unexpected blow. Balbo, the commander in chief of the Militia, was forced to resign by the disclosures made during his libel action against the *Voce Repubblicana*. Mussolini, himself implicated, accepted his resignation in a comradely letter, which increased the scandal. He had probably decided to replace Balbo by an ex-general of the regular Army in any case; but instead of gaining credit for a 'normalizing' initiative, he now appeared to have acted only under constraint.[19] Within the fascist movement, Balbo had great popularity and prestige: the repercussions of his resignation were serious, especially in the Militia, which had an important and distinctive role in the events leading up to 3 January.

The Balbo affair accentuated the previous contradictions in Mussolini's policy. To appease conservative opinion it was necessary to give the Militia a national and military role, but this needed the co-operation of the Army, which was not prepared to agree without obtaining safeguards. Consequently, Mussolini found himself caught in a crossfire from his military and conservative critics in the Senate, and the powerful vested interest of the Militia officers. The urgency with which influential representatives of the Army, such as Generals Giardino, Zupelli, and Caviglia,[20] pressed their demands, reflected a serious alarm at the existence of a very considerable armed force which had, in reality, emancipated itself from all effective control. Could even Mussolini be sure of controlling his undisciplined private army? Even if a successful *coup* remained improbable, it was not beyond the power of the Militia, with support from the rest of the fascist movement, to create a violent interregnum. Public opinion, Giardino said, was alarmed by the possibility of an armed reaction, 'even if limited to a few provinces . . . in the case of political change, or even of a radical purge'. The last phrase showed the fear that Mussolini himself would not have the power to discipline the fascist movement even if he had the will: which was no more than realistic. Consequently the demand for the purge of the higher ranks of the Militia no longer reflected merely an exclusive professional jealousy, but also the urgent need to bring the corps under control. 'The Army must always be the strongest force of all the forces which exist in the Nation', the General continued. 'What guards against even the most unexpected conflict, indeed even the notion of any conflict whatsoever, and therefore assures the peace of civil society, without the actual employment of force, is simply and exclusively the just proportion of forces.' The problem was not only one of status but of power.

The opposition of the Militia officers to the new directives, adopted in response to Army pressure,[21] can neither be reduced to a mere matter of salary and status, nor seen apart from such pedestrian considerations. Its motives were not only material but psychological (the refusal to abandon political violence as a way of life), sociological (the dislike of impersonal, bureaucratic organization), and political (in common with other extremist fascists, the belief that the time had come to cut short discussion). This mixture appears in a letter written by the Milanese Militia Consul, Carini; 'If instead of consuming litres of ink we took up the *manganello* again . . . how much good would result. With opponents of such a quality the most valid, calm, elevated, convincing argument is worth the same as a dry fig . . . General Radini has been transferred to Bologna and a brave but completely unknown General is coming here. This way of treating the [Militia] zones like regiments or brigades of the Army is a real absurdity, and these provisions will inevitably lead to the death of the Militia – to say nothing else. General Radini is a likeable and intransigent *fascist*, and absolutely OK. He doesn't want to go to Bologna . . . and I think he will finish by offering his resignation. If his example is imitated by others of us and the same kind of attitude is taken up at Bologna, we will see the Militia disintegrate and perish. It is necessary that you should recall this state of affairs to him who has not well understood what the Militia is, and has equally not well understood that we hope that the Voluntary Militia for National Security will remain just that.

I am writing this . . . with a feeling of true desperation in my heart (and I speak only of desperation because discipline forbids me to mention different feelings) . . . I who for two years have eked out a living with my family on 793 lire and *nothing else* except the modest pension won by 26 years of fearless sacrifice . . . If we act in this way I foresee that at the right moment (which has perhaps already arrived!) the instrument of defence might not respond to the final appeal.'[22]

Such a mixture of motives probably lay behind the so-called 'movement of the Consuls' in December 1924. The culminating event in this story is fairly well known: on the last day of the year thirty or so Consuls of the Militia called on Mussolini, with the pretext of wishing him a happy new year, but with the real object of protesting against the changes in the command of the Militia and of warning him that if the Government did not act to suppress opposition criticism, the 'second wave' would begin.[23]

Much remains obscure in this story: the account of a violent altercation between Mussolini and the spokesman of the Consuls has been described as a 'pre-arranged comedy'.[24] But, at least in its origins, the 'movement of the Consuls' would seem to have been the product of a genuine dissatisfaction with Mussolini's leadership, and probably envisaged an action of the kind Giardino had feared. One would assume that action against or without the powers of the State would have figured only as a desperate last resort: the intention would rather have been to make impossible a policy of accommodation and compromise by a St Bartholomew's night of terror, thus compelling Mussolini to throw the Government's weight behind the movement.

According to some versions, the movement was organized and led, at least in its earlier stages, by Balbo himself.[25] This is not improbable, but the evidence is not conclusive. Mussolini was acutely nervous of the repercussions of Balbo's resignation among the officers of the Militia.[26] Balbo advised his supporters 'to give proof of our discipline one last time . . . The Government of our Leader has ordered us not to hold demonstrations either for or against the Government itself. We obey, but if even this last message of peace is not accepted by the opposition, let it be known that we are ready to make the war-cry of the first days of fascism sound again'.[27] The fascist regional assembly of Emilia elected Balbo chairman; the Prefect of Bologna reported that Mussolini's message was 'received with notable coldness by the Assembly and there were even some expressions of disagreement'. In the heated discussion which followed, 'two tendencies were affirmed: one for the possibility of a second wave and the other for normalization. However, in the afternoon that for normalization prevailed. The first tendency was sustained by the representatives of Ferrara and Ravenna who demanded the reconstitution of action squads; the other tendency demanded legislation which would safeguard the claims of fascism. The state of mind of the representatives of some provinces must be seen in relation to the request made by the generalissimo that the present commanders of the Emilian Militia should be maintained . . . It was affirmed that illegalism can disappear only if the Government dictates laws which impress the fascist spirit as capable of defending the results of the revolution

... the Militia, held to be the true and only guard of the fascist revolution, must include the best *squadristi* as it must be the *squadrismo* of Fascism.'[28]

On 21 December 1924 the *Voce Repubblicana* reported 'the more or less clandestine meetings of the higher officers of the Militia, presided over by Balbo'; the same paper (17 December) had reproduced a significant telegram from Grandi to Balbo: 'Yours received. Remain Ferrara. Keep very calm. Show yourself able to wait in silence. This is what one must do at the moment. Your faithful friend Grandi embraces you.' At this point the indications of Balbo's activity disappear; he was certainly silent, but whether out of obedience or conspiratorial secrecy it is hard to say.

There is no mention of his presence at the meetings of Militia leaders at Ferrara on 9 December and at Bologna on the 10th. According to the vigilant and usually well-informed Prefect, Bocchini, the Ferrara meeting dealt only with the difficult personal situation of Consul Forti, one of Balbo's chief friends and subordinates in Ferrara province, implicated in the murder of Don Minzoni. The Bologna meeting, attended by all the Consuls of Emilia and Romagna, was presumably official in character; similar meetings were held in other regions on the initiative of the *Comando Generale* to discuss the new directives. Bocchini reported that 'the discussion was extremely animated, reflecting the very depressed state of mind not only of officers but also of *capi-squadra* and *militi*. With the exception of the two Consuls Borghi and Diamanti, all the others showed hostility to the proposed settlement, noting among other considerations that the Militia in Emilia and Romagna is formed by old *squadristi* who obey none but their present officers because they were once the leaders of the old action squads. Even Consul Zunini, Reggio Emilia. Legion, a Colonel of the Army, fully agreed, indeed threatening resignation.' However, the participants agreed to 'undergo' the settlement, provided it had 'definitive and unmodifiable sanction so as to constitute an irrevocable right for the present officers who will be enrolled', in other words, given security of tenure.[29]

But this request was not so easily granted. Gandolfo's decision to replace all zone commanders who had not attained the rank of brigadier in the regular army left the Consuls untouched, but not exactly secure. Although the replacement was officially announced on 20 December, the new commanders were not due to take up their posts until 1 January. Here is one explanation of why the movement came to a head on 31 December.

The zone commanders reacted to their forcible retirement by turning to clandestine activity. The commander of the zone of Umbria and the Marche, Lt.Gen. Agostini, was in a particularly awkward position; the *Voce Repubblicana* (29 November) had revealed that he had organized and personally led an expedition of the *squadraccia Perugina* against the dissident fascists of Ferrara, in the interests of Balbo. He could expect no help or support from the local leaders of the party, with whom he had quarrelled.[30] This quarrel went back to late June, when he had favoured the use of force against the opposition. On 17 December the Prefect of Perugia reported that Agostini had gone to Rome 'to reach agreement with those who find themselves in an identical position, and to regulate his conduct in conformity with theirs'; it was said that he intended to put his command at Mussolini's disposition, but the Prefect recommended the Government to consider 'what other position could be found for Agostini if necessary outside the Militia. This so as not to leave the impression that it is intended to harm or abandon him and to avoid the possible repercussions consequent on such a state of mind.'[31]

At this point matters became more serious. With the Giunta episode in the Chamber the disagreement between Mussolini and some of the leading members of the party became public. As fascism threatened to split into two or more factions, it was natural that the discontents of the Militia Consuls should receive fresh impetus and political backing. According to Montagna, thirteen Consuls met at Florence in the days before Christmas, and it was then that the decision was taken to go to Rome on the 31st to demand the 'second wave'.[32] The *Voce Repubblicana* (25 December) again gives some confirmation; it revealed that 'immediately after the Giunta episode in the Chamber, three important and highly secret meetings were held at Ferrara, Bologna, and Florence, each of which was attended by numerous officers of the Militia as well as by several deputies'. But the *Voce* went on to give warning that the pretended disagreement between the Duce and the *ras* was a 'low manoeuvre', and that in fact in these meetings provincial fascism had shown itself in perfect agreement with Mussolini, directing criticism exclusively at revisionists, Liberals, and Combatants.

This raises the central question of whether the movement of the

Consuls was planned in collusion with Mussolini. The *Voce*'s testimony is impressive, but there is one piece of direct evidence to contradict its interpretation. The republican journal refused to believe the report that Mussolini had ordered police surveillance of the secret meetings; however, on the 23rd Mussolini telegraphed to the Prefect of Bologna, 'Comandante Generale Militia Gandolfo reports to me movement several Militia officers your zone which is said to be headed by Consul Silingardi and lesser figures. Please watch situation discreetly and make understood supreme reasons which impose silence and obedience on all.'[33]

It is not clear if or when the movements of the Consuls were co-ordinated from a single centre. However, they were certainly extensive. Silingardi and Zappoli, an old fascist who commanded one of the Bologna legions, conferred with Agostini on the 22nd; the Prefect of Perugia added a more urgent note to his earlier warnings.[34] Finally, on the 28th a meeting of high officers of the Militia of North and Central Italy was reported to have taken place at Florence, with Agostini again present.[35]

It emerges from this account that the movement of the Consuls undoubtedly existed as an independent, semi-clandestine conspiracy, to which the Prefects and police were not party.[36] However, the problem of Mussolini's relation to the movement cannot be settled so easily. Before evaluating the last act, it is necessary to consider the evolution of the general situation in the fascist party.

Mussolini's circular to the party on 30 November had been accompanied by stern warnings against indiscipline.[37] The circular itself recommended conciliation towards possible allies, condemned illegalism and the continuance of *squadrismo*: this was nothing new, although it sanctioned the move away from the intransigent line adopted at the *Consiglio Nazionale*; but both the political context and the reception of the message show that these were more than just conventional expressions. Particularly ominous to many fascists was the suggestion of a purge: 'It is necessary to liberate the party from all the elements unfitted for the new settlement; those who make violence a profession.'[38]

The reception of the message in Emilia has already been described; it was no better in the two other most fascist regions, Tuscany and Lombardy. At Florence, the Prefect reported that 'All the speakers declared acceptance of the message and desire to make act of devotion to Duce but showed state of mind tending to extremism out of fear that opposition parties will gain upper hand . . . The rt. hon. Lupi appealed to concord and discipline dissenting from the other speakers. The rt. hon. Morelli turning to the rt. hon. Ciarlantini asked him to draw attention to perplexity and sorrow of Florentine fascism and in concluding demanded complete amnesty for fascists condemned for political crimes. The meeting closed without voting any motion.' Meanwhile about 500 fascists collected in S. Maria Novella and advanced on the Palazzo Vecchio, where the meeting was taking place, but were turned back by the police; others tried to break into the offices of the Liberal *Nuovo Giornale*. The demonstration was organized and led by the Consul Tamburini, the most influential of the Florentine fascists; he headed a delegation which was received by Ciarlantini (the representative of the Fascist Party Direttorio), to whom 'it manifested extremist intentions, making it known that discipline would not be maintained if some leaders of Florentine fascism were attacked'.[39] Tamburini's record was a particularly black one; the Florentine fascists were extremists out of a sense of self-preservation. But the 'parade-ground populism' of Tamburini, in alliance with the armed squads of the *agrari*, represented an organization of great destructive potentialities.[40]

The account of the Lombard regional meeting confirms the rumours of a disagreement between Farinacci and Mussolini.[41] After the *Popolo d'Italia* had declared that 'there are no *ras*. They are fantasies', it cannot have been welcome when the next day Farinacci's leader in *Cremona Nuova* carried the headline 'Long live *rassismo*', even if, according to him, the *ras* desired nothing except peace and harmony. On 30 November he had something of a triumph.

'Maggi [Federale of Milan province] although submissive to the Duce said it was necessary to follow a direct path and not a zigzag, not to exalt Farinacci one day and then throw him overboard as had been done during the last days. This mention provoked applause for Farinacci . . . Farinacci spoke next welcomed by great applause. He said that although having every intention of obeying the Duce it must be kept in mind that since the opposition aims high and at putting fascism on trial a policy of force without weakness or compromise is necessary. Teruzzi spoke in the same sense. Finally Arnaldo Mussolini much applauded said that the party should be guided by its Directorate and not by the Government. That this Directorate has failed to have a precise political line. That everything must not be demanded from or imputed to the Government and that if the party zigzagged the fault must be attributed to the Directorate . . . all were concerned to demonstrate their feelings of absolute loyalty by accepting the message. However agreement with the thesis of a strong government has prevailed and a certain preoccupation is to be noted among those present with being abandoned especially by the magistracy which is said to have exceeded in ordering arrests and invoking the intervention of the Government to prevent persecution.'[42] The speech of Arnaldo Mussolini deserves attention. It was clearly a hastily improvised attempt to shift the responsibilities for failure onto Farinacci and his fellow-members of the Direttorio, and as such unconvincing, given that on the same day (30 November) the *Popolo d'Italia* was proclaiming the necessity for the absolute obedience of the party to the Government. However, the idea that the party should have a certain autonomy, adopted by Arnaldo so hastily, had serious support. There was a curious apparent convergence between the 'revisionist' and the 'integralist' or revolutionary points of view; for either, it seemed that fascism, as a political force, could recover its vigour (whether as a legal or a revolutionary movement), only if it regained its independence from the Government. Thus the complaint of the revisionist Bottai that the 'confusion, rather than connection, between the actions of the party and the Government, has caused the party to be corrupted, in ideals and practice, by the necessary diplomacy of the art of government',[43] was taken up by the extremist *Battaglie Fasciste*.[44] Later, the 'revolutionary' Suckert's demand that Mussolini should abandon the Government and fight the elections 'as the head of a revolutionary political movement',[45] can be confronted with de Stefani's letter to Mussolini, protesting against the speech of 3 January: 'My deep and mature conviction is that fascism should affirm itself in free political competition, freed from the responsibility of supreme power. This will increase the strength of fascism and its training for command. The work begun will be resumed by the will of the Italian people.'[46] The sincerity of de Stefani's recommendation is beyond doubt. What legalitarians and extremists really had in common was a distrust of Mussolini's authoritarian and ambiguous leadership, the feeling that he had subjugated the movement to his personal caprices. But it must be asked whether (obviously only up to a certain point) Mussolini himself did not see some advantage in the party's desire for greater independence at this stage; if his right hand, the Government, did not know what his left hand, the party, was doing, so much the better. It would make it easier for him to play a double game, as he was so fond of doing.

Mussolini continued to zig-zag for some weeks after the regional meetings. It is arguable that he had been preparing to purge fascism and reduce it to the adjunct of a new bloc of order; but the attitude of fascists and liberals alike gave little encouragement to the project. This left only one-party dictatorship as a true political alternative: however, Mussolini continued to hesitate before committing himself, and his policy was reduced to a series of expedients. Consequently the crisis of fascism continued to develop.

A serious open division of opinion among the fascist deputies first appeared over the attempt to pass a new bill for press censorship; the moderates agreed with Liberal criticisms, whereas the extremists demanded that the bill should be passed before Christmas by summary procedures. The withdrawal of the bill was a grave sign of the political weakness of the Government, and seemed to be the prelude to disintegration. The crisis appeared irreparable; and at about this time the search for a government that could take the succession became more urgent. Senator Pompeo di Campello, one of the gentlemen of the King's household, approached the fascist deputy Paolucci and asked him to write to the King, recommending the formation of a 'government of national concentration . . . of which all the Prime Ministers would form part, including Mussolini if he accepted, without him if he showed himself intransigent'.[47] Paolucci did not ask whether Campello was speaking on Victor Emmanuel's behalf; he was known to sympathize with the opposition.

The Giunta episode brought the split in the Fascist party further into the open. The magistracy requested permission to open proceedings against Giunta, one of the vice-presidents of the Chamber, for his part in organizing the attack on the dissident fascist Cesare Forni. The fascist deputies staged a demonstration in his favour and when a Liberal, Boeri, showed his disapproval by leaving the Chamber, Mussolini called him back and told him that, since he had been elected on the Government list, he ought to resign. This unconsidered outburst nearly led to the secession of the Liberals from Parliament; Mussolini retracted, and imposed the acceptance of Giunta's resignation. In the meantime Giunta himself, Edoardo Torre, and others, had organized a meeting of the deputies of their way of thinking.[48] Giunta himself backed down and maintained his resignation, but in the Chamber next day the extremists, led by Michele Bianchi, who was angrily interrupted by Mussolini, made their rebellious attitude plain. The formation of the extremist caucus precipitated a similar move by the moderates; 44 deputies met at the house of Paolucci and agreed, with one exception, to support 'a policy of conciliation and normality within the Constitution', and to send a delegation to Mussolini to demand the end of the Militia's public order functions, the purge of the party, 'greater respect for the constitutional forces', and the restoration of single-member constituencies.[49] Salandra called a meeting of his group and it was feared that he would announce his opposition to the Government.[50] At this point it was necessary above all for Mussolini to gain time, and to avoid the threatened convergence of moderate fascists and right-wing liberals: Paolucci relates (p. 259) that, coming to the Chamber, 'I found myself faced with a masterly *coup*: Mussolini deposited on the bench of the Presidency the bill for the return to single-member constituencies'. This unexpected move disconcerted everyone. It was read as yet another sign of the disintegration of the Government, especially since Mussolini had evidently acted without consulting the majority of the Cabinet: it dismayed the extremists, who took it as yet another concession to liberalism; but it was successful in disrupting, at least temporarily, Paolucci's following, and in preventing a possible hostile vote by Salandra and his group. However, Mussolini's brusque dismissal of Paolucci himself suggests that he was already meditating an abrupt change of course.

Mussolini's passage to action was determined, first of all, by the publication of the Rossi memorial; the comment of the *Giornale d'Italia* (31 December) explains clearly enough why the Government could not continue as it was: 'We have a Prime Minister inculpated in common crimes. No nation can tolerate that such a situation be protracted . . . Whoever helps him today to subtract himself from the regular course of justice becomes his accomplice.' But there were also other events which narrowed Mussolini's choice to two alternatives: resignation or reaction. The first was the attitude of Salandra, who had resigned from the Presidency of the *Giunta del Bilancio* on 26 December, although his letter was made public only on the 31st.[51] Therefore it was necessary for Mussolini to take the initiative; only an aggressive action could restore confidence and avoid the disintegration of the Cabinet. The parallel with the March on Rome is instructive: then the King refused to give special powers to a Cabinet which was in crisis. Mussolini's timing, and the efficacy of his threats, enabled him to begin the reaction, on 30 December, with the apparent agreement of a united Cabinet, and this gave him a great advantage.[52] His manoeuvre was to have it believed that the repression was underwritten by the Liberal ministers, authorized by Salandra to remain in the Cabinet, and then to split the latter's group against him.[53]

Simultaneously the extremist revolt was coming to a head. This was true not only of the movement of the Consuls, but also of the activities of the extremist deputies[54]; the discussion of the new electoral law when the Chamber reopened threatened to be the occasion for a revolt against Mussolini's policy. The spokesman of their discontents was Curzio Suckert (Malaparte). An opponent contrasted the revolutionary extremism of Suckert with that of 'persons who fear to lose the positions they have conquered by violence', but the distinction, if partially valid on the plane of motive, obscures the convergence possible on the plane of political action. The ambience of Florence, where the most violent *squadrismo* had always found sympathy and encouragement from a certain literary and artistic *bohème*, specially favoured such an alliance; and Suckert in spite of the disparity in culture and intelligence could boast of the friendship of a man like Tamburini. In his article, 'Fascism v. Mussolini?', alongside the assertion that 'Mussolini got his mandate from the fascist provinces . . . a revolutionary mandate . . . hence the absolute duty of the rt. hon. Mussolini to realize the revolutionary will of the people', there was the recommendation to the party's deputies that 'the immunity which you enjoy should be extended, in just measure, to all fascists. . . . Either everyone in prison, or no one'.[55]

This slogan was the true rallying-cry of provincial fascism; it was echoed by Tarabella, if we are to believe the accounts of the meeting, during the Consuls' altercation with Mussolini.

In an interview with Mussolini, Suckert explained that the extremist revolt took the electoral reform only as a pretext, or more precisely as the symptom, of 'a policy of the liquidation of fascism as a doctrine and as a party'.[56] It is also related that the latter replied, 'My dear Suckert – if we weaken now, we will never come back, never. Do you understand, yes or no ?'[57]

Suckert's exaltation of the revolutionary provinces bore fruit in the *fatti di Firenze*, on 31 December.[58] Several thousand fascists from all over Tuscany were brought to Florence for a mass rally; after this had ended, parties of the Militia and irregular squads, armed with shotguns and pitchforks, wrecked the printing presses of the *Nuovo Giornale* and the Combatant weekly, *Fanteria*, and devastated the Masonic lodge, the *circolo di cultura*, and the offices of a number of opposition lawyers. It was the first general punitive expedition directed mainly against middle-class anti-fascism.[59]

The rally was attended by Renato Ricci, a member of the *Direzione*; he 'recalled to the fascists . . . that we are henceforward at the end of the opposition campaign, as the national Government has shown that it is taking energetic steps to meet the situation. It is necessary to wait in discipline . . . at the orders of B. Mussolini'; but he then agreed to read a motion expressing the will of the assembly: 'The Florentine fascists, assembled to affirm the precise intentions of the party, faced with the hostile offensive . . . declare their loyalty to the Duce . . . but make their obedience and their discipline conditional on the decisive action of the Government, which must be demonstrated, if necessary, by dictatorial action.'[60]

The official fascist version of the events made out that the provincial Federation had taken the initiative in organizing the rally. Farinacci wrote that, 'Judging this important event in the quality of a member of the Directorate of the party, we should have to pronounce words of regret and repudiation; but we cannot: we would go against our thoughts and our conscience; if our followers rebelled against the *Direzione* of the party and the Government in order to defend fascism with devotion . . . the fault is not ours'.[61] But such a simple version of the events cannot be believed. The Liberal minister Casati told Salandra 'that he knew for certain that the happenings of Florence were organized by Suckert, the envoy of the Palazzo Chigi, or of the *Direzione* of the party, which is the same thing, with the agreement of Mussolini'.[62] The source of Casati's conviction is unknown, but clearly his view demands respect. However, it is only in part confirmed by other evidence. Certainly the official version cannot be sustained; Suckert himself wrote that 'it is no longer a mystery to anyone that the motion pro-claimed by the rt. hon. Ricci in the Florence assembly . . . and enthusiastically acclaimed by the immense crowd . . . in the Piazza della Signoria, was compiled not at Florence in the seat of the Provincial Federation, but at Rome in the seat of the *Direzione* of the party. This signifies that the *Direttorio Nazionale* itself was with the revolutionary provinces against the normalizing Govern-ment'.[63] But was Casati correct in assuming that the *Direzione* had acted with the prior approval of Mussolini ?

To answer this question, it is necessary to return to the 'move-ment of the Consuls'. One of the accounts relates that Mussolini asked why Tamburini was not among the Consuls, whereupon Tarabella gave him a letter from the former, which said that he had started the reaction himself.[64] Now Tamburini's letter does exist:

To the Duce,

I am at Florence to prepare and effect the rally that the *Direzione* has requested, otherwise I would be at Rome to wish you well, but also to say to you that now is the hour for the Man worthy of comparison with Napoleon to send all good men to drive out and suppress those in the pay of foreign nations to ruin Italy.

I, and with me all the fascists of the province of Florence, have toler-ated every insult to ourselves and to the other leaders, *but* absolutely will not tolerate those addressed to you, so the possibilities are two: either you, guided by God, pursue a grandiose programme, as we hope, or *we* before becoming an object of ridicule will engage battle because it is a fine thing to win or die as a soldier . . . With intransigent loyalty, Tullio Tamburini.[65]

This was a private and unpublished letter, and it is unlikely there-fore that it was written to provide Mussolini with an excuse. More-over, evidence of Tamburini's real attitude can be gained from a letter he wrote to Michele Bianchi several months previously: 'If the Duce wishes to be again what he was up till the Matteotti murder, he will certainly have to send to the devil some exponents of collaboration and take back the old fascists. We wish that at all costs the Ministry of the Interior should be in the hands of a fascist, and not of one who mines the ground under the Duce's feet.'[66]

This letter suggests that the governmental reaction, started on 30 January and entrusted to Federzoni as Minister of the Interior, would have appeared insufficient to Tamburini, even if, which is doubtful, he knew of the decisions of the Cabinet when he wrote the letter.

It remains to explain the attitude of the *Direzione*. It is possible that, as Casati suggested, they obtained Mussolini's approval for the rally, but did not inform Tamburini. It is also possible that they were pursuing the tactic of independent party action. The start of the reaction on 30 December must have suggested that the initiative would in any case meet with retrospective approval.[67]

The precise position of Farinacci is difficult to determine. Probably, after a period of doubt, he decided to serve as the instrument for regaining the support of the extremist group for the Government. Certainly his recommendation of discipline contained a barely veiled threat: 'If Mussolini were disposed to give way, only then would we rebel and abandon the supreme hierarchies':[68] but the next day he argued that the opposition owed their safety to Mussolini, as 'once he had to abandon power no force could any longer hold back the fascists and the nation would be plunged . . . into the horrors of a struggle whose consequences can be foreseen.'[69] One can certainly doubt whether, in his case, the threat of revolt was not mainly a device to impress outsiders with the conviction of the Government's moderating function.

There is no evidence linking Farinacci with the movement of the Consuls, and there is no reason to believe that their embassy was endorsed by the *Direttorio*. There is, instead, evidence that a dissident group within the party knew of it and tried to exploit it. At first sight, the most improbable aspect of the story is that after their interview with Mussolini, some of the Consuls, at the instigation of the deputy Edoardo Torre, went to the house of a prominent member of the Freemasonry of the Piazza del Gesu, Vizzoni, where he proposed to them that they should try to replace the Duce by a leader who belonged to his organization.[70] As a result, Tarabella and Galbiati founded an 'anti-masonic order'.[71] But the episode seems less unlikely in the light of a reference by Mussolini to 'the attempt made by them [Torre and the dissidents of Alessandria] to disintegrate the party *in the whole of Italy*'.[72]

In retrospect, the decisions of the Cabinet on 30 December can be clearly seen as the beginning of the drive towards dictatorship. But several of the Cabinet, which had refused Mussolini his demand for full powers, probably did not share this view of what they had done; rather they consented, reluctantly, to authorize temporary measures to reduce tension. So Casati, and Sarrocchi, could nevertheless believe that in exchange for delaying their resignation, they had exacted a promise from Mussolini to employ only legal means of repression.[73] The fascist ministers Oviglio and de Stefani, who both disapproved of the speech of 3 January, had probably the same opinion. Thus the offensive of the extremists which began in Florence on 31 December, and was soon followed up in Pisa, Bologna, and elsewhere, really modified the position and prepared the way for the much more comprehensive repression inaugurated on 3 January and confirmed by the reconstructed, all-fascist Cabinet on the 7th.

However, the illegal reaction of the *squadristi* was second not only in time but in importance to the semi-legal repression by the State organs. Suckert protested that 'Fascism must recall to its leader that the Ministry of the Interior is the least suitable organ for carrying out a revolution', and appealed to his 'friends of the *Direttorio Nazionale* . . . to show that the *Direzione* of the party is not a dependency of the Viminale but a real revolutionary committee, which intends finally to realize, against all comers, the will of fascism'.[74] But the fascist masses had played their essential role in intimidating the King and public opinion and could now be put back in the box: the *Impero* (8 January 1925) could legitimately accuse Suckert of illogical 'demagogy'.

Only too much had been gained by the extremists; the reconstitution of the action squads (even if unofficial), renewed immunity from prosecution, the co-operation of the other organs of the State with the Militia; not to speak of the second-stage consequences, the appointment of Farinacci as party secretary and the final advent of the long-promised fascist legislation. Nevertheless, the events of January prefigured the absorption of the party by the State, and not in the sense that Farinacci or the integralists wished. On the face of it, certainly, the integralists saw their legislative measures enacted: but in practice these resolved themselves into the creation of additional bureaucratic mechanisms which took their part in the suffocation of the autonomous life of the party, as of the other and worthier currents of national life. The extremist programme proved inadequate for the real renewal of the State, even as the fascists themselves understood it. The 'dynamism' of the movement could in reality be maintained only by continued terror; this was the true character of extremism. But after 3 January it lost, along with its last pale pretensions to 'heroism', its necessity or relevance.

When the Chamber re-opened on 12 January a fascist deputy, Maffei, declaimed: 'The blackshirts are ready for all the manoeuvres of their opponents. They are in a state of complete efficiency.' Federzoni interjected, 'One *carabiniere* is enough'.[75]

## REFERENCES

[1] Mussolini, *Opera Omnia*, ed. G. Pini and E. Susmel (Florence 1951–), Vol. 21, pp. 238–9. Subsequent references to Mussolini's speeches or writings are, unless otherwise stated, taken from this source.

[2] Ibid. Vol. 20, pp. 61–2. See also his speech to the Assembly of the Fascist party 28 January 1924: 'The fascist revolution is not bedecked with human sacrifices; it has not created special tribunals; the rattle of the firing-squads has not been heard; terror has not been exercised; emergency laws have not been promulgated.' Ibid., p. 164.

[3] *Popolo d'Italia*, 5 August 1924, speech of V. Pellizzari.

[4] C. Pellizzi, *Problemi e realita del Fascismo* (Florence: 1924), pp. 103, 164.

[5] ACS (Archivio Centrale dello Stato), Carte Michele Bianchi, fasc. 43, 1 May 1923.

[6] *Pagine di critica fascista* (Florence, 1941), p. 221.

[7] See G. Lumbroso, *La crisi del fascismo* (Florence, 1925), *passim*.

[8] Head of Mussolini's press office and a member of the Direttorio of the PNF. Arrested for complicity in the murder of Matteotti.

[9] ACS, *Min. Interno, Gabinetto, Uff. Cifra*, tel. in partenza, 30 May 1924, n. 12000.

[10] G. Salvemini, *Scritti sul fascismo*, vol. 1, ed. R. Vivarelli (Milan, 1963), p. 219.

[11] *St Antony's documents*, 14 June 1924 (correspondence relating to Cabinet changes). Ibid., reference of Acerbo, 18 September 1924, to the 'conspirators . . . of the 14th of June'.

[12] *Giornale d'Italia*, 30 December 1924. This count included the Liberals Casati and Sarrocchi, the two moderate Fascists de Stefani and Oviglio, the ex-Nationalist Federzoni, the Catholic Nara, and the two military ministers.

[13] M. Rocca, *Come il fascismo divenne una dittatura* (Milan: 1952), p. 124.

[14] G. Sarrocchi, *Ricordi di un esule da Palazzo Madama* (Florence: 1950), p. 27 n. On 1 January 1925 *Popolo d'Italia* wrote: 'The government is fascist and Mussolinian, because no one can govern against fascism and against Mussolini.'

[15] *Opera Omnia*, Vol. 21, p. 240. *Popolo d'Italia*, 3 January 1925: 'to restrain the fascists it is necessary to restrain the press which provokes them . . . the Government's order prohibiting rallies and meetings and promoting an enquiry into the Florence incidents, is a new proof of the intentions of the rt. hon. Mussolini and his collaborators . . . The Government desires a legalitarian settlement.'

[16] *La Nazione*, 25 November 1924: 'If the creature did not obey its creator it might even happen that the latter would leave it to its destiny.'

[17] *Popolo d'Italia*, 29 November 1924.

[18] ACS, Carte Michele Bianchi, fasc. 2, Arnaldo Mussolini to Bianchi, 27 November 1924.

[19] Balbo's successor was General Gandolfo; he was an ardent fascist who had

previously been Prefect of Cagliari. Balbo had been appointed 'temporary' C in C of the Militia on the resignation of De Bono.

20 *Atti Parlamentari, Senato, Discussioni, 27 legisl. sessione* 1, pp. 379–85 (4 Dec.), (Giardino), pp. 485–8 (9 Dec.), (Zupelli), pp. 415–6 (5 Dec.), (Caviglia). For Mussolini's reply see *Opera Omnia*, Vol. 21, pp. 197–9.

21 See *ACS, Min. Interio Gabinetto Uff. cifra*, 8 Dec. 1924, n. 26,409: General Gandolfo asks the Zone Commanders to report the impression made on the Consuls 'by the new directives of the Militia'.

22 ACS, Carte Farinacci, fasc. 3, 1924, s/f C., 26 Dec. 1924.

23 E. Galbiati, *Il 25 Iuglio e la MVSN* (Milan: 1950), pp. 37–9; R. Montagna, *Mussolini e il processo di Verona* (Milan: 1949), pp. 22–9; A. Tamaro, *Venti anni di storia*, Vol. 2 (Rome: 1952–4), pp. 60–2; E. M. Gray, 'La genesi del 3 gennaio', *Il meridiano d'Italia*, 23 January 1949. The Militia Consul commanded a Legion, at full strength about 1500 men.

24 L. Salvatorelli and G. Mira, *Storia d'Italia nel periodo fascista* (Turin: 1956), p. 330.

25 Gray, *loc. cit.*; G. Pini and D. Susmel, *Mussolini, l'uomo e l'opera* (Florence: 1953), Vol. 2, p. 403.

26 *St Antony's documents*; ACS, *Min. Interno, Dir. Gen. P.S. AGR* (Affari Generali e Riservati), 1924, b. 91 fasc. *Ferrara*, 29 Nov. 1924, b. 95, fasc. *Ravenna*, 30 Nov. 1924.

27 *Corriere della Sera*, 30 November 1924.

28 ACS, *Min. Interno Dir. Gen. P.S. AGR*, 1924 b. 89 fasc. *Bologna*, 1 Dec. Prefect of Bologna to Mussolini.

29 ACS, *Min. Interno, Dir. Gen., P.S. AGR*, 1924, b. 87, fasc. MVSN, s/f, Sistemazione dei gradi nella Milizia, Prefect of Bologna to Mussolini, 11 December 1924.

30 ACS, *Min. Interno Gabinetto Uff. cifra*, Tel. in arrivo, 10 Dec. n. 39997, Prefect of Perugia to Min. Interior; ibid. *Dir. Gen. P.S. AGR*, b. 95, fasc. *Perugia*, 15 Dec. ibid.

31 ACS, *Min. Interno Gabinetto Uff. cifra*. Tel. in arrivo, 17 Dec. n. 40680.

32 R. Montagna, *op. cit.*, p. 23. According to Gray six Consuls obtained an audience with Mussolini on the 23rd: but this is probably a confusion, as the other versions do not mention the fact. Or the meeting may have taken place, but have had no significance.

33 ACS, *Min. Interno Gabinetto Uff. cifra*. Tel. in partenza. 23 Dec.

34 Ibid. tel. arrivo, 23 Dec. Prefect of Perugia to Mussolini: 'For the reasons I explained to you personally permit me to insist on the most rapid possible settlement for Gen. Agostini.'

35 Ibid. 29 Dec. Agostini's enemy, the *federale* of Perugia, Felicioni, was the source of the information: this suggests it was thought to be compromising.

36 See also, in *St Antony's documents*, report of 28 March 1925 from Prefect of Milan to Mussolini describing Tarabella and Galbiati as the leaders of that part of the Militia which resented the appointment of Generals to the zone commands and feared that the system might be extended to the legions. They wanted instead to give the Militia 'a squadrist character with its own leaders'. Their associates were Moschini (Mantova), Testa (Mirandola), and Candelori (Rome). This corroborates the later accounts, which mention Testa and Candelori as among the leaders, with Tamburini, Tarabella, and Galbiati.

37 *Popolo d'Italia*, 30 November 1924. 'Fascism-Government should be like a general staff, which should never be put into the difficult position of thinking that its will is not respected by the soldiers, or even discussed.'

38 Ibid. 1 December 1924.

[39] ACS, *Min. Interno Gabinetto Uff. cifra.* Tel. in arrivo, 1924, n. 39048, 30 Nov. Prefect of Florence to Mussolini.

[40] Salvemini, *op. cit.*, pp. 134-6; C. Ronchi Bettarini, 'Note sui rapporti tra fascismo "cittadino" e fascismo "agrario" in Toscana', in *La Toscana nell Italia unita* (Florence: 1962), p. 372.

[41] *Giornale d'Italia*, 27 November 1924.

[42] ACS, *Min. Interno Dir. Gen. P.S. AGR*, 1924, b. 93 fasc. *Milano*, 30 Nov. Prefect of Milan to Mussolini.

[43] G. Bottai, *Pagine di critica fascista*, p. 325.

[44] 6 December, A. Luchini: the delimitation between party and government was necessary as the government 'shows itself . . . extremely ill-adapted, we do not say to realize the postulates of the fascist revolution, but even . . . to direct the movement'.

[45] Interview with *La Stampa*, 23 December 1924.

[46] *St Antony's documents*, de Stefani to Mussolini, 5 January 1925.

[47] R. Paolucci, *Il mio piccolo mondo perduto* (Bologna: 1947), p. 256.

[48] *Giornale d'Italia*, 19 December, quotes their circular: 'some deputies who are old fascists have felt the necessity for an exchange of ideas among those who are best able to understand the absolute necessity of the defence of the ideals, and the political and moral programme of fascism.'

[49] Paolucci, *op. cit.*, pp. 257-8.

[50] *Resto del Carlino*, 20 December 1924.

[51] Salandra resigned before the publication of the Rossi memorial. For its motivation, see G. B. Gifuni, *Il Risorgimento*, Feb. 1962, 'Dalla crisi Matteotti alla proposta liberale delle dimissioni di Mussolini nella seduta del Consiglio dei ministri del 30 decembre 1924'.

[52] The actual measures taken were: (1) an instruction by Federzoni to the Prefects to apply the press censorship decree with rigour; (2) the arrest and search of the organizers of *Italia Libera*. (ACS, *Min. Interno, Gabinetto, Uff. cifra*, Tel. in partenza, 30 Dec.).

[53] See G. B. Gifuni, *Il Risorgimento*, Oct. 1962, 'Verso la dittatura. Il Diario Salandra del gennaio 1925', pp. 196-7; 52-3. The Milanese Liberal associations, led by De Capitani, voted a motion of 'absolute collaboration' with the Government on 28 Dec.; ACS, *Min. Interno Gabinetto Uff. cifra*, Tel. in arrivo n. 41560, Prefect of Milan to Mussolini.

[54] *Giornale d'Italia*, 25 December, reports that the extremist deputies were to hold a meeting on 28 December and the moderates on 2 January.

[55] *La Conquista dello Stato*, 21 December 1924.

[56] Suckert commented that 'Devotion cannot be carried to the point of suicide'. *La Stampa*, 26 December 1924.

[57] *Giornale d'Italia*, 30 December 1924.

[58] The journal of the Florentine fascists, *Battaglie Fasciste*, published Suckert's next attack: 'All, even Mussolini, must obey the warning of integral fascism.' *La Conquista dello stato*, 28 December 1924.

[59] Salvemini, *op. cit.*, pp. 111-2; ACS, *Min. Interno Gabinetto Uff. cifra*, tel. in arrivo 31 Dec. 1924 n. 41835, ibid. n. 41867, ibid. 1 Jan. 1925 n. 23. *Battaglie Fasciste*, 4 January 1925; *Nuovo Giornale*, 31 December 1924.

[60] *Battaglie Fasciste*, 4 January 1925.

[61] *Cremona Nuova*, 2 January 1925; *Popolo d'Italia*, 1 January 1925: 'The fascist assemblies, summoned by local initiative and not that of the *Direzione* of the party, have been provoked by the perfidy of the opposition.'

[62] G. B. Gifuni, *op. cit.*, p. 199; Sarrocchi, when he saw Salandra on 5 January, 'did not dissent from my opinion concerning the responsibility of the Govern-

ment for, or rather their direct instigation of, the Florence disorders'. Ibid., p. 200.

63 *La Conquista dello Stato*, 18 January 1925.

64 Montagna, *op. cit.*, p. 24.

65 *St Antony's documents*.

66 ACS, Carte Michele Bianchi, fasc. 6, 17 Sep. 1924.

67 Even at Florence, the 'second wave' was preceded by a number of arrests carried out by the police (Salvemini, *op. cit.*).

68 *Cremona Nuova*, 23 December 1924.

69 Ibid. 24 December 1924.

70 Montagna, *op. cit.*, pp. 28–9. Besides Torre, Acerbo and Balbo had been members of the Piazza Gesu freemasonry. (A. Tasca, *Nascita e avvento del Fascismo* (Florence: 1965), p. 504. Tamburini and Suckert are also listed, but the source is dubious.

71 Galbiati, *op. cit.*, pp. 47–62; *St Antony's documents*.

72 My italics. ACS, *Segreteria Particolare del Duce, Carteggio riservato*, 242/R, *Roberto Farinacci*, Chiavolini to Prefect of Cremona, 20 February 1925.

73 *St Antony's documents*, 4 January 1925, Sarrocchi to Mussolini. A concern with legality is apparent in Federzoni's instructions to search the houses of *Italia Libera* leaders, 'deputies excluded'. (ACS, *Min. Interno, Gabinetto, Uff. cifra*, Tel. in partenza, 30 Dec. Federzoni to Prefect of Genoa.)

74 *La Conquista dello Stato*, 4 January 1925. Ibid, 18 January, claimed that Mussolini's measures were essentially directed against the fascist movement, and to frustrate an integralist *coup*.

75 *Giornale d'Italia*, 13 January 1925.

# The Men of the Archangel

## Eugen Weber

We are often told that fascist movements recruit most heavily among the middle or lower middle classes, a point which is supposed to show their essentially conservative or reactionary nature. This raises several questions. First: is the assertion factually correct? Do fascist or fascist-type movements actually draw their leaders and followers in significantly high proportions from the middle sections of society? Second: is the concept of middle classes a meaningful one in this context? And last: is there something particularly reactionary about those groups among whom fascism recruits most heavily and, indeed, what are the particular characteristics of such groups?

If questions of this nature are more easily asked than answered, it is because information is thin on the ground. Analytical studies of party membership and party leadership are very scarce indeed. No study like Daniel Lerner's *Nazi Elite* has been devoted to other movements. Harold Lasswell and Renzo Sereno on 'Governmental and Party Leaders in Fascist Italy', published nearly thirty years ago,[1] is not very helpful; Dante L. Germino's *Italian Fascist Party in Power* adds little on this score; the NSDAP has fared a little better, with Hans Gerth's essay (in Robert K. Merton, ed., *Reader in Bureaucracy*), Rudolf Heberle's studies of Schleswig-Holstein, written in the thirties and gathered in a slim but useful volume, *From Democracy to Nazism*, and Theodore Abel's very suggestive inquiry among Nazi Party members, *Why Hitler Came Into Power*. But that is about all. And in the absence of evidence, especially such evidence as would allow us to compare the recruitment and motivations of fascist movements in different countries and conditions, we are thrown back on guesswork, which can be very useful, but also misleading – according to one's prejudices. We may assume, for instance, that shop-assistants, being 'lower middle

[1] *American Political Science Review*, October 1937.

class', will go fascist rather than socialist or communist; although Hans Fallada's little man goes the other way and, in Belgium, the white collar unions are social-democratic. We may assume that peasants will be conservative, perhaps reactionary, irrespective of particular conditions, and cite fascist successes in the Po valley, while forgetting that they were won against the obstinate resistance of peasant communes whose red flags held out for a long time against the black; or, in France, we may cite Henri Dorgères while forgetting Renaud Jean.

Only more precise studies will tell us who has inclined to what, in what proportions and in what circumstances. And, while in no position to contribute more precision to the debate, I should like, at any rate, to establish that the matter is still controversial. I shall try to do this by introducing a certain number of facts about one of the lesser known fascist movements of the thirties, and then using that and other data in an attempt to begin a comparative discussion of fascist sociology and fascist appeal. The foolhardiness and imperfections of this course will have been warranted if it succeeds in sparking further studies that can correct its errors and introduce some order into a realm where today only inference and opinion reign.

The third strongest party to come out of the Romanian general elections of December 1937, was a movement best known in the West as the Iron Guard. The electoral label under which it campaigned, All for the Fatherland (TPT), was the last of a series devised to cope with the vagaries of governmental disfavour, but which never concealed the continued existence of one enduring body founded in 1927 – the Legion of the Archangel Michael – and of its founder, Corneliu Codreanu.[2] Its first contact with universal suffrage, in the general elections of July 1931, had brought what was then called the Codreanu Group less than 2 per cent of the total votes cast (34,183) and, under the Romanian system, no seats. In the ten months that followed, Codrenist candidates had been successful against Liberal opponents in by-elections fought in two Moldavian counties. They retained these seats and added to them when new general elections held in July 1932 brought them 70,674 votes and five seats in the Chamber. Dissolved by govern-

<hr/>

[2] For the story of Codreanu's movement and its antecedents see my *Varieties of Fascism* (Princeton: 1964), *passim*; and, in greater detail, 'Romania' in Hans Rogger and Eugen Weber, *The European Right* (Berkeley: 1965).

ment fiat on the eve of new elections in December 1933, the elections of 1937 were the first opportunity they had of re-entering the competition at the polls. They won 478,378 votes, 15·58 per cent of the ballot – 4·82 per cent less than the largest party, the National Peasant Party, and 6·43 per cent more than their runners-up and immediate competitors of the National Christian Party, and they elected 66 deputies in a Chamber that numbered 390.

In the electoral campaign that followed almost immediately, when the newly-appointed National Christian government dissolved a parliament which had had no time to meet in order to seek an improbable working majority, the TPT was expected to improve its already strong position. But elections were never held. February 1938 brought a royal coup d'état that did away with the party regime, instituted a new Constitution, and suppressed further political – let alone electoral – competition. Arrested shortly after, murdered at the end of the year,[3] Codreanu would not see his movement come to power when King Carol was forced to abdicate in September 1940, nor watch its popularity collapse in the months that followed. After January 1941, when its bid to retain power collapsed, the Legion became a rump of voluble exiles squabbling over the causes of their failure. But between 1930 and 1941 it had been a major factor in Romanian politics, a force whose popularity is reflected in the attention with which the present Romanian regime still treats it today.

As the only 'fascist' movement outside Italy and Germany to come to power without foreign aid, the Legion would repay investigation by scholars curious to explain its success in a society very different from those of the west and central European lands where fascism first appeared and prospered: a peasant country, underdeveloped, underindustrialized, where no working-class parties threatened the vested interests of the bourgeoisie, where the bourgeoisie itself in its classic commercial and industrial form was weak or absent,

---

[3] Codreanu's arrest in April 1938 did not come as Ghita Ionescu avers in *Communism in Rumania*, p. 55 'after a new outbreak of terrorism', but after Codreanu's calling for and maintaining his followers' complete submission to the government. Codreanu's murder on 30 November 1938, did come after such an outbreak which the imprisoned leader had struggled to prevent, and which served to justify his elimination. He and the thirteen legionnaires who died with him were not shot, as Ionescu says, but first garrotted and only then 'shot while trying to escape'.

where nationalism was not an issue of party politics but part of the general consensus, and where therefore a radical nationalist political movement could not succeed either by recruiting nationalists against anti-nationalists or by mobilizing social reactionaries against organized workers, because there were neither anti-nationalists nor organized workers to justify such appeals.

A widespread view holds fascism to be the ideology of a declining bourgeois society. Yet in Romania no bourgeoisie comparable to those of western or central Europe ever developed, and the Legion never pretended to defend what bourgeoisie there was, but attacked it and condemned the corrupt ways which it connected with bourgeois values and institutions. In this it resembled other fascist movements which never appear as the last weapon of liberal finance capitalism, but rather as its doom. All over Europe, throughout the twenties and the thirties, from Finland down to Spain, the fascists saw themselves as revolutionaries and, what is more, their conservative critics accused them of it. Some liked to think of the fascist revolution as perfecting the principles of 1789, a point of view that Marcel Déat developed at some length in his *Révolution française et révolution allemande* (Paris: 1943) and that we find again in Ruggero Zangrandi's *Il Lungo Viaggio attraverso il Fascismo* (Milan: 1962).

The organic view of the nation led easily towards collectivism and to emphasis on the most neglected and productive sections of the national community. This was the socialism of national-socialism, the inspiration of its anti-bourgeois and anti-capitalist orientation. Looking back on the twenties and thirties, on the *embourgeoisement* and governmentalization of contemporary socialists, it is easier to understand why fascists attacked them not only for dividing the nation but also for forgetting their revolutionary spirit.

So, fascists were or wanted to be revolutionaries. Yet they found themselves opposed to rival revolutionary parties with which they disagreed on an absolutely vital issue: that of class warfare or, from their point of view, of national unity. This fundamental disagreement, and the rivalries, competition, and manoeuvring that followed, cast the fascists as the unlikely allies of the forces of order or reaction; it made sure that their violence would serve against their revolutionary competitors and, at least to start with, preserve much of the system (if not the order) which they rejected.

Inevitably, in the circumstances, those fascists who stood for revolution were overtaken and overborne by those who stood more for national unity, with the anti-Marxism and the opportunistic alliances this implied. In the hierarchy of priorities, power and anti-Marxism came to stand before revolution. Even though these were temporary developments, they necessarily altered the physiognomy of the movements they affected until, in the West, fascism came to appear (though only temporarily) as the preserver of the society against which it had rebelled.

In other societies, however, where significant movements of the revolutionary left did not exist, where the working classes were not organized, where the socialists were inaudible and communists invisible – except across the border, as an alien, hostile power – the fascists faced no radical competition. Their radicalism was able to develop without need to guard itself on its left, or compromise too much with the forces of moderation. In countries like Romania, and even Hungary, fascist movements appear in quite a different guise from that with which we are familiar in the West: not because their slogans or their activities were very different, but because their role was different. They were free to act as the radical and revolutionary movement they never clearly became in the West. This is what happened in Romania, in the case of Codreanu and his Legion of the Archangel Michael, and it becomes apparent when one looks at the particular public to which they appealed.

Codreanu's followers have been described by their own country-men as 'made up largely of pseudo-intellectual riff-raff unable or unwilling to make a decent living, and who sought refuge in a mystic nationalism, the only reality of which was a ferocious anti-Semitism'; as mostly 'white-collar workers, unsuccessful students, and various dilettanti transformed into political zealots'; or again as a conjunction of déclassés and *lumpenproletariat*.[4] Yet, in the nearest thing to a free election since 1928, this unprepossessing gang managed to garner nearly 16 per cent of the popular vote and to enlist the hopes of several hundred thousand people for their 'mystic nationalism' which aimed, although Cretianu does not say so, not only to destroy existing authorities but also to renovate them

---

[4] Alexandru Cretianu, *The Lost Opportunity* (London: 1957), p. 20; Ionescu, *op. cit.*, p. 37; Lucretiu Patrascanu, *Problemele de baza ale Romaniei* (Bucarest: 1946), pp. 259–62; compare the more nuanced and perceptive discussion in Henry Roberts, *Rumania* (New Haven: 1951), pp. 231–2.

and to create a 'new man' endowed with all the virtues Romanians lacked: honest, responsible, industrious, reliable, above all *correct*.

It was this vague but not altogether unfocused reaction to the prevailing slackness and corruption, and the hope of a better world that went with it, that helped the Legion win not only the leadership of the country's student movement, but a dominant influence which most observers note.[5] The rather vague élan of romantic nationalism did not exclude a very utilitarian and didactic moralism, which should remind us that in countries like Romania objectives we may consider bourgeois can play an essentially revolutionary role, and that it was only by using terror to suppress corruption and to impose simple bourgeois virtues like honesty, punctuality, responsibility, and hard work that the communists actually rationalized and revolutionized the economy of countries from Romania to China, and introduced their own version of *une juste inégalité* and *la carrière ouverte aux talents*.

That this began in student circles is highly symptomatic. Where representative institutions do not exist or, existing, do not really function, schools and universities provide almost the only and certainly the most convenient platform for public discussion of national and international issues, and students are bound to form the vanguard of all radical movements. The more backward the country, the greater the part that students play in its political life, if only because, in the absence of other agencies of human concentration such as factories, schools will take their place, gathering a similarly uprooted and concentrated public, facilitating the formation of groups and the preparation of action, creating a student self-consciousness and solidarity before the appearance of other politically significant class solidarities.

Until the middle twenties, the Romanian student movement had turned on bread and butter issues. It was Codreanu, from the University of Iasi, and his henchman Mota, from the University of Cluj, who taught the students to subordinate material to political demands and turned them into a politically significant force. Thus, the part played by students in Romanian politics in general and legionary politics in particular, the role of legionnaires in politicizing the student movement and then mobilizing the students in their

---

[5] E.g., Roberts, *op cit.*; Henri Prost, *Destin de la Roumanie* (Paris: 1954) and *Les Mouvements nationalistes en Roumanie* (Bucarest: 1948), MS in the author's possession.

campaign to make over and take over the country, indicate their 'superior' dynamism and their understanding of a new kind of politics appropriate to the society to which they addressed themselves.

The possibility remains that a political movement starting from such a base would reflect interests as particular as those of the other groups that preyed upon the country. And it may well be that they reflected the mind and needs of the stratum from which most student militants had stemmed. But the first thing we can say about this is that it was hardly bourgeois in any sense of the word. The second, less definite, is that it seems highly representative of the masses of the population and especially of the peasantry which accounted for four-fifths of it; witness the Legion's strength in the theological seminaries and agronomical faculties where most of the peasant students went, its popularity with village priests and those village teachers who did not lean towards the Peasant Party, and the number of legionnaires who were country born.

Like Codreanu, son of a small-town high school teacher, like Ion Mota, son of a country priest, like Constantin Papanace, son of Macedonian settlers in Dobrogea, legionary leadership came from the provincial, only-just-urbanized intelligentsia: sons or grandsons of peasants, school teachers, and priests. But the very fact that their bastion was in the schools, and that they soon attracted or at least affected an important portion of the country's youth and of the intellectuals, meant that the Legion's social make-up would become broader with time.

A nominal roll in the possession of Mr Constantin Papanace gives the age and professions of 251 legionnaires, most of whom had taken refuge in Germany after the unsuccessful rising of January 1941, and who were interned in Buchenwald between 1942 and 1944. This is not a representative group: it includes a number of boys who were studying in Germany at the time and who sided with the Legion, it does not include women (some of whom were quite active in the Legion), it does not include priests (who played an important role in the rural leadership, with one even becoming a County Prefect in the period of the National-Legionary state, and 218 charged with participation in the rising of January 1941). It would be most likely to reflect the legionary leadership in Bucarest and a few other centres, whom the Germans helped to leave the country. Which may explain the absence of priests, the paucity of peasants, and the strong representation of the educated professions.

The most numerous group by far are the sixty students accounting for 26 per cent of the total, followed at a distance by thirty workers, twenty-nine lawyers, twenty-six public servants (including four policemen). Education accounts for 10·8 per cent, and the professions, other than law, for about 10 per cent more. (See table 1.)

PAPANACE'S ROLL

| Table 1 | | Table 2 | |
|---------|---|---------|---|
| *Professions* | | *Age* | |
| Student | 60 | Born in 1880 | 1 |
| | | 1896 | 1 |
| Worker | 30 | 1898 | 2 |
| | | 1900 | 2 |
| Lawyer | 29 | 1901 | 2 |
| | | 1902 | 3 |
| State employee | 22 | 1903 | 2 |
| | | 1904 | 2 |
| Tradesman or shopkeeper | 13 | 1905 | 3 |
| | | 1906 | 6 |
| Professor | 13 | 1907 | 9 |
| | | 1908 | 5 |
| Schoolteacher | 12 | 1909 | 10 |
| | | 1910 | 17 |
| Engineer | 12 | 1911 | 17 |
| | | 1912 | 24 |
| Commercial employee | 10 | 1913 | 28 |
| | | 1914 | 18 |
| Journalist | 8 | 1915 | 16 |
| | | 1916 | 10 |
| Police | 4 | 1917 | 7 |
| | | 1918 | 6 |
| Agriculture | 4 | 1919 | 17 |
| | | 1920 | 5 |
| Doctor | 3 | 1921 | 8 |
| | | 1922 | 2 |
| Officer | 3 | 1923 | 2 |
| Other | 8 | 1924 | 1 |
| | | Total who give age | 226 |
| Total | 251 | Average age in 1940: 27·4 | |

### Table 3
### Legionnaires executed at Vaslui, 21 September 1939*

| | |
|---|---:|
| Students | 14 |
| High-school students | 1 |
| University graduates | 5 |
| Lawyers | 4 |
| Engineers | 4 |
| State employees | 2 |
| Officers | 1 |
| Journalists | 1 |
| Total | 32 |

* C. Papanace, *Martiri Legionari* (Rome: 1952), p. 19. The sample, too small for statistical use, is given for comparative purposes. It represents known leaders imprisoned in the concentration camp at Vaslui, and executed as part of the reprisals for the legionary murder of Prime Minister Armand Calinescu. Of forty-four men similarly executed in another camp, Miercurea-Ciuc, twenty were university or high-school students.

It is interesting that, while there are four policemen, there are only three officers (whom discipline must have kept at their posts), only three doctors (whose profession may have kept them busy), and only four peasants. So this is not a representative cross-section of the movement's membership, only an indication of the make-up of its leadership which we may compare with the figures of the country's active population in 1930, of which 78·2 per cent was engaged in agriculture (as against only 1·7 per cent in Buchenwald), 9 per cent in industry and transport (as against 13 per cent or more in Buchenwald), 3·2 per cent in commerce (as against three times that many in Buchenwald) . . .

What we have here at first sight is the predominance of salaried employees, professionals and members of that 'new middle class' in which Ralf Dahrendorf sees 'one of the main sources of support for the Nazis, and possibly for the Italian Fascists too'.[6] But it can be judged in proper perspective only when correlated with the age of these men, which is uniformly very low (see table 2): in 1940, 21·2 per cent of them were under twenty-five, nearly 40 per cent under thirty – a factor which brings out their marginality, their restlessness, their lack of integration in the existing order of things,

6 See his 'Recent Changes in the Class Structure', in S. R. Graubard, ed., *A New Europe?* (Boston: 1964), p. 317; and his *Class and Class Conflict in Industrial Society* (Stanford: 1959).

altogether their availability for radical visions and enterprises before which their elders might be inclined to hesitate.[7]

That the Legion was a young movement is clear from the age of its leaders: in 1931, at the time of their first electoral enterprise, Codreanu was thirty-two, his second in command, Mota, twenty-nine; other leading figures, Vasile Marin – twenty-seven, Mihail Stelescu – twenty-four. It is not clear, for lack of data, whether their studies had been as unsuccessful as Ionescu claims, but incidental information shows that the leading figures had completed their university studies and that those who failed to do so, like Stelescu who became a deputy in 1932 at the age of twenty-five, did so because they turned into directions more fascinating and perhaps more rewarding. In any case, only 8 per cent of students registered in Romanian universities during the years 1921–32 ever graduated, a fact which indicates that graduation from one's studies (at all levels) was in Romania the exception rather than the rule, and that it would be hard to draw particularly illuminating conclusions from the number of legionary militants who abandoned their academic endeavours.

We might do better by turning squarely in the one direction which critics of the Legion have ignored – that of their electoral activity. There is good reason for ignoring it, since detailed data of Romanian electoral results is scarce and I have had to make do with superficial indications gleaned from the press, from Codreanu's circulars and memoirs, and the announcements of the Romanian Ministry of the Interior. The results, such as they are, may be seen in Map 1, which shows not a total picture of Legion support but those areas where it seems to have been most active and most successful. Until 1933, these centred in South Moldavia (Putna, Tutova, Covurlui), South Basarabia (Cahul, Ismail, Tighina), with one bastion in central Transylvania (Turda) and two outlying counties in North Moldavia (Neamt, Campulung).

The first thing to be said about this distribution is that it was primarily the result of chance and of the private predilections or connections of Codreanu and his friends. The mountains, the

---

[7] We might compare this with the situation in the NSDAP, in which 7·82 per cent of the membership was under twenty-five, 18·16 per cent under thirty, and the average age of thirty-four Reichsleiter cited by Franz Neumann, *Behemoth* (London: 1944), pp. 374–6, is 39·5. In his study of the *Nazi Elite* (*op. cit.*, p. 10), Lerner places its average age about 48.

monasteries, the forests and the rushing streams of Neamt and Campulung are the cradle and the core of Moldavian history. Codreanu was fascinated by them, liked to retreat there, and cultivated the local people who repaid the unwonted interest shown in their isolated lives with an interest of their own. The same was true of the arid mountains of the Moti, in the county of Turda, whence Mota liked to trace his descent and where he led many a student march.

Then, like all Romanian nationalists, but more than most, Codreanu was interested in the peculiar historical survival of the *Razasi* – free villages whose inhabitants traced their descent from a common free (noble) ancestor and claimed a customary freedom to run their own affairs through a council of village elders. Some of these village-aggregations are mentioned in seventeenth-century charters as 'Republics'.[8] Those razas communities which lasted into the 1930s were marked by a highly integrated society, collective organization, and a long tradition of struggle, first against encroaching landowners, then against the forestry trusts which devoured the common forests and destroyed local secular customs. These regions attracted Codreanu's attention, and a glance at the map will show that counties like Tutova and Covurlui, where razas villages account for 45 and 44·5 per cent of the population respectively, were among those where Legion activities first began, while all three of the famous seventeenth-century 'Republics' – Vrancea (Putna), Tigheci (Cahul) and Moldavian Campulung – appear on the Legion map.

So, on one hand historical affinities, on the other the predilections of a romantic nationalist. Last, but not least, chance: personal contacts of an earlier day which led to Codreanu's very first rural propaganda tour in 1929, in the God-forsaken north-east corner of Covurlui county, where he went invited by a local acquaintance and whose peasants never forgot him.

If we now turn to seek less subjective criteria, we find that these are all poor, isolated, predominantly agricultural counties, which makes them no different from many other parts of Romania, except that they are more so than most. Neamt, Tutova, and Putna had an unusually high incidence of pellagra (between thirty and sixty cases per thousand inhabitants), second only to one other county.

---

[8] See H. H. Stahl, in *Enciclopedia Romaniei*, I (Bucarest: 1938), pp. 563–75.

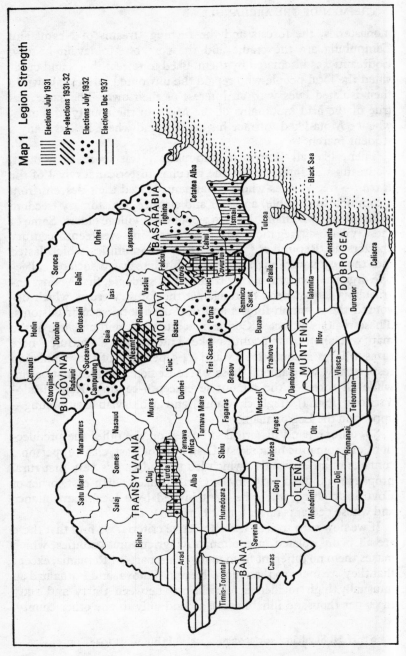

Map 1  Legion Strength

Elections July 1931
By-elections 1931-32
Elections July 1932
Elections Dec 1937

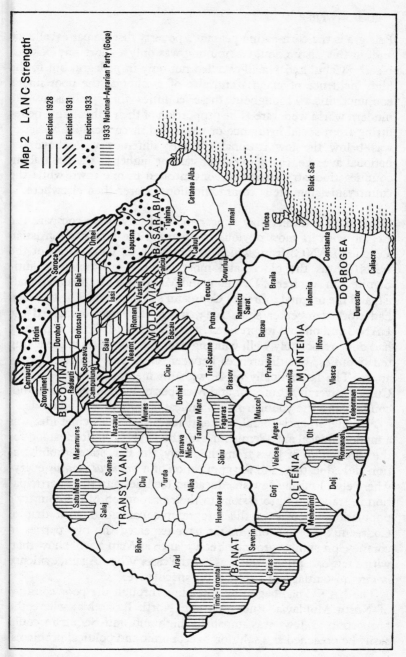

Map 2  LANC Strength

‖‖ Elections 1928
⧄ Elections 1931
⠿ Elections 1933
‖ 1933 National-Agrarian Party (Goga)

Pellagra is the corn-eating peasant's poverty disease par excellence and, in this distinction, Campulung was only a short way behind. Nearby Cahul and Ismail excelled not only in pellagra, but in the high incidence of malaria and also of trachoma, the poor man's conjunctivitis. Throughout these counties the symbols of the modern world were rare. The proportion of their inhabitants benefitting from social insurance or organized in cooperative societies was below the low national average; illiteracy well above the national average, rising to 60 per cent or higher in the Basarabian counties; industry absent or concentrated in one town while the countryside stagnated; communications poorer than elsewhere.

What all this means may appear more clearly if we compare the Legion with its most obvious competitor: the National Christian League (LANC) from which it sprang. A.C. Cuza, head of the LANC, was the oldest and most virulent of Romanian anti-Semites, an admirer of Drumont and Maurras, a patented nationalist, and the original source of Codreanu's inspiration. The two men had worked together since 1923, when Codreanu organized the LANC and offered its presidency to Cuza. In 1926, the new party had done reasonably well, winning over 120,000 votes and electing ten deputies, but differences between Cuza and Codreanu grew apace. The latter finally broke with his mentor in 1927, because Cuza, University Professor and Member of Parliament, would not countenance the younger man's radical objectives and methods.

Nationalist, anti-liberal, and anti-marxist, Cuza's chief idea was a monomaniacal anti-Semitism, and the LANC platform stood for the elimination of Jews from the Army, the Bar, state administration and education, and the application of a *numerus clausus* everywhere else, limiting Jewish education facilities and their participation in trades and professions to their proportion of the country's population. Insofar as this programme coincided with that of Codreanu's Legion, one might have expected the two parties to compete on similar ground. Yet a glance at Map 2 will show that, with a few exceptions, this was not the case. Why? Again, evidence is circumstantial and explanation speculative.

The LANC had begun by spreading through the poor counties of North Moldavia, Bucovina, and North Basarabia, where the proportion of Jews was unusually high and anti-Semitism could easily be preached as a solution to economic and political problems.

Throughout Bucovina, especially, the greater part of industry, particularly the important lumber business, was in foreign, mainly Jewish, hands. The countryside, sometimes very poor, always over-populated, where older home industries were wilting under the impact of machine-made goods, looked to the towns for work. Yet the little country towns, once reasonably prosperous centres of local commerce, wasted away for lack of railroads or because one city (here, Cernauti) monopolized all industrial and commercial activities. The peasant looking for work, the small urban bourgeois trying to compete with more modern enterprises, found themselves facing Jewish entrepreneurs, large and small, whose most striking characteristic was less their money power than their foreign-ness.

Jews, who accounted for only 4·2 per cent of Romania's population, made up 23·6 per cent of Moldavia's urban population, 27 per cent of Basarabia's urban population, 30·1 per cent of Bucovina's urban population. Most of them (two-thirds in Moldavia, almost five-sixths in Bucovina, almost all in Basarabia) spoke Yiddish as their first, sometimes as their only, language. Their dress, their language, and their ways designated them as a separate national group, which is what they insisted they were. Refusal to assimilate made this highly compact Jewish population more visible, and concentrated upon it the wrath of cultural and economic nationalists. To the peasants, the Jews represented the farm-stewards or farming trusts exploiting their labour, the innkeepers and shop-keepers lending them money at usurious rates (because the state refused to lend them any at all), the mills and timber companies milling their grain, milking their income, cutting their forests, refusing them work or giving it them at starvation wages. To the people of the market towns they represented competition, on the spot or in the larger urban centres. To the new aspiring bourgeoisie they were the men who stood in their way in the schools, the courts, the money market, the professions. To idealists, they were resident foreigners who spurned the national culture, rejected national unity, threatened national being and integrity.

These were the sentiments to which the National Christian League appealed; but it could do this best where its argument reflected local experience: in Storojinet where 46 Synagogues faced 77 Orthodox Churches, in Radauti where 49 Synagogues faced 71 Orthodox Churches, in Botosani where 66 Synagogues faced 109 Orthodox Churches, in Iasi where 108 Synagogues faced

239 Churches; in towns like Suceava or Botosani, skirted by the new railway lines and thus decaying; in regions like Soroca which once shipped its fruit and wines and grains down the Dniester to the Black Sea but now decayed for lack of roads or railroads; in a poor county like Baia where peasants could not make ends meet on the great estate lands divided among them after the first world war, and blamed the Jewish usurers and timber merchants; in Falciu, crossed by erstwhile-busy roads, now deserted for railways that avoided the region, where once-prosperous markets had shrunk to nothing and drought had come to finish what the communications catastrophe began.

There is a line from a Romanian song which embodies the whole ethos of the LANC: 'As they come with rails and trains/There is not a song remains!' But the nostalgic resentment, the backward-looking bitterness of Cuza's party, does not go far in describing the atmosphere of Codreanu's new movement. Where the typical LANC stronghold was poor because decaying, the typical legionary stronghold was poor because it had never been better off. In South Basarabia, Ismail and Cahul are and always have been economically isolated[9]; the same holds good for Tutova and for the notoriously poor land of the Moti, in Turda, on which the Legion concentrated its attention.

More important, perhaps, the Jewish problem was less acute in legionary counties than in those of the LANC. In Putna or Ismail, anti-Semitism made a less effective battle cry than in the Bucovina counties. When one leaves the North-East, the Jewish question diminishes in intensity and anti-Semitism loses its edge. The most striking thing about Map II is the regionalism of the LANC. Cuza's anti-Semitic party could not spread beyond the borders of the region where anti-Semitism answered local problems and realities. When it sought to become a national party, it had to ally itself with the National Agrarian Party of Octavián Goga, a nationalist from Transylvania who brought with him a breath of populism and an appeal less regionally restricted. Even so, flying the anti-Semitic flag above all others, the coalition Cuza and Goga

9 South Basarabian land had the lowest average price per hectare of any in Romania, markedly lower (by over 30 per cent) than land values in North Basarabia where the LANC predominated, and less than one-third the value of land in wealthier provinces. The same applies to Southern as compared to North and North-West Moldavia.

formed in 1935 continued to do best in the North-East that still furnished Cuza's firm base. Between 1932 and 1937, while Codreanu's movement grew sixfold, the Cuza-Goga group hardly advanced at all. This indicates the Legion's superior dynamism, but also the limits of the anti-Semitic appeal, limitations which Codreanu recognized both in theory – by acknowledging that Romania's problems went far beyond Jewish ones – and in practice by adapting his propaganda to provinces with other problems and another mentality. The results of 1937 are proof that he did this successfully; but his success was not unconnected with methods the legionnaires developed in the areas where they first started out.

When comparing the areas of legionary and Cuzist strength, another difference appears which may be relevant in this connection. Where Romania's average population density in 1930 was 61·2 per square kilometer, the average of LANC counties was 73, that in the Legion counties 54, falling as low as 40 in some places. This suggests that the older party had established itself in more populous areas where it found a more accessible public. The new movement had to seek followers in less densely populated areas, in communities that were less accessible and more neglected. It had to work harder to win, and to the extent it won, its exertions served as useful training. The tale of legionary electioneering is one of arduous marches or rides into the countryside, over hill and dale, through snowdrifts, across precariously frozen rivers or along dusty, muddy trails to villages that politicians never saw, to mobilize a peasantry untapped or forgotten or disillusioned at the failure of soliciting politicos in whom it had put its trust. Legionnaires continued to apply the methods evolved in these early campains, going to the peasant and winning his trust by working in his fields and staying in his home, when they moved out of the East after 1934, establishing new bastions among the peasants of Muntenia and Oltenia in counties with an old tradition of peasant socialism, like Vlasca and Teleorman, and generally in areas where, once more, the very high incidence of malaria (Vlasca, Teleorman), pellagra (Braila, Prahova), or syphilis (Dolj), reflected the prevailing misery and malnutrition.

The method worked because of the enthusiasm and dedication of the militants, because of Codreanu's insistence on effort and discipline, but also quite simply because these students and other 'riff-raff' were very close to the peasants, as we have seen; able and willing to talk the language, dance the dances, and work the fields of the men to whom they addressed themselves.

Far from being a bourgeois or petty-bourgeois movement in the sense such words suggest, the Legion was a popular and populist movement, with a programme which the masses (in the Romanian context of peasants and workers) recognized as radical enough for them, and which the representatives of the established order, from Cuza to the King, recognized as revolutionary. It may be significant in this connection that the only other party with populist velleities, the Peasant Party, was very weak in those North-Eastern provinces where Codreanu started out, or else lost the peasants' trust (as happened in Muntenia and Oltenia after 1933) by abandoning its more reformist activities. Equally interesting: the only region where the Legion did not implant itself as a protest movement, Maramures in the North and North-West, was also the only region where the small Social-Democratic Party showed some activity, which suggests once again that the Legion prospered where it filled a need some other movement failed to fill, where it found an available public.

The same holds good of Codreanu's appeal to industrial workers who, in the absence of an effective labour movement, turned to the one leader who offered solutions more extreme than those of the established parties. A special Legionary Workers' Corps, founded in 1936, soon boasted eight thousand members in Bucarest alone. Disbanded from 1938 to 1940, by October 1940 it counted thirteen thousand militants.[10] Electoral successes in industrial counties like Prahova and Hunedoara suggest that recruitment was not limited to the capital.

Codreanu's radical nationalism was calculated to appeal to all who put their hope in radical changes. His anti-communism would not bother them. Insofar as workers or peasants noted it, it would appear as a form of anti-Russianism and hence acceptable. Insofar as communism or socialism was identified with Jewish leadership, the social anti-Semitism of the urban poor, the economic anti-Semitism of the peasants, were sufficient to discredit them. Codreanu offered a doctrine of radical reform which neither clashed

---

[10] *Buna Vestire*, 19 November 1940; *Corneliu Zelea Codreanu: 20 Ani dela Moarte* (Madrid: 1958), p. 65.

with their nationalistic prejudices nor aroused their suspicion of city slickers out to use and discard them. Neither the appeals of class consciousness nor those of bourgeois liberalism could wake much of an echo in the Romania of that day. If we are to look upon his ideas as a class doctrine, it would be one similar to the social nationalism of many underdeveloped countries today, violently opposed to internal and external oppressors, and appealing to all for whom the established order represented the fount of injustice, oppression, and opportunities denied: peasants, workers, and those whose patriotic and moral principles were offended by the impurities of the ruling system.

Economic factors were less important in recruiting the dissatisfied (who could have turned towards reaction and Cuza as easily as they turned towards revolution and Codreanu), than in establishing a degree of isolation, in keeping certain groups and areas outside the swim, uninvolved in the current political process, uncommitted to given political attitudes, and thus open to legionary appeals. Hence the inordinate role of youth in a movement that began by mobilizing schoolboys and students, admitted no men over thirty in its elite formation (the Mota-Marin Corps, founded in 1937) and always relied heavily on its network of youth clubs (the Brotherhood of the Cross, or FDC, founded in 1924).

But a movement that rests on youth faces a major problem, which is that youth does not last and that, sooner or later, the normal conflict of generations will be aggravated by ideological references and recriminations. Most fascist movements resolved the problem by elimination, expulsion, or encouraging hegiras, which rid the leadership of younger challengers and the movement of its more radical elements. In the Legion, the problem was solved when the original group of leaders was decimated in the persecution of 1938–9. In 1940, Codreanu would have been 41, Mota 38, Marin 36, and their friends to scale: which is quite young enough. But most of this group was dead, all of its leading personalities had disappeared, and it is interesting to see that, of the 226 men interned in Buchenwald whose age we know, only fifteen belonged to Codreanu's generation. The average age of these men in 1940 would have been 27·4, with more than three-quarters of the group still in their twenties. Which means that, politically speaking, they had not even existed in the early thirties, and that they represented a new generation, a new *promotion*, who had replaced their fallen elders.

So the Legion always remained a very young movement, and thus supremely available for every kind of revolutionary action. And it is significant that, in the conflict that opposed moderates and radicals within the Legion after Codreanu's death, and especially during the period of the National-Legionary State, the older men stood largely for temporizing and compromise; they opposed the January rising and in some cases even sided with General Antonescu (like Codreanu's own father): facts which may explain the small proportion of older men in Buchenwald and also the swashbuckling spirit, the brutal, reckless, and inexperienced kind of politics which marked the Legion's brief spell of power.

All of which suggests that the major factors in a radical or revolutionary orientation are less strictly sociological than psychological: those cultural and, above all, chronological factors which make for greater availability, greater restlessness, greater receptivity, at least, to possibilities of change and of action to secure change.

I started out by asking three questions. First: do fascist-type movements recruit most heavily from the middle sections of society? While the leaders, like those of most political movements, come from the middle sections, this in itself proves little more than the similar origins of left-wing leaders. Their following, on the other hand, in a country like Romania, included a significant portion of peasants and manual workers.[11]

The same seems true, *mutatis mutandis*, of other countries. Thus, Hans Gerth's study of Nazi party membership in 1933 shows almost one-third to be manual workers and 21 per cent white-collar workers. Then, in descending order, come artisans, merchants, and professional men who together account for 17·6 per cent; peasants, 12·6 per cent; and others (domestic servants, taxi drivers, and so on), about 10 per cent.[12] When we remember what we are told about the petty-bourgeois nature of the NSDAP, this seems a pretty fair spread, even though manual workers, who made up 46 per cent of the German working population, are under-represented.

[11] Cf. Hungary, where industrial workers accounted for 40 per cent or more of the membership of the National-Socialist coalition formed round Szalasi, while only 23 per cent of the active population was engaged in industry and mining. Istvan Déak, *National Socialism in Hungary, 1920–1938*, p. 101.

[12] Cf. the slightly different figures in Wolfgang Schafter, *Entwicklung und Struktur der Staatspartei des Dritten Reiches* (Hannover, 1956), p. 17.

THE MEN OF THE ARCHANGEL

We must bear in mind that classes with less education and less leisure are generally under-represented in politics; that industrial labour was solidly organized in unions and in the Social-Democratic Party; and that it was being solicited by a rival protest party (KPD) which could appeal to sentiments of class-consciousness laid down for generations. In the circumstances, Nazi success in attracting as many of that group as it did seems impressive, and the accepted identification of fascism and the middle groups of society less than overwhelming.

In any case, is the concept of middle classes a meaningful one in this context? I think it is misleading because, by association, it suggests orientations and interests which are not typical of fascist movements. In the Marxist view, such people fight to preserve their existence as members of the middle class and thus, whether deliberately or not, provide the last weapon of finance capitalism. This is hardly true of the Romanian peasants; and fascists in general attack finance capitalism, repudiate the idea of the middle class as a separate class, and reject its values. Where they do not reject what we call 'bourgeois' values, it is precisely where their application, as in Romania, would have the least conservative effects.

In political terms, economic and social class seem less relevant to political orientation than ideological conditioning and the existence (or absence) of strongly structured parties. Where such parties exist, Catholics, peasants, or industrial workers are not available to the appeal of other ideologies. Where such parties are absent or weak, these groups are just as open as all others. To the extent that Western industrial workers are well organized and that, at the other end of the political spectrum, the small but significant minority of the rich and secure maintains its self-confidence, doctrines of violent protest and radical change will necessarily do best among the remaining groups. To the extent that those least committed to the established order are most available, the radicals will do best among them. It is only in this sense that we can say that fascists recruit their troops among the middle classes – and especially from the section which a German sociologist has revealingly described as the quasi-proletariat.[13]

[13] Theodor Geiger, *Die soziale Schichtung des deutschen Volkes* (Stuttgart: 1932); Robert Waite, *Vanguard of Nazism* (Harvard: 1952), finds that most men in the Free Corps came from lower middle class and peasant backgrounds. The

The third question – are these people especially reactionary? Do they embody, does their activity express, tendencies which we should describe as politically or socially retrograde? The answer to this question depends upon one's views of the regimes attacked or displaced by fascism; and, in the Romanian case at least, Codreanu's Legion appears as a distinctly radical social force.

Students of fascism have pointed out that the exigent code and high idealism of such groups must be related to the baser reality of their activities in the service of a ruthless cause or in the enjoyment of their short-lived triumphs. The point is well taken and the failure well known. But it might be suggestive to compare this fracture between dream and deed with the fate of children who are taught one set of values at home and at school and then, in due course, warned that these cannot be integrally applied in the world – that, in other words, integrity is not a social virtue. Protests against surrenders and compromises, against the slackness of current morality, are considered evidence of immaturity, a state out of which they will grow to accept the world as it is rather than as it should be according to proclaimed theory but not to current practice. In effect, most people do just that, and adolescent revolt is generally succeeded by more or less reluctant, more or less contented, adjustment. Inability or refusal to adjust, albeit for the best of moral reasons, is then considered a sign of weakness, of incompetence, and finally of failure. On reflection, this is an odd state of affairs; and it is only our resolute inconsistency that enables us to avoid the implications of a situation in which the wheels of society turn only at the expense of its avowed principles.

It would be possible to argue, as Roger Caillois has done in his essay on 'L'Esprit des sectes',[14] that the discrepancy between principles and practice drives not the weakest but the strongest into intransigent positions where criticism of worldly laxness resolves into a new rigour, an idealistic and puritan reformism which

labouring classes, he says, did not tend to join even the volunteer army of the Republic. Why? 'Men with a job and a family did not feel disposed to risk their economic position.' They would not even risk it to join the Socialist Security Force which had to recruit the same buccaneer types as the Free Corps. So, when a miner or a factory worker has a job and sticks to it, he counts as *labour* and we understand why he will not join a Free Corps. When he is out of a job, he becomes lower middle class and is free to join, because we all know the link between lower middle class and reaction.

[14] *Instincts et Société* (Paris: 1964).

turns into rebellion and (given an unusual conspiracy of events) even revolution. *Ich kann nicht anders!* is the cry of the ill-adjusted: it may become the starting point of a crusade to readjust society.

The worldly equation between idealism and childishness may break down when grown men refuse to put away childish things, not because the men are puerile but because the things seem valuable – more valid than the ways for which they are to be discarded. This begs a question as to the nature of the things, and when we look we find that they are the very commonplaces of moral education: truth, justice, industry, love of the fatherland, loyalty, courage, fair dealing – all virtues which the world consistently teaches in its schools and just as consistently tones down, a situation whose exasperating features most of us manage to ignore.

There is no space to go into the wider aspects or the philosophy of such compromise; only into its relevance to fascism and to the rise of such intransigent and 'pure' movements as the Legion of the Archangel Michael. And there we might consider that the stronger the moral teaching, the greater the shock of the discrepancy between principles and practice, the stronger the inclination to rebel. In France, where young people were early introduced to a rather sceptical view of the world and its ways, such intransigence would be less widespread than in a Germany where education, at school and in the home, was much more fundamentalist in matters of morality and patriotism. In a country like Romania, where official education was highly moralistic and patriotic, the difference between lessons learnt at school and the corruption and opportunism of urban or public life would be extraordinarily shocking. Naturally, the shocked would be a minority and those proceeding to rebellion even fewer, for few can or care to stand against current practice, and the particular values on which such reaction is based are not inculcated in all.

They have little currency among the very poor and educationally neglected, whose inclination is to take things as they come (albeit with ill grace) without arguing that they should be otherwise, especially not on principle. They find little echo in an industrial working class which has been persuaded that injustice is inherent in a society where the dominant classes use words as they use their power, in the service of their particular interests. From the Marxist point of view, public hypocrisy in a non-Marxist society is un-avoidable: it would be its absence that seems shocking. It follows from this that rebellion must be directed not against superficial moral flaws, but against the power structure of which morality is merely the (corrupt) expression. This is why idealistic reaction appears so frequently among middle-class intellectuals and among young men brought up in social groups with a simple fundamental-ist moral code: either trained to place principles above practice, or deeply shaken to see practice flout and stain principles so recently and authoritatively inculcated.

Whether in disillusion or righteous indignation, one may find here the origin of the impulse to establish 'the foundations of an ideal alliance in the midst of a sordid world'.[15] Such an alliance be-comes a school of virtue, of initiative and discipline, of hardness and loyalty, a training ground for the service of a transcendent cause which emancipates the zealots from a society they now accept only to conquer and change.

There is nothing intrinsically evil about this. A society whose balance is one of selfishness and habit, whose tolerance is laxness or lethargy, where prudence is the mistress of decision, can benefit from an infusion of fervour, from a reaffirmation of the principles on which it claims to stand. The intransigence of the zealots, their activity, even their violence, may act as a sharp and bitter tonic to a flabby public morality, a challenge to which some may rise by dis-carding the lazier compromises, the softness, the permissiveness not of strength but of doubt. And, to go no further, it does appear as if much of the European Left between the wars defined itself against the challenge of fascism in terms of the challenge of fascism, and the process was a natural one since the sources of dissatisfaction were the same for both sides, lying in both cases in a moral revolt against existing society, against the hypocrisy and soft-ness of the Establishment, against a decadent economic liberalism and the overweening power of capital. The sources of dissatis-faction were similar, the radical conclusions were similar, only the directions in which people followed their conclusions were differ-ent, and even these were essentially a combination of populism and sectarian elitism. And here we must repeat the argument of this essay: that where no Left existed, the protest, the politicalization of the unpoliticalized, the cowed or ignorant, the resigned or

[15] Ibid., p. 93.

124

indifferent – their *nationalization*, with all its revolutionary implications – all this was left to movements like Codreanu's.

There were cold technicians or profiteers of power in both camps, whose populism was as superficial as their idealism. What proved more important was that both populism and elitist zeal altered with the achievement of power, and they altered because the movement itself changed from an alliance of critics and rebels to a coalition of defenders and exploiters of what had been won. Such change was inevitable and goes far to explain the performance of idealists in power, much farther than the inference that the oppressed dream only of becoming oppressors.

In their war against society the zealots had called for change, had cultivated violence and the heroic virtues which both justified and made it possible, had prided themselves on being an elite of the initiated, the virtuous, the brave. Society once conquered, the erstwhile rebels became governors. The only change now wanted was such as they themselves would bring, the violence they practised was no longer excusable or heroic but tyrannous and mean, the elite they constituted aspired to include society as a whole, so that whatever virtues it once possessed dissolved in the mass and what had been the deliberate commitment of the few became the forced or managed conformity of the many.

The greater the victory, the less resistance was left in the way of those absolute principles which once furnished the dynamic and inspiration of action. Intransigence turned into intolerant persecution and the heroic content of the movement into posturing. The movement itself remained in motion partly by substituting sham aims for real ones, or, losing impetus, degenerated into a defence organization for the vested interests of a new power clique.

Success, it seems, is the worst enemy of fascism. Of the three European movements which achieved power by their own efforts, the Italian fascists recovered some of their original radicalism only in defeat; the Romanians, who had little time to show their salt, were first decimated, then swamped by incompetent and greedy opportunists; and the Germans who did best (from their own point of view), began by eliminating their radicals and ended by producing a generation of power technocrats and political engineers, uninterested in principle or doctrine and utterly indifferent to the motives of their elders, except as factors in their own careers.

This is not because, as has been said, the only aim of fascism is power, but because the true aim of fascists which, in one guise or another, is to effect a national revival and regeneration, contradicts not the means they use to get to power, but those they use once they are in power. The ruthlessness, the passion, the fierce resolve which mark the struggle for power become poor counsellors when power has been grasped. The personalities best suited to the struggle are not always best suited to rule. The movement which thrived on the availability of an uncommitted public now rests on rigidity and regimentation. And the contradictions of the situation make it virtually certain that it will fail, either to its opponents or to its ideals.

# The Austrian Heimwehr

## Ludwig Jedlicka

The years of authoritarian rule in Austria ushered in by the Chancellor Dr Dollfuss and the Heimwehr movement in 1933, and continuing after the Chancellor's murder at the hands of national-socialists by the government of Dr Kurt Schuschnigg, are sometimes described as a period of fascism or clerical-fascism. The term 'clerical-fascism', however, hardly stands up to scrutiny, for the system in question consisted of a mixture of the most varied right-wing ideas, ideologies, and tendencies which had been trying to make headway in Austrian home affairs since 1920 and which, by the middle twenties, had taken shape within the so-called Heimwehr movement. The term 'clerico-fascism' appears in Charles A. Gulick's *Austria from the Habsburgs to Hitler* (German ed., Vienna, 1948). The German historian Ulrich Eichstädt wrote that after the events of March 1933 Austria ceased to exist as a democracy and took the path towards Austro-fascism.[1] Ernst Nolte, in his comprehensive survey of the history of fascist thought, comes to the conclusion that Austrian 'Heimwehr-fascism' succeeded in putting the state on a new basis, but was not identical with the 'Austro-fascism' which had superseded the parliamentary system of government. In evaluating the personalities who dominated the Austrian scene from 1933 to 1938, he suggests that Prince Starhemberg, the leader of the Heimwehr for many years, was probably more of a fascist than an aristocrat, but that the same cannot be said of either Dollfuss or Schuschnigg.[2] Given these differing views about Austrian fascism, about its origins and its effect on political events, the present study will be confined to the Heimwehr, that is, to the movement which is still regarded as the sole repository of authoritarian and fascist thought in recent Austrian history. It is unfortunate that of the existing studies of this movement there are only a few which can be called scholarly.

[1] Ulrich Eichstädt: *Von Dollfuss zu Hitler* (Wiesbaden, 1955), p. 17.
[2] Ernst Nolte: *Der Faschismus in seiner Epoche* (Munich, 1963), p. 41.

The Austrian historian Adam Wandruszka deals with the Heimwehr in his admirable essay on the political structure of Austria, but he was unable to consult sources which have since come to light.[3] Three studies breaking new ground have been made by members of the younger generation of Austrian historians. They deal with the ideological history of the Heimwehr and its precursors, as well as with the 'Fatherland Front' which was in some ways its successor.[4] A Hungarian, Dr L. Kerekes, has made a study of the Heimwehr that is of special importance for the light it casts on the support which that movement received from Italy.[5] His work is based mainly on material in the Hungarian state archives.

The Austrian Heimwehr movement came into being during the winter and spring of 1918–19. In the rural districts of Austria voluntary defence units were formed as guards for homes, farms and railways. They were fitted out with weapons of the former imperial army and acted in support of the as yet feeble state administration set up at the end of the war. Similarly, so-called workers and factory guards were formed in the towns, which, unlike the more conservative country districts, were for the most part controlled by the social-democrats. These organizations were thus from the very start divided into adherents either of the Right or the Left. Both were issued with arms by the Austrian government, and these were never called in.[6] When in 1919 the Allied Commission demanded the surrender of weapons, these

[3] Adam Wandruszka, 'Österreichs politische Struktur', in: *Geschichte der Republik Österreich* (Vienna, 1954).

[4] F. Schweiger: *Geschichte der niederösterreichischen Heimwehr von 1928–1930*, phil. Dissertation (Vienna, 1965); Irmgard Bärnthaler: *Geschichte und Organisation der Vaterländischen Front*, phil. Dissertation (Vienna, 1964); Ingeborg Messerer: *Die Frontkämpfervereinigung Deutsch-Österreichs* (Vienna, 1963).

[5] Lajos Kerekes: 'Italien, Ungarn und die Österreichische Heimwehrbewegung 1928–1931' in: *Österreich in Geschichte und Literatur* (Vienna, 9 Jg. F. 1, January 1965).

[6] The political significance of the *Bauernwehren* and *Heimwehren* in the event of a left landslide is brought out in a report of 8 July 1919, by the British military attaché, Colonel Cunningham, *Documents of British Foreign Policy, 1919–1939*, First Series, vol. VI, no. 22, p. 37 ff.   An official report dated 30 November 1918 (*Österreichisches Kriegsarchiv, Waffenstillstand und Interall. 1919–21* B.M.f. Heerwesen, Sektion 2), gives the following figures for weapons issued to the various defence units: 1156 machine guns, 80,345 repeating rifles, 13,627 carbines, 3967 hand grenades, 888 side-arms, 8,702,640 rifle cartridges, 72,891 pistol cartridges. The treaty of St Germain limited the size of the army to 30,000, to which can be added 10,000 police troops, armed only in part with rifles. This indicates roughly the number of weapons remaining in the hands of the civilian population.

considerable stocks found their way into the various secret depots of the defence units and also played their part in a short interlude of frontier warfare. In Carinthia large sections of the population were determined to take up arms against the encircled Yugoslavs. The fighting which followed showed the voluntary organizations, which since the spring of 1919 had borne the name of *Heimatschutz*, fighting shoulder to shoulder with detachments of the regular army. The sequel to the use of these voluntary formations was the first big expansion of the Heimwehr. It developed into a para-military organization for the defence of Austria against foreign enemies, but also against 'marxism' as the foe within, and this, in its turn, led to significant political, military and ideological re-lationships with similar movements in Germany.

Contacts with German formations were made via the Tyrol and Upper Austria. In 1919 and 1920, citizen defence units sprang up in Upper Austria, organized in the main by members of the landed gentry and the lower middle classes to deal with disturbances created by the workers in the industrial districts of Linz and Steyer. Similar developments took place in the Tyrol, where there was fear of an Italian invasion. The initiator here was the Christian-Social politician and lawyer Dr Richard Steidle, a native of South Tyrol, who was to become the most extreme supporter of fascist ideology within the Heimwehr movement. At first, however, it was from Bavaria that the groups in the Tyrol, Upper Austria, and Carinthia were most strongly influenced. The Bavarian defence unit set up by Dr Escherich, which has come down to history under the name of 'Orgesch', became the patron and arms supplier of the Tyrolean and Upper Austrian formations. After the collapse of the Kapp *putsch* in Berlin in 1920, one of its leading participants, Waldemar Pabst, a Prussian and former major on the General Staff, came to the Tyrol and there took up Austrian citizenship under a false name. Soon, as their chief-of-staff, he became the organizational driving force behind the Austrian Heimwehr, and attracted the attention of those, particularly in Bavaria, who were interested in the possibility of getting reinforcements in the event of a general show-down with marxist opponents in Germany and Austria.

The Heimwehr and its backers in Austria directly or indirectly supported every radical movement emanating from Munich. Contact with Hitler was maintained between 1920 and 1923, and although there were no ideological ties between Heimwehr and national-socialism, numbers of the *putschists* of 9 November 1923, among them Goering, found refuge in the Tyrol.[7] In view of the relative stability of conditions in Austria between 1924 and 1926, these developments were of negligible ideological importance, but it is interesting to note that in Upper Austria it was the emergence of Prince Starhemberg which built the first bridge between the Heimwehr and the political parties. Princess Fanny Starhemberg, a prominent representative of the christian-social outlook, was the intermediary between the Heimwehr and Hauser, a church dignitary and the governor of Upper Austria. He declared his readiness to have discussions with the leaders of the Heimwehr, particularly with Ernst Rüdiger Starhemberg, the princess's son. This was the beginning of the steadily growing support given to the Heimwehr by the leading bourgeois political party in Austria. Documents recently unearthed in the Hungarian archives show that even at this early stage an intense interest in the Heimwehr was awakening in Hungary and Italy, and among the most influential bourgeois politicians in Vienna.

Much clearer-cut in its ideology was the organization emerging in the eastern districts of Austria, above all in Vienna. Here was the most powerful group of military and semi-military organizations, the Frontkämpfer Association of German-Austria. This had been founded by Colonel Hermann Hiltl, formerly on the Staff of the imperial army. He had at first intended it merely as an association to foster comradeship among ex-soldiers. Soon, however, the association developed into an aggressive political force of a para-military type, and on 20 May 1920 it published as its programme a four-point declaration of principle:

1. The Frontkämpfer Association is a completely autonomous and independent organization.
2. Its guiding principle is: 'The general good must be placed before petty party politics.'
3. It is aryan in character, stands outside party politics, and has no

---

[7] For the early history of the Heimwehr movement see the official publication: *Heimatschutz in Österreich* (2nd ed., Vienna, 1935), and Hans Arthofer: *1918–1936. Vom Selbstschutz zur Frontmiliz* (Vienna, 1936).

truck with international, subversive elements such as social-democrats and communists.

4. Its ideal is the unification of the entire German *Volk*.[8]

The Frontkämpfer soon acquired para-military features. Field-days, tactical exercises, alerts during strikes and demonstrations, offers of support to the administration, feelers put out to the army on every conceivable occasion, these were the hallmarks of a de-velopment which at first prevented the Heimwehr from making headway in Vienna, Lower Austria, and the Burgenland. Never-theless, the Association adhered to its radical programme. At a conference in 1926 it adopted a number of principles which amounted in substance to opposition to the marxist ideology, the demand for a reduction in the number of seats in the national and regional legislatures, for a strengthening of the powers of the presi-dent, and for a change in the electoral law (this last, interestingly enough, mooted the idea of corporate representation).[9]

Although, at a lecture given in Vienna on 8 March 1926 on 'Fascism and Frontkämpfer Association', Colonel Hiltl refused to have his organization put on a par with fascism, giving as his main reason the behaviour of the fascists in South Tyrol, the ideological development of the Association continued to be marked by its obvi-ous borrowings of fascist ideas. The concept of strong leadership was advanced more and more forcefully:

Iron nerves and self-confidence undreamed of by the average man are the hallmarks of the true leader, who in the terrible loneliness of the strong is ready to oppose a whole world of hostile forces. Since the *Volk* is no longer a spiritual entity, every leader needs a minority on whom he can rely. These men, moulded by his will and welded together in spirit and purpose, will exercise the kind of authority which ... unites the soul of a nation. This minority must be supported by the traditions of the fatherland, must look backwards to the heroes of the *Volk*, and must draw its strength from the great past of its *Volk* and its native land.[10]

The formation of an elite which was to mould the 'new state' was another question taken in hand – at any rate theoretically – at an

---

[8] Oberst Hiltl: *Ein Gedenkbuch* (Vienna, 1931), p. 79 ff.

[9] Reproduced in *Die neue Front* (Journal of the Frontkämpfer Association), 1 June 1933.

[10] I. Messerer, *op. cit.*, p. 119 ff. (from the report of a participant at the conference in 1926).

early date. Not only did the Association engage actively in *Wehrsport*, but secret courses were also instituted to train a group of young people to become the 'iron kernel' of the organization. In these exercises, the instruction sheets of which have been preserved, there are unmistakable suggestions of the ideology of the SS of the future. An instruction sheet of the so-called 'iron kernel' declares:

The Iron Kernel is the heart of the Frontkämpfer Association, the centre from which the power streams out that permeates the whole organization. The Iron Kernel is the lever of the highest leader, his secret right hand, his support. The leader is the head, the Iron Kernel the heart of the Association. The Iron Kernel does not itself lead; it is the executive organ of the leader and carries out every service that is necessary in the interests of the Association. The Iron Kernel is the soul of the organization – a soul imbued with the spirit and will of the leader.

'Iron' signifies hard, unbreakable, firm. A sword is made of iron! The Iron Kernel is the leader's sword. 'Kernel' means that which is inmost, the invisible, the steadfast centre. From this is derived the concept Iron Kernel.[11]

The ideology of the corporate state, which the Heimwehr later took over from Italy and propagated so intensively, had already been proclaimed by the Frontkämpfer Association before 1927. It is therefore no coincidence that the first serious internal upheaval of the young republic of Austria came about through an affray between the Association and the Social-Democratic party. In January 1927, in the little town of Schattendorf in the Burgenland, there were violent clashes between Frontkämpfer and members of the social-democratic defence union, the Schutzbund, resulting in a number of dead and severely injured among the adherents of the Left. On 15 July 1927, in a trial by jury held in an atmosphere of high political tension, the accused Frontkämpfer were acquitted. A day later fighting broke out in Vienna, the law-courts were burned down, and the police attacks on the demonstrators caused almost a hundred deaths and even more severe casualties. The wound inflicted on the young republic was not healed. The Christian-Social and the Greater Germany groups, in short the whole of the Right, accused the social-democrats of being Bolshevists and of preparing for revolution. Throughout Austria the

[11] Ibid, p. 101.

Heimwehr now began to spread and advance vigorously; supported by considerable financial resources supplied mainly by industry, they became a power to be reckoned with. This was first noticeable in respect of the armed forces, but very soon the Heimwehr set out to influence the parties of the bourgeoisie both ideologically and politically, and to overtrump them. It is noteworthy that in the years 1927 to 1933, during this tempestuous phase of development, the Frontkämpfer Association in eastern Austria lost every vestige of importance; gradually it broke up and was absorbed by the Heimwehr and from 1932 onwards by the National-Socialist party as well.

The rise of the Heimwehr in 1927 was more than a reaction to the events of July or a counter-offensive by the anti-marxist front; it represented also the breakthrough of modes of thought partly borrowed from fascist ideology and admittedly very much akin to it. Indeed, the material support which the Heimwehr received could not alone account for its rise. Chancellor Seipel, completely misinterpreting what was happening, presented the Heimwehr as a force protecting democracy. In one of his celebrated speeches (at Tübingen, 26 July 1929) he defended it, with deliberate ambiguity, against those critics both at home and abroad who, at this early stage, recognized that the movement represented a danger to democracy:

In our land of Austria there exists a mighty mass movement which wants to liberate democracy from party rule. The pillars of this movement are the Heimwehr. My criticism of pseudo-democracy is not directed against one particular party only, but against all those which follow its lead. All parties in Austria have their doubts of the rightness and lawfulness of our present system of government except the Social-Democratic party, which refuses to listen to criticism and regards as sacred precisely those aspects of our democracy which are not good. It is actually for this reason, and for this reason only, that the Heimwehr movement is in conflict with the social-democrats. This has nothing to do with class warfare. The Heimwehr includes citizens of every class among its members and supporters. The world has probably heard very different verdicts on the Heimwehr. Quite understandably there has been a deliberate campaign to give a false picture of the movement. It is true that the Austrian Heimwehr exerts a form of military discipline over its members. This is not a sign of militarism; it is done for the sake of discipline. The main danger which it faces, and of which its best members are well aware, is that while engaged in a struggle against the predominance of parties, it may itself degenerate into a mere political party. Only a discipline similar to that of an army will save them from this danger. It is true that the Heimwehr cultivates a spirit of combat in its ranks and that this spirit has time and again been manifested in defensive struggles against the terrorism which the social-democrats deny in theory, but which unfortunately they again and again exercise in practice. It is true that the Heimwehr has occasionally also fallen foul of administrative bodies and functionaries of the majority parties. But this has happened only when these clearly displayed the influence of undemocratic party rule. That is the truth.[12]

Seipel believed, wrongly, that when the moment came he would still be in a position to keep the movement within bounds. He failed to realize that the Heimwehr detachments were growing stronger month by month, and that they were constructing for themselves a doctrine fed by many streams, which would in the end overthrow the democratic constitution by extra-parliamentary means. The watchword soon became not anti-marxism, but war against democracy in general.

This sharp break in the ideological development of the Heimwehr is of the utmost importance. From out of the ranks of an armed host of peasants led by members of the petty-bourgeoisie and pensioned-off officers, there arose a movement which tried zealously to equip itself with an appropriate ideology, but which, subjected as it was to a wide variety of influences, never succeeded in achieving a coherent programme. Although Italian fascism was most unpopular in Austria on account of South Tyrol, nevertheless Italy and above all Mussolini were intensely interested in the Heimwehr movement. Recent research has shown that both moral and material support was given by Italy from 1928 onwards. Kerekes' study, based on the files of the Hungarian ministry of foreign affairs, shows that already in 1928 Mussolini was engaged in far-reaching political and military schemes in the Danube basin. A memorandum by the Hungarian prime minister Bethlen indicates the ends Mussolini was pursuing.[13]

I consider it necessary that we should first discuss the whole situation and agree on the common aims as well as on the political methods and paths we should follow. In this regard there are two directions in which common action by Hungary and Italy can be envisaged. One aim should be

[12] H. Arthofer, op. cit., p. 39.
[13] Lajos Kerekes, loc. cit., pp. 3 ff.

to ensure that in Austria, with the help of the Heimwehr, a government of the Right should take over. The present government's aims in the field of foreign affairs do not in all respects resemble ours and they follow a policy of friendship with Czechoslovakia and indeed with the whole Little Entente which much displeases the government of Hungary. In my view, Seipel's foreign policy is more or less in accord with Benes' ideas. He is an opponent of the *Anschluss* and he would like to set up in the Danube basin, if not a confederation of states, at least an economic block. This policy makes him a friend of the Czechs. He does not believe that a strong and independent Hungarian state, which could be driven to enter this block only by force of arms, would be advantageous for Austria. A regime of the Right, which would come to power with the help of Italy and Hungary and which would lean on these two countries for support, would insofar benefit Italy as it would harp less on the Tyrol question. It would even delay the *Anschluss*, for in internal affairs it would have a totally different outlook from the present German government – a government which might be even further to the left after the next elections – and these opposing policies in home affairs would certainly postpone the *Anschluss*. For Hungary, too, a government of the Right in Austria would be advantageous, because communications and the trade in arms between Hungary and Italy would be safeguarded.

In my opinion, the setting up of a government of the Right has now become easier, because the Heimwehr has extended its organizational network and has established certain contacts with the Vienna chief of police and with several army leaders. In the event of their taking action, they can count on the goodwill of these bodies. According to my information the Heimwehr would need about 300,000 schillings to complete the building up of their organization as well as a certain amount of help in procuring arms. I am in contact with them and have been informed that provided they receive adequate assistance they are prepared to go into action at an appropriate time. They have suggested that I should act as their intermediary. I would therefore propose that Italy should give them the assistance they request and furthermore should accept me as the recognized go-between.

On Friday, 6 April I again met Mussolini and he gave me a precise answer, namely: 'I am ready to place at your disposal for transfer to the Austrian rightist organizations one million lire, either in a lump sum or in instalments; I am also prepared to hand over to them at the frontier the arms they require, provided that they give an undertaking about when and in what measure they will seize power in the foreseeable future. Yes, when this has been accomplished, I shall also be ready to treat with the new government about improvements in the lot of the German minority in South Tyrol.'

Early in June 1928, Richard Steidle, the leader of the Heimwehr in the Tyrol, addressed to his Hungarian friends a memorandum on the secret political aims of the Heimwehr. This too is in the Hungarian archives:

The Heimwehr is at present in a state of transition; from being an organization purely for defence it is becoming an organization with national and political aims. The momentum generated by the intense anti-marxist outlook of its members must and will force the so-called ruling parties to alter the semi-bolshevist constitution which came into being under pressure from the Reds of the Wiener Strasse, no matter what resistance or other reactions this provokes.

The 150,000 men now organized in the ranks of the H.W., who are prepared to stake their lives on the triumph of their beliefs, cannot and will not be satisfied with the role of a growling dog, crouching and keeping watch until his owner, in this case the government parties, lets him off his chain, as happened on 15 July 1927, only to tie him up again as soon as his job has been finished against the thief who has broken in. They insist on having their share in the fashioning of the state.[14]

Mussolini had a good understanding of Austrian political conditions, acquired before 1914 when he was a social-democrat. His accommodating attitude had a realistic background. In the event of its seizing power, the Heimwehr was to renounce South Tyrol and to change the Austrian constitution at the earliest possible date, at the outside not later than 15 March 1930. A series of mass demonstrations and protest marches by the Heimwehr, above all the famous rally of 7 October 1928 in Wiener Neustadt, a citadel of the Social-Democratic party, was intended to drive the hesitant government, and above all Dr Seipel, into altering the constitution, perhaps by some kind of *putsch* or *coup d'état*. Mussolini's main object, which he pursued steadfastly until 1934, was the elimination of the Social-Democratic party of Austria, whose leaders were personally known to him and which he hated with the single-mindedness of a renegade.[15]

These secret contacts with Italy, hidden from the public eye, but nevertheless every now and again arousing suspicions that were strenuously denied by the Heimwehr, brought in their wake the

14 Ibid. p. 4.
15 For Mussolini's activities in pre-war Austria see the instructive essay of Hans Kramer, 'Die Versammlungsreden Mussolinis in Deutschtirol im Jahre 1909', in: *Historisches Jahrbuch* (Munich), 1955, p. 765.

ready acceptance of purely fascist ideas. In 1926, when the law on syndicates was introduced in Italy, the Heimwehr journals openly praised 'fascist socialism':

One thing is certain, that Italy today, thanks to tightly controlled trade unions, is spared serious economic conflicts, and that fascism is therefore able to use all its energies for carrying through such internal and external policies as it considers advisable.[16]

Even more important was the fact that there existed in Austria itself a doctrine which could provide the ideology of the Heimwehr with a groundwork of theory. It had found some favour among the intelligentsia – from the National Liberals to the Catholics – and could easily be adapted as an Austrian version of fascism. It was the universalist philosophy of Othmar Spann, a professor at the University of Vienna. Both Spann's book *Vom wahren Staat* (first published in Leipzig in 1921) and his lectures furnished the Heimwehr with a part of its ideology. Above all else, it seized upon the concept of the corporate state. In a very amateurish fashion and without a proper understanding of Spann's meaning, the Heimwehr movement thought it had discovered in the ideology of the corporations or *Stände* a panacea for the future and an Austrian complement to the fascist ideas which had already been taken over. Groups of influential intellectuals, such as the German Club in Vienna, intervened in this discussion about the Heimwehr programme. The Club, a meeting place for business men and academicians belonging to radical and German-national groups, arranged a series of lectures in which both Professor Spann and Dr Richard Steidle, as well as representatives of the German *Stahlhelm* took part to discuss a programme. Its first objective was to alter the constitution; the ultimate aim was to set up a new type of state. Even before this the programme of a revival of the *Stände* had been proclaimed, particularly by Pfrimer, the leader of the Styrian Heimwehr. Walter Heinrich, a colleague of Spann's, was the main proponent of the idea of a corporate state.[17]

Even at the time of its greatest expansion in 1928/9, the Heimwehr was not immune to altercations within its own ranks. In Lower

16 *Alpenländische Heimatwehr*, No. 5, May 1926.
17 Cf. Schweiger,'*op. cit.*, p. 225, also the writer's study: 'Zur Vorgeschichte des Korneuburger Eides', in: *Österreich in Geschichte und Literatur*, April 1963. Vienna, pp. 146 ff.

Austria and the Burgenland especially, the Heimwehr was closely associated with the Christian-Social party and refused to accept accretions of fascist and German-national theories. Julius Raab, a Christian-Social member of the legislature, later to become prime minister, played an important part in these disputes. He had joined the Lower Austrian Heimwehr at Seipel's request but dissociated himself more and more from the radical wing under Steidle and Pfrimer.[18]

It was not until about 1930 that Prince Starhemberg, at that time regional leader in Upper Austria, committed himself to the ideology of the new fascist course. Starhemberg's activities in *Freikorps Oberland* and in national-socialist groups in Munich in 1923 had bound him closely to Hitler's way of thought. Mussolini's massive support of Starhemberg increasingly moulded the Heimwehr into a political instrument which, in the elections of 1930,was able to operate at a parliamentary level. Starhemberg stood as candidate of his own new party, the *Heimatblock*. In spite of Mussolini's support, the block obtained only 228,000 votes (the social-democrats got one and a half million), so it was with a contingent of only eight members that Starhemberg entered Parliament.[19] Before this, an attempt had been made to resolve internal dissensions by the solemn proclamation of a programme. This was done on 18 May 1930, at a conference of Heimwehr leaders in the small town of Korneuburg in Lower Austria. The programme became famous as the 'Korneuburg Oath'. The text – a conglomeration of German-national, patriotic Austrian, and fascist ideas – deserves to be given in full:

We are determined to rebuild Austria from its foundations!

We are determined to bring into being the Volksstaat of the Heimatschutz.

We demand of every comrade:

undaunted faith in the fatherland,

untiring zeal in service, and

passionate love of his native land.

We are determined to take over the state and to remould it and its economy in the interests of the whole *Volk*.

We must forget our own advantage, must subordinate absolutely all

[18] See Kerekes, *op. cit.*, p. 9, and Starhemberg's unpublished memoirs, p. 33 (facsimile in the Vienna Institut für Zeitgeschichte).

[19] See the writer's 'Julius Raab', in: *Neue österreichische Biographie*, Vol. XVI, Vienna, 1965.

party ties and party interests to the aims of our struggle, for we are determined to serve the whole community of the German *Volk*!

We repudiate western parliamentary democracy and the party state!

We are determined to replace them with government by the corporations (*Stände*) and by a strong national leadership which will consist, not of the representatives of parties, but of leading members of the large corporations and of the ablest, most trustworthy men in our own mass movement.

We are fighting against the subversion of our *Volk* by marxist class-struggle and liberal and capitalist economics.

We are determined to bring about an independent development of the economy on a corporate basis. We shall overcome the class struggle and replace it by dignity and justice throughout society.

We are determined to raise the standard of living of our *Volk* by fostering an economy based on the soil and administered for the good of all.

The state is the personification of the whole *Volk*; its power and leadership ensure that the interests of the *Stände* are contained within the framework of the needs of the whole community.

Let every comrade realize and proclaim that he is one of the bearers of a new German national outlook, namely:

> that he is prepared to offer up his blood and his possessions, and that he recognizes three forces only: Faith in God, his own unbending will, the commands of his leaders![20]

The programme thus proclaimed was generally judged – by the Heimwehr itself as well – to be completely fascist in conception. Dr Pfrimer, who a year later was the first of its leaders to attempt, by means of a *putsch*, to realize the programme, declared in a speech about the Korneuburg programme given on the very day of its announcement:

On all sides the conviction was evident that here in Austria only fascism could now save us. (Loud and enthusiastic applause.) We must make an attempt to seize power; then the leaders of our movement will be able to take the business of government in hand. We already have the power to seize the initiative and the strength to change Austria into a true people's state.[21]

Despite this bombast, and its efforts in the 1930 elections, the Heimwehr increasingly lost political influence at home. The danger

---

[20] Reproduced in *Heimatschutz in Österreich*, p. 43.

[21] Schweiger, *op cit.*, p. 210, quoting the Heimatschutz journal *Der Panther*, 24 May 1930.

that power would be seized by violence receded with Dr Johann Schober's able handling of the negotiations concerned with bringing the constitution up to date, and his unyielding attitude in face of the threats of a Heimwehr *putsch*. It was becoming obvious that the Heimwehr was breaking up into separate ideological groups. The Styrian Heimatschutz was being steadily infiltrated with national-socialist ideas. On 13 September 1931 Dr Pfrimer attempted a *putsch*, but it collapsed in face of resolute government resistance.[22] For the Heimwehr it was a catastrophe, for it had been made plain that many of its sections, particularly in Lower and Upper Austria, had refused to take any part in it. The whole movement was being transformed. Those led by Starhemberg now tried to join forces with the Christian-Social party and with patriotic Austrian groups. The Styrian Heimwehr, on the other hand, found an heir and later an ally in the National-Socialist party, now entering the Austrian scene in force. When the severe economic and political crisis broke in 1932, the Heimwehr disintegrated into a number of fragments, each following a direction of its own. It was one of Chancellor Dollfuss' tactical achievements that in his struggle against the national-socialists he succeeded in winning over a section of the Heimwehr movement to his side.

The turning point was the elections of April 1932, as a result of which national-socialists entered the regional legislatures of Lower Austria, Salzburg, Carinthia, Styria, and Vienna. Even if the big parties, especially the Social-Democrats and to a somewhat lesser degree the Christian-Social party, had as yet little to fear from the increase in national-socialist votes, it was obvious that the smaller parties, such as the *Grossdeutsche Volkspartei*, the *Landbund*, and above all the *Heimatblock* (the parliamentary representation of the Heimwehr) had lost a considerable number of votes. The Styrian Heimwehr went over to the national-socialists. The Styrian Heimatschutz entered into a pact with the Austrian NSDAP. On 19 June 1933 both bodies were banned by the government. (After the *Anschluss*, a number of prominent Heimwehr leaders, such as Kammerhofer and Rauter, were given important commands in the SS.) The remaining groups, particularly those led by Starhemberg and Major Emil Fey, the leader of the Vienna

[22] See Josef Hofmann: *Der Pfrimer-Putsch*, published by the Österreichisches Institut für Zeitgeschichte, Vol. 4 (Graz, 1965).

Heimwehr, whose patriotism was of a more purely Austrian character, became allies of the Chancellor. Dollfuss had managed to scrape together a coalition consisting of the Christian-Social party, the *Landbund*, and the *Heimatblock* which provided him with a majority of one vote. This situation, which gave them the power of tipping the scales, brought great advantages both to the Heimwehr and its foreign backers, especially Mussolini. The Chancellor, who at first had no intention of becoming a dictator, and whose origins in Lower Austria as a peasant democrat had made even the social-democrats consider him for a short time a suitable candidate for the post of prime minister of a grand coalition, was now faced with a terrible choice. He had either to yield to the national-socialist assault or seek allies wherever he could find them. As we know from the Hungarian files, it was principally Gömbös, the Hungarian prime minister, who at the end of 1932 or the beginning of 1933 once more brought in Mussolini. This step was taken because of Hungarian fears of a powerful democratic front, including the Social-Democratic party, in Austria. But because of the Social-Democratic party's tactically foolish opposition to the Lausanne loan, Dollfuss slowly reached the decision to conciliate both the Heimwehr and Mussolini, and to govern with the aid of emergency decrees.[23]

On 17 October 1932 Major Fey, known to be an intransigent opponent of the social-democrats, became secretary of state for security in the Dollfuss government. Soon he had organized the Heimwehr into an armed auxiliary police force. Mussolini followed developments in Austria with great attention, for Hitler's accession to power and the challenge presented by the ever-increasing numbers of the national-socialists made that country a European problem. The chief aim of Dr Dollfuss, whose determination to stand up to Hitler-Germany should on no account be doubted, was to preserve the country's independence. Italy, a neighbour of Austria both well disposed and militarily prepared, stood ready to help. The Hirtenberg arms affair in January 1933 had already shown the world that Italy was ready to use any means to promote a fascist regime in Austria. On 4 March 1933, the more or less accidental resignation of all three chairmen of Parliament gave Dollfuss the

23 For the growing Italian-Hungarian influence in Austria see: L. Kerekes, 'Akten des ungarischen Ministerium des Äusseren zur Vorgeschichte der Annexion Österreichs', *Acta Historica*, vol. vii, no. 3–4, Budapest, 1960.

opportunity to set up an authoritarian regime, and Austria began the journey which with the aid of the Heimwehr led to the so-called corporative State.

The National-Socialist party in Austria was banned following their murderous assaults on 19 June 1933. The Social-Democratic party, enjoying the support of over 40% of the voters, was waiting passively, to see how matters would develop. The driving force behind Dollfuss, who in the spring of 1933 had not yet formed any settled plan, was undoubtedly the Heimwehr under Starhemberg. The latter, at Mussolini's request, placed himself at the Chancellor's disposal for the experiment in authoritarian rule. The great Heimwehr demonstration on 14 May 1933 put a seal on the alliance which, under the name of the Fatherland Front, was to combat national-socialism. This was to develop into a totalitarian government party on the lines of the fascist and national-socialist parties and was to last until the loss of Austrian independence in March 1938.[24]

Dollfuss' purpose in founding the Front was the subjugation of the parliamentary parties and the creation of a united front of patriotic Austrians. He had first obtained Mussolini's support through the efforts of Gömbös and Starhemberg, who twice made the journey to Rome on his behalf. In the notes he made in London, Prince Starhemberg mentions that it was he who, shortly after Hitler's seizure of power, had drawn Dollfuss' attention to the possibility of defeating the national-socialist terrorists by organizing an Austrian counter-terror and by activating Austrian patriots. The gist of the proclamation of 21 May 1933, announcing the formation of the Front, consisted in a declaration of war against all who threatened Austria's safety. It concluded with the following words:

All groups, all party organizations, all associations and societies that want to serve their fatherland must join together to form one great and vigorous army united in one great and common aim: Austria and her right of existence; Austria and her duty to survive so that her mission in Central Europe may be accomplished for the future good of every German.

Men and women of Austria!

It is the duty of every upright Austrian to offer his services to the Fatherland Front. Everybody, organizations and individuals, men and

[24] For the history of the Fatherland Front see Irmgard Bärnthaler, *op. cit.*

women, the old and the young, in fact all who love Austria will join the Front. Hail Austria! Hail Dollfuss our leader![25]

The correspondence between Dollfuss and Mussolini, found after the end of the war, clearly proves that Mussolini was using the Heimwehr as a weapon with which to coerce Dollfuss, who was still hesitating, into setting Austrian internal politics on a fascist course.[26] In a speech of 11 September 1933, Dollfuss made an attempt to conform to Mussolini's wishes by repudiating not only marxism but also the democratic and liberal ideologies of the past. Gradually, too, the Fatherland Front made its mark, for, partly in competition but at times in partnership with the Heimwehr, it became the instrument through which the increasingly authoritarian regime exercised its control. The system was copied from the methods used in Germany and Italy, but it differed in that the radical aims of the Heimwehr were blocked by Dollfuss, who preferred to develop the corporative state according to the maxims of the papal encyclical *Quadragesimo Anno*, rather than follow the path of fascism.[27] After the events of 12 February 1934 which, as we know today, followed strong pressure by Mussolini, the Heimwehr, incorporated into the Fatherland Front as a 'shield for its defence', was for a short time in the ascendant. Its Vienna leader, Major Fey, seemed to be on the way to succeeding Starhemberg as the 'ideal dictator' of Austria. It even looked as if he might one day become a danger to Dr Dollfuss and his christian-social followers. Indeed, just before his murder, the Chancellor tried to turn the rivalry between Starhemberg and Fey to his own advantage by depriving the latter of his powers.

The events of 25 July 1934 shook the newly-established regime to its foundations. It was only support from Mussolini which saved Austria from the threat of destruction. After the murder of Dollfuss, Hitler was forced to draw back.

The years of Schuschnigg's government were marked by struggles between the various factions supporting the regime. During

[25] Arthofer, *op. cit.*, pp. 41 ff.

[26] *Geheimer Briefwechsel Mussolini-Dollfuss* (Vienna, 1949). Particular importance attaches to Mussolini's letter of 9 September 1933, in which he recommends that Austria should turn fascist as a means of defence against national-socialism.

[27] Alexander Novotny: 'Der berufsständische Gedanke in der Bundesverfassung des Jahres 1934', in: *Österreich in Geschichte und Literatur*, 5 Jg., F.5, 1961, pp. 209 ff.

1935–6, Schuschnigg and the Fatherland Front were able to hold back the Heimwehr and the smaller para-military organizations and to isolate Starhemberg. The authoritarian state and strong leadership were embodied in the Fatherland Front itself. The type of military politician represented by the Heimwehr could not be allowed to lead an independent existence outside the state party. The end of the militant wing of the fascist movement in Austria followed grotesquely enough upon Starhemberg's last overt effort to make certain, in all circumstances, of Mussolini's support. On 13 February 1936, at the end of the Abyssinian campaign, he sent the following telegram to Mussolini:

In the consciousness of the close bonds of sympathy which involve me as a fascist in the destiny of fascist Italy, I congratulate Your Excellency with all my heart both in my own name and in the name of all those who are fighting for the triumph of the fascist idea, on the glorious and wonderful victory of Italian fascist arms over barbarians, on the victory of the spirit of fascism over dishonesty and hypocrisy, and on the victory of fascist devotion and disciplined determination over mendacious demagogy. Long live the clear-sighted leader of victorious fascist Italy; may the fascist idea triumph throughout the world![28]

Schuschnigg was unwilling to tolerate this denigration of the League of Nations, on which Austria was dependent financially. He excluded Starhemberg from the government and from the Fatherland Front. The Heimwehr was silently absorbed into the Front militia, which had been taken over by the army. It was only just before the fateful events of 12 February 1938 – Schuschnigg's meeting with Hitler at Berchtesgaden – that former Heimwehr circles became politically active once more, but they were no longer in a position to exert any significant influence on the tragic developments that followed.[29]

28 Charles A. Gulick, *Österreich von Habsburg zu Hitler* (Vienna, 1948), p. 442.
29 See the writer's study: 'Ernst Rüdiger Fürst Starhemberg und die politische Entwicklung in Österreich im Frühjahr 1938', in *Österreich und Europa* (Vienna, 1965).

# Quisling's Political Ideas

## Paul M. Hayes

*There they stand, he said within his heart, they laugh: they understand me not: I am not the mouth for these ears. – NIETZSCHE*

Attempts have already been made by historians, psychiatrists, and journalists, to examine Quisling's political ideas, but none has produced a satisfactory analysis. Each has used his own formula, and each has failed to evaluate the problem. All have been confronted with the same inconsistencies which broke the logical pattern of Quisling's ideas. Yet the belief persists that if only a missing link in his character could be discovered, then all Quisling's actions would fall into place and all his ideas appear consistent.[1]

Since the attempt to explain how a man who was passionately devoted to his country could commit high treason, the attempt to reconcile the naivety of many of Quisling's actions with his high intelligence, has proved unfruitful, it may be more profitable to assume that a logical basis for Quisling's ideas did not exist. In this case any attempt to impose a pattern on his actions becomes redundant. The only criteria for analysis adopted here are those which require no pre-ordained pattern for Quisling's ideas and actions; little more than an examination of the more important elements in his political philosophy will be attempted.

Perhaps the most important trait in Quisling's character was his sense of dedication. He believed that he was born to lead Norway, to guide the Norwegians (and the rest of the Nordic race) from darkness into light. The necessity of this mission was only too clear to him and to his small band of devoted followers. His convictions

---

[1] Recent analyses have been made by Dr Johan Scharffenberg, Sverre Hartmann, Viktor Mogens, and Ralph Hewins. Ralph Hewins has tried to prove that Quisling did not commit treason. The basis for my own view was suggested by a talk with Professor Magne Skodvin of Oslo University and Dr Olav Riste of the Norwegian War History Department.

were easily confirmed by chance occurrences. For instance, the fact that he had been born on 18 July was especially important to him since it was the anniversary of the battle of Havsfjord (circa 872) as a result of which Norway had become united. For Quisling this was not a mere coincidence but a clear indication of his destiny.

In this belief Quisling constructed his plans on a much larger scale than other politicians. His ambitions were readily communicated to his lieutenants, who in many cases lacked the ability to see where Quisling was leading them. Blind faith in his powers replaced reason. Despite his scientific training, Gulbrand Lunde was capable of writing complete nonsense about Quisling's 'mission': 'in our time our leader, Quisling, has tried to complete what Ibsen outlined so clearly – Norway has been a state, it shall yet become a people.'[2] Such an ambition was too nebulous and insubstantial to make an extensive political appeal. Because his beliefs formed an article of faith, Quisling naturally refused to compromise with the beliefs of others. He was not prepared to give up a single portion of his creed in order to attract support. He always believed that, provided he held to his task, he would be victorious in the end.

Prophets, whether true or false, seldom seem to make successful politicians. Quisling was no exception. He was absolutely inflexible as a politician and in consequence never mastered the art of compromise which usually forms the essence of the successful politician's craft. His ideas were rarely adjusted to the needs of a given situation, and consequently the vast majority of the Norwegian people found nothing of value in the sentiments he expressed. That this was the case made no difference to Quisling, who pursued his course resolutely despite all setbacks. If he failed to gain extensive popular support, at least his few followers were confirmed in their faith in him as an idealist, a visionary in pursuit of a lofty goal.

Quisling's range of interest in the political sphere was, as might be expected from a man with these characteristics, exceedingly narrow. He was indifferent to issues which were of vital importance to others. He showed little concern for economic and social affairs,

---

[2] *Quisling har sagt.* Introduction to Vol. I. This collection of extracts from Quisling's speeches and writings was published in four parts, 1940–4, by the Nasjonal Samling Press (Oslo).

and his political programmes give slight evidence of attention to practical matters. Quisling was nearly always preoccupied by more abstruse questions such as the conflict of ideologies or the influence of religion on history.

His lack of success Quisling attributed not to his failure to appeal to the people but to a conspiracy between the other politicians to conceal his ideas from the public. His party's disastrous election results in 1936 were attributed to a massive front constructed by a collusive action ranging from the communists to the Hoyre. Thereafter bitterness against the parties and the politicians became a dominant factor in his attitude; he seemed to consider himself in some way above political life, though eager to enter and reform it. From his violent antipathy to Norwegian politicians there gradually developed a profound distaste for the system which allowed these men to gain and retain power. In 1937, for example, after learning the results of the Oslo municipal elections, Quisling declared: 'Today the financial power of the party politicians triumphs ... Oslo has chosen Marx and Mammon. But we continue the fight. We do our duty. Our cause will be victorious in the end.'[3] Two years later he went even further; 'Democracy is a gigantic international system of exploitation.'[4] It was in this way that Quisling's practical experience of politics turned him away from the Norwegian parliamentary system. The fight which he henceforth envisaged had little connection with electoral battles.

Nevertheless he continued in his belief that one day he would be recognized by the Norwegian people as their saviour. A fundamental change had, however, taken place in his attitude towards his anticipated success. Observing the ability of the established parties to hold the support of the vast majority of voters in Norway, he rightly concluded that he and his party were unable to compete on the same terms. The Norwegian people needed guidance until it became obvious to them that Quisling's ideas would produce the best results. In other words, he decided that it was essential to have leadership from above, and particularly from himself. There lay before him two excellent examples of 'enlightened direction' in Italy and Germany, and it was easy for Quisling to conclude that Norway required a similar system.

[3] *Fritt Folk* (Quisling's paper), 23 October 1937.
[4] Quisling's speech at Hamar in August 1939. It was entitled 'Democracy is collapsing – a new era is developing'.

To suggest that this development in Quisling's attitude towards Norwegian democracy can be traced entirely to the years immediately before the Second World War would be inaccurate. Although circumstances favoured the adoption of new plans only in these later years, Quisling had in fact held most of the ideas on which they were based for many years. For example, when he founded Nasjonal Samling early in 1933 he soon took the title of 'Forer' or leader, in direct imitation of Hitler. He also attempted to raise a small private army with the dual function of guarding his own person and providing a party elite – the similarity to the SS is obvious. Like Hitler, Quisling tried the procedures of democracy, and when they failed to install him in power was equally ready to abandon them in favour of more drastic means. These actions suggest that the affection which Quisling professed to hold for democracy when he first entered Norwegian politics at the end of the 1920s did not go very deep.

It was one of his blind spots that he could never understand the deep dislike which he so often aroused among his fellow countrymen. Though not wholly unfortunate from his own point of view, this did little to improve his grasp of political realities. Despite all setbacks and rebuffs, Quisling did not abandon his cherished hope that he would be called to lead Norway when the hour of crisis came. Eventually his genius would be recognized, and until that day dawned it was essential that he should not compromise with weaker spirits for the sake of arriving at his goal sooner than had been intended. Such ideas were wholly fantastic, but the evidence that Quisling held them seems irrefutable. Even in 1945 he had not given up hope that Norway would unite behind him.[5] This total lack of realism was at the same time his strength and his greatest weakness. The highly individual brand of fascism which Quisling advocated had its parallels in other movements. Quisling's political ideas were similar in many ways to those of Alfred Rosenberg. Both were composed of a strange amalgam of romanticism and authoritarianism, although Quisling's views were never clearly defined as Rosenberg's were. Until he was actually awaiting trial, Quisling never completed a major political work[6] explicitly stating

[5] See his notorious talk given on 1 January 1945.
[6] This was the famous treatise which he entitled Universalism. Rosenberg was the author of, inter alia, Der Mythus des 20 Jahrhunderts and Ordenstaat, both of which contained themes central to Nazi ideology. Quisling read them with considerable interest.

his aims and intentions, whereas his German mentor was an exceedingly prolific author. Although in the formulation of his ideas Quisling undoubtedly owed a great deal to Rosenberg, in essentials he had held them long before he met the Nazi leader.

To a large extent Quisling's political ideas were moulded in his youth. His home and his country were two major influences in his life. The years he spent in Fyresdal taught him to love nature and to distrust mankind which polluted nature in attempting to improve upon it. Quisling's ideal society was a simple association of peasant farmers working together to promote the good of the community. This romantic image was somewhat modified by the second important influence in his life, love of his country. He was a patriot who believed that Norway had a useful part to play in the world, and he sought means to enlarge its power. Although he believed that this might best be achieved through the development of his simple society, he was sufficiently realistic to appreciate that this was impossible in the existing circumstances. But if the existing structure of power in the world were suitably changed, then the desired modification of society could take place. From a traditionalist ideal of stability was born a revolutionary doctrine, inherently and from the outset self-contradictory. The confusion may be ascribed in part to the romanticism which was an essential part of his nature. He invariably enlarged the significance of events or of personalities which had played a dramatic though not necessarily important part in history. In examining his political thought, therefore, it is essential to remember that to him the logical consequences of a particular belief were never as significant as its emotional content.

One of the most consistent elements in Quisling's political philosophy was his belief in the importance of the individual. He felt that mankind was best able to fulfil its potential through individual action, unregulated by a strict, institutionalized society. This did not mean that he was in any sense an anarchist; actions needed guidance, but in a manner which left room for individuality to emerge. Perhaps the closest parallel to Quisling's ideas on this point was provided by the actions of Himmler, who wished to encourage the development of 'natural leaders', but was obliged to create the elaborate organization of the SS in order to further his plans. Quisling's speech at Hamar in August 1939 contained a

PAUL M. HAYES

similar inherent contradiction when he declared that what he sought was 'a social individualism based upon national ideas'.

The sources of his belief in individualism are to be found chiefly in his childhood experiences. He spent his youth in the remote valley of Fyresdal, where children were quick to learn the value of self-reliance. In a community of individuals with strong personalities such a development was almost inevitable. The wild aspect of the countryside emphasized the need to develop a strong will if man was to struggle successfully against his environment. It was here that Quisling developed respect for the peasant farmer who wrested a living from the soil. From respect it was a short step to the fabrication of an ideal.

Other elements contributed to the development of this belief. Quisling's long stay in the Soviet Union during its formative years taught him how oppressive a bureaucratic state could be. At this time he was working under Fridtjof Nansen for the League of Nations Relief Commission, and he came to hate all those who put obstacles in the way of his work. Although Quisling occasionally grumbled about the malicious inefficiency of Western officials, most of his anger was directed at the communists, for whose cause he had originally been most enthusiastic. He realized that only a strong man such as Nansen was capable of overcoming these obstacles. Leadership thus provided the best guarantee of human rights. The preservation of individualism was for Quisling the only barrier to the collapse of freedom. Democracy was no safeguard. 'Democracy', he proclaimed, 'is theoretically individualism – the right of each man. But in practice it is the right of the strongest.'[7] In this fashion yet another curiosity was added to his personal beliefs, for he deduced from experience that individualism and democracy were incompatible. It did not apparently occur to him that in the absence of democracy individualism in many of its forms was less likely to find tolerance.

Despite this enthusiasm for individualism, Quisling did not approve of unrestricted political choice for individuals. It was here that his bitter political experiences reshaped his earlier thought, with the result that his theories became an inextricable tangle of conflicting ideas. Although he was in most issues opposed to the idea of state control, he advocated a form of 'guidance'

[7] *Quisling har sagt*, Vol. I, p. 93.

which, correctly given, would enable individualism to develop on desirable lines.[8]

From this position he argued that education was essential to help people think clearly. Society required educated men to deal with and eliminate its undesirable institutions, an educated elite to assist in the completion of the development of the rest of society. They would be all individualistic but would share a common purpose.[9] They would not become an oligarchy, for they would be dedicated, not merely desirous of retaining power. The aim of the elite was service, not mastery. This implied the necessity for different classes of citizen within the state. Although he never made any attempt to define the exact relationship which should be maintained between these grades, Quisling did make certain general suggestions. None was in the smallest way relevant to democratic government.

In the course of this search for a free society of individuals, Quisling outlined a totalitarian system of government. He assumed that the actions of the elite would be correct simply because they were the elite. He never examined the possibility of serious disagreement among them. It was the duty of the elite to protect the people from themselves. The people had no right of redress since, until they were educated, they were incapable of knowing what was in their best interests.

The existence of this inferior class in the 'ideal society' would have to be accepted for some time. Although education by the elite would eventually be almost completely successful, there were certain groups which would be unable to respond to this system because of their inherent inferiority, and these had no place at all in Quisling's society. They lacked the 'basic urge towards individuality'[10] and this deficiency usually arose out of impurity in racial ancestry. The race which he deemed to be particularly impure were the Jews, and their existence was consequently an obstacle to the fulfilment of his ideal society. This conclusion was to lead Quisling to uncritical acceptance of Nazi doctrines.

[8] In some ways Quisling's 'guides' were the direct descendants of Plato's 'guardians'.

[9] In a talk at Lillehammer, on 6 October 1933, Quisling made it clear that the purpose of the Hird was more far-reaching than the creation of a personal bodyguard. The Hird was to help 'provide a new way'.

[10] Speech during the Oslo municipal election, 1937.

The belief in Nordic superiority, and the contempt for 'inferior races', had developed into a full-blown theory of race by the time Quisling came to power in 1940. Earlier, as Minister of Defence,[11] he appears not to have held these beliefs; at any rate he did not openly express them. Nevertheless, their origins may be traced back to his youth and early manhood,[12] and particularly to the years he spent in the Soviet Union.

It is difficult to understand why Quisling held his views on racial superiority so strongly. Norway was not a country where such sentiments were likely to engender enthusiasm. In central and eastern Europe there was a tradition of anti-semitism; but until the establishment of Quisling's party there seem to have been few, if any, problems concerning the Jews in Norway.

In 1851 the constitution of 1814 had been amended to allow practising Jews to enter Norway. Subsequently they were given full citizenship rights. Even before 1851, however, there had arisen a relative concentration of the Jewish population in Bergen and other important ports on the west coast. In many cases these closely related families had been in Norway since the heyday of the Hanseatic League. The immigration of Jews after 1851 was certainly not large and the Norwegians found no difficulty in absorbing them. Complete equality had been achieved by 1870, and by 1900 all suggestion of prejudice appears to have vanished.[13]

By 1939 the Jews were virtually indistinguishable from the rest of the community, and played a full part in public affairs. Their position in Norway was resented only by the small body of fanatics who followed Quisling, whose hatred of them was unbridled. He usually referred to Carl Hambro (leader of the Conservative party, and later President of the League of Nations) as 'that plotting Jew, Hamburger-Levy'. Once he came to power, the fate of the Jews was sealed. He himself had had no unhappy encounters with Jews in his childhood or early schooldays, nor was his military career in any way affected. The earliest date at which his anti-Jewish senti-

[11] In the Kolstad and Hundseid governments, from 1931 to 1933.

[12] Quisling frequently said that all his ideas had been formed before he entered politics in 1930. While such statements should not be accepted uncritically, of many of his ideas they were certainly true.

[13] Hilberg, in *The Destruction of the European Jews* (p. 355) wrote: 'Henceforth the Jews were not merely undergoing emancipation, they were being absorbed into the Scandinavian way of life, and that was a process from which the North was reluctant to retreat even under Nazi pressure.'

ment was made manifest was after his return from the Soviet Union. His original enthusiasm for the new regime in Russia had been turned into its opposite, and in seeking an explanation of communist excesses, he concluded that the high aims of communism had been perverted, and that this perversion was the work of the Jews. It seems probable that he read some anti-Jewish work – perhaps the *Protocols of the Elders of Zion*. (Later he was to quote extensively from this fantasy.) He clearly believed that the chief figures in the communist hierarchy were Jewish or half-Jewish, and that they were responsible for the decline of communist ideals. In after years, Rosenberg's racial philosophy became the centre and the basis of most of Quisling's political theories.

Quisling's racial theory was much more elaborate than the mere advocacy of anti-semitism. He believed in Nordic supremacy, and his definition of Nordic included the inhabitants of most of Northern Europe. In addition there were the Germanic colonies in Austria, the Ukraine, and Transylvania. There were also certain races of basically sound stock which had been 'polluted' by the Jews. Among these he numbered the Dutch and the English. His aim was to purge these races of the inferior elements living among them and then create a vast union of peoples of Nordic descent. War between Germany and England was to be avoided because it would decimate the Nordic race and ruin his vision of a 'Greater Nordic Peace Union, based on all the states bordering on the North Sea'.[14] It was here that Norway's statesmen, in particular himself, had a special task – 'to work together to promote peace between England and Germany is our chief task in international politics today'.[15] During the 1939–45 war his ideas on these points were drastically revised, for the participation of England was rejected. Quisling had discovered that the Jewish stranglehold there was too strong and that in consequence England had become hopelessly corrupt. Norway's new aim should be 'to come to an understanding with our Germanic fellow race; and in the Greater German community we shall have a leading position in the working of the New Order'.[16]

Closely connected with this concept of Nordic unity were his ideas on nationalism. These were not aggressive in character, but

[14] Statement of 21 June 1945, p. 3.
[15] From a talk in Oslo, 8 April 1938.
[16] From a talk at the Kringkastingen, 26 September 1940.

in many ways merely ultra-conservative. It was the nationalism of a national revival which would lead to a new national order, both politically and socially. That his ideas on the reforms required to produce the new order were completely inconsistent was unimportant. Quisling picked up any plan that took his fancy. The details were irrelevant – he would know which plan to adopt when the time came for decision. That these details might be of greater practical interest to people, and therefore of greater appeal, than his visionary schemes, did not concern him at all.

The need for a national revival in Norway was derived from the difficulties of the years after the 1914–18 war. The bitter class struggle that followed its conclusion would, he believed, destroy all that he valued in Norway. 'The old parties are worked out . . . they are all more or less class parties.'[17] There had to be a new party which would rise above the old class struggles. Quisling therefore broke with the Agrarian Party, which he had joined in late 1929 or early 1930, and founded his own party, which he called Nasjonal Samling (National Unity).

Some of the means which Quisling proposed to use to promote national unity were far from new. They were often old conservative ideas decked out in ostensibly more radical clothes. 'Our party,' declared its leader, 'will not be a party in the same sense as other parties, but a party beyond party, an organized revival. In it farmers, workers, and burghers will be able to find a part to play in the national task. This will promote a national sense of purpose and will increase determination and strength.'[18] The aim of the NS was to unite Norway behind a new national government, the motto of which was to be 'Peace, Order, Justice'. To judge from the character of the wartime Quisling government it seems unlikely any of these lofty goals would have been reached in any national revival led by his party.

As a promising young politician, Quisling was given the Ministry of Defence in 1931. During his tenure of office he became the most unpopular politician in Norway. In the course of a strike at the hydroelectric works Quisling (with Government approval) sent troops to 'restore order', and to protect the peace of Norway against

---

[17] *Oppfordring til Nasjonal Samling*, 1933.

[18] From the introduction to a Nasjonal Samling pamphlet distributed in the 1933 election.

'the Red revolutionaries'. The Labour Party never forgave him, though Quisling always insisted that his action was aimed at communist *agents-provocateurs* and not at the workers. His quarrels with the Labour Party made him a hopeless liability to the Agrarian Party, which was rather pleased to lose him in 1933.

It is evident, however, from all that Quisling wrote or did, that he had little sympathy for the urban working class. Certainly when he became Minister-President his main activity in regard to the workers, apart from depressing their standard of living and shooting two of their leaders, consisted in an attack on the trade unions. He proposed to replace them by a National Labour Front, as Ley had done in Germany. This was characteristic of his peculiar brand of nationalism. He made national unity the rallying call of his party, but was not actually ready to do anything to promote it.

Although traditionalist in his appeals to nationalism, Quisling was not unaware of the pressures which could be brought to bear on the working class on behalf of a new form of nationalism – national-socialism. 'Over the whole world nationalism is on the advance – nationalism is the political philosophy of the twentieth century and is pre-ordained to be victorious.'[19] But it was in vain that Quisling sought to revive a more aggressive nationalism after the collapse of his scheme for national revival. He referred always in militant phrases to the need for a strong, prepared Norway. He even tried to create a national issue by reviving the dispute with Denmark over the ownership of Greenland.[20] This appeal fell as flat as its predecessors, and as his chances of gaining power grew more remote and improbable, so the policies he advocated became more unrealistic. At the same time many of his early adherents were transferring their support to other parties, and the NS fell into a decline from which it recovered only with the entry of a considerable number of time-servers in 1940 and 1941. More and more Quisling began to refer to the missionary task of his party – an implicit recognition that he was working in a hostile environment. His remedies for the serious state in which he found the Norwegian nation changed with every new event. By 1939 few Norwegians took him at all seriously.

[19] *Fritt Folk*, 9 April 1938.
[20] One of the first things that Quisling did when he met Hitler was to give him a memorandum in which he insisted that Iceland, Greenland, and the Faroes were all Norwegian by right.

As hopes of power receded, Quisling came to emphasise that the prime goal of his party was to exercise a moral influence. This theme had been apparent from its foundation, but did not emerge fully until after 1936 when the party was under pressure. In 1931 Quisling had demanded 'a political and religious party'. During the war his ideas increasingly acquired a semi-religious content. In 1941, speaking of the German crusade on behalf of the Nordic races, he said: 'National-socialism must be united with Germanic radical thinking in a political-religious party.'[21] As the war went increasingly badly for Germany, so did Quisling become more eager to establish his political position in Norway by claiming to be the guardian of moral and religious standards. In 1943 he insisted that his programme was 'a guarantee to the Norwegian Church that God's word will be preserved whole and untainted'.[22] By 1945 all he wanted to do was to retire to Fyresdal as the local pastor. It was in that year that he completed his vast work on 'Universalism', which consisted largely of moral and religious, rather than political, dissertations.

It is clearly impossible to detect any clear and unambiguous line of thought which can be followed through from the earliest days of Quisling's political career to its ignominious end. He was a political phenomenon rather than a politician; a collector of ideas rather than creator of a new system. He was not a political thinker in any constructive sense; he introduced no new ideas and developed no coherent analysis of the state and its functions. The measures he occasionally advocated were designed for immediate adoption – he had no well considered long-term plans.

It has been a source of perplexity to many analysts of Quisling's character that it has proved difficult to reconcile his intelligence with his actions. How could a man with a brilliant academic record adopt such irrational ideas and perform simple tasks so badly? The answer lies, perhaps, in two limitations of that intelligence. First, Quisling found it impossible to make decisions – choice was imposed on him by the progress of events which he made no attempt to control. Second, although he loved to argue and to speculate about intangible matters, he was always uneasy in his encounters with reality. He saw events in stark black and white, and this inability to compromise caused difficulties both in his personal

21 Speech at the Colosseum, 1 February 1941.
22 Speech of 1 February 1943.

relations and in his public life. He withdrew into a world of speculation, whence he expected to emerge like a *deus ex machina* at the
critical moment. As the moment was deferred, so Quisling's faith
in other men diminished, and his faith in his own mission grew.
In this lonely and introspective world no healthy and constructive
political philosophy could develop, and his ideas and actions thus
became centred exclusively on himself and a few friends. His
abstract intelligence availed him nothing, for he never learned how
to apply it.

# The All-Russian Fascist Party

## Erwin Oberländer

On 30 August 1946 *Pravda* gave prominent place to a report on
'The trial of the leaders of the anti-Soviet white-guard organizations and agents of the Japanese intelligence service Semenov,
Rodzaevsky, and others', in which the former leader of the All-
Russian Fascist Party (VFP), Konstantin Vladimirovich Rodzaevsky, was condemned to death. This was the final and macabre
event in the history of a movement which in the 1930s, encouraged
by the successes of Italian fascism and German national-socialism,
had entertained serious hopes of becoming successor to the
CPSU.

Certainly there were few readers of the Moscow paper who knew
anything of that history, and *Pravda* had no intention of enlightening them. The Russian fascist movement had fallen into complete
oblivion, yet in any comprehensive study of fascism reference
should be made to those Russian emigrés who sought in 'Russian
fascism' an alternative to bolshevism; the former they defined as 'a
synthesis of the lessons to be drawn from the failure of the White
movement, the experience of Italian, German, and Japanese
fascism, Russia's glorious past and the present post-revolutionary
Russian reality'.[1]

Since we are dealing here with an emigré movement that was
scattered over the entire world, it is peculiarly difficult to trace its
activities. Only a few issues of the newspapers and periodicals put
out by the Russian fascists are still in existence, and they are distributed among a number of different libraries.[2] Given that the source
material is so inadequate, the present essay does not claim to be
anything more than an initial review of the Russian emigré fascist
movement which reached its highest point in the foundation of the
All-Russian Fascist Party.

[1] *Natsiya*, 1932, 1, p. 1; 1934, 5, p. 7.
[2] I have been able to consult the issues of *Fashist* (Putnam, Conn.) for 1933–8,
copies of *Natsiya* (Shanghai), and *Nash Put* (Harbin).

## The rise of the movement

After the triumph of the Red Army in the Civil War, the Russian emigrés were confronted, in the words of the fascist journal *Natsiya* (1932, No. 1) with the question 'what must happen if the walls of the Russian prison are to fall, if the tri-coloured flag is to wave proudly over the liberated Kremlin, if an end is to be put to the communist destruction of national consolidation, if, in brief, Great Russia is to re-enter the family of nations ?'. The answers given to this question differed so widely that the various political groups in the emigration, some of which maintained the traditions of the pre-revolutionary parties while others represented new trends, came into violent conflict with each other. The younger people among them were the first to tire of these internal feuds, and to feel themselves betrayed by their leaders. They began to look for new ideas, around which the emigrés could unite and the Russian people be summoned to active struggle against the Soviet regime.

Among the discontented there were many who were fascinated by Mussolini's success in his struggle against the socialists and communists of Italy. The fascist concept of the corporative state seemed to them a genuine alternative to the proletarian class dictatorship, and so to offer an effective weapon against the Soviet regime. 'The tragic catastrophe of the White movement teaches us how not to fight bolshevism; the experience of Italian fascism teaches us how we have to fight the bolsheviks.'[3] Equally attractive to the emigrés was the 'universal character' of fascism, which was gaining a growing number of adherents, and not only in Italy. They regarded it as a stage in world history 'through which the whole of humanity must inevitably pass'. By joining the 'world fascist movement', they hoped not only to avoid the suffocating narrowness of the emigré circles, but to be in a position to put before the Russian people prospects for the future with which no other emigré group, still less the communists, could compete.

Thus Russian fascism arose in the first place as a reaction against the shortcomings of the older generation, who in the opinion of the fascists neither knew how to fight the bolsheviks nor had any clear picture of Russia's future: 'The old parties have not stood the test of life. The pre-revolutionary aspirations of the intelligentsia have

[3] *Natsiya*, 1932, 4–5, p. 2.

led Russia and the Russian people to the abyss. The emigré groups are stuck fast in endless quarrels and fruitless attempts to unite. For all those who love Russia not only in words but in deeds, who are prepared to make sacrifices to patriotism and . . . really want to fight, there is only one road – into the ranks of the Russian fascist blackshirts.'[4] It was this kind of thinking which led Russian emigrés to found the Russian fascist movement, which had its chief centres in Manchuria and the United States; in almost all the other countries where there were Russian emigrés, small sections of the movement's adherents were set up.

## Russian fascists in Manchuria

The first and largest Russian fascist organization arose in Manchuria.[5] Along the course of the Chinese Eastern Railway, which remained in Russian hands until 1935, there had long been a fairly numerous Russian colony, most of them employed by the railway or engaged in trade. The majority had settled in Manchuria before 1917, and became Soviet citizens while continuing to work in Manchuria. According to Soviet sources they numbered 150,000 in 1932. The revolution added a new group to the Russian colony, estimated by the League of Nations in 1921 to number a further 150,000. The existence side by side of these two groups generated a good deal of tension, not least in the Russian law faculty of Harbin University, where before long a pro-Soviet and an anti-Soviet students group were formed. From the summer of 1925 there existed among the latter a small fascist group, impressed by the successes of the Italian fascists, which called itself the Russian Fascist organization (RFO). It conducted a lively agitation among the students, and in January 1927 brought out the 'Theses of Russian Fascism', obviously inspired by Italian ideas of the corporative state, which are reflected also in the name of the 'Union of the National Syndicate of Russian workers', founded in the same year. This association, whose chief was Professor N. I. Nikiforov, undertook as its first task the 'study of the various political trends of an anti-communist character'; it soon became a fascist organization, established a number of fascist circles along the Railway, and be-

[4] *Natsiya*, 1932, 1, p. 2.
[5] Cf. Peter Balakshin, *Final v Kitae* (2 vols. San Francisco, Paris, New York; 1959), 1, pp. 112–16.

gan to smuggle propaganda material into the USSR.[6] This brought the Soviet consul in Harbin on to the scene – and the Chinese authorities prohibited any kind of fascist propaganda.

Nevertheless, in May 1931, the first congress of all Russian fascist groups was held, in strict secrecy in Manchuria. It decided to found the Russian Fascist Party (RFP). Major-General Vladimir Dmitrievich Kozmin, no doubt because of his impressive appearance, was elected president.[7] Supreme direction of the party was invested in a central committee; its secretary, and hence in effect leader of the party, was the twenty-four year old Konstantin Rodzaevsky. Born in 1907 of poor parents in Blagoveshchensk, he had fled from the Soviet Union in 1925 and made his way to Harbin, where he joined the young fascist movement. Gifted as organizer and journalist he was to remain its leader until its end in 1945.

This congress also adopted the first party programme. Unfortunately, the writer has been unable to obtain a copy, but it no doubt corresponded in essentials with the ideas advanced by Rodzaevsky in his first article for *Natsiya* (1932, No. 1). He started from the assumption that 'tremendous historical events' were about to occur for dark clouds were moving towards the Soviet Union from the west and the east, while within the country itself the isolation of the rulers from the people was becoming more marked and nationalist trends steadily more powerful. These developments, which he considered favourable for fascism, provoked the question: Can we tell the Russian people what these developments portend, or shall we repeat the mistakes of the Whites by leaving the question unanswered? Rodzaevsky maintained that the RFP, whose motto was 'God, Nation, Labour', had to come out unambiguously for 'solidarism' on the Italian model as the new social order. On the other hand, it would be unwise at that stage to determine the specific legal form of the future state which was to embody that order; what they needed was a platform around which the most varied tendencies, sharing a common hostility to communism and capitalism, could unite. This tactical consideration obviously reflected his

[6] It was claimed (*Fashist*, 1934, 8, p. 7) that 14,000 copies of fascist leaflets were smuggled into the USSR in 1927–8.

[7] Kozmin's role was only representative. He resigned in 1933. Since no successor was appointed, Rodzaevsky took over the formal leadership as well.

intention of winning as many members of right-wing circles as possible for his party. A Russian fascist, he said, could in no circumstances be a democrat or republican, but he could be a 'monarchist, legitimist, Bonapartist, etc.'. In each of these groups the RFP sought to kindle the hope that in the fascist Russia of the future their form of state would prevail.

But it was not only from the conservatives in the emigration that the RFP hoped for support. From the outset of their struggle against bolshevik Russia, they and their predecessors had looked to Japan, the strongest power in the Far East, as a potential ally. When, in the winter of 1931–2, the Japanese occupied Manchuria (they reached Harbin on 5 February 1932), and in March 1932 proclaimed the independent state of Manchukuo, the RFP, thanks to its pro-Japanese attitude, reached the high point of its existence and became the most influential emigré organization in the Far East.

Its activities were at first unquestionably consistent with Japanese policy, which made no attempt to conceal its anti-Soviet direction. All over Manchuria, and elsewhere in China as well as in Japan, RFP sections were established, some of which also set up fascist organizations for women, students, and young people. From April 1932 *Natsiya*, the theoretical journal of the party, appeared in Shanghai; in Harbin, from 3 September of the same year, its daily paper *Nash Put*. On 5 August 1932 a party school was organized in Harbin, designed to train economists, administrators, and social workers for the fascist Russia of the future.

The new party, which according to Rodzaevsky numbered 4000 members, sought to establish contact with other Russian fascist groups, particularly those in the United States. On 28 October 1933 Rodzaevsky wrote to the leaders there and proposed the amalgamation of their organizations into an All-Russian National Labour Party of the Third Russia.

## Russian fascists in the United States

The foundation and structure of the Russian fascist movement in the United States was in essentials the work of its leader Anastasi Anastasievich Vonsiatsky. He was the son of a colonel in the gendarmerie who had been murdered by Polish revolutionaries in 1910. In November 1917, as a junior officer in the Nikolaevsky Cavalry School, he joined the Volunteer Army then being formed and fought throughout the Civil War until the Army's evacuation of the Crimea in 1920. As emigré he attached himself to the militant anti-communist Brotherhood of the Russian Truth, for which he provided funds after his marriage to a rich American. In the early thirties he became convinced that the existing political emigré organizations no longer met the requirements of the day, largely because the older generation were unable to show the younger people a promising road to the liberation and transformation of Russia. But he did not differentiate his movement from that of the Whites as sharply as did the Russian fascists in the Far East. He and his party did indeed wish to learn from the mistakes of the Whites, 'who never found real contact with the people', but he was also anxious to establish that Russian fascism was 'the heir of the White movement'. Heroic deeds, such as the legendary march across the ice to Ekaterinodar, in which Vonsiatsky had himself taken part, seemed to him peculiarly well suited to inspire the fascists with militancy.[8] When, in May 1933, impressed by the spectacular Nazi triumph in Germany, he founded the All-Russian Fascist Organization (VFO), he looked on it as the continuation of the White movement. The new party had its headquarters in Putnam (Connecticut), and soon built up an entire network of branch organizations throughout America. In August 1933 the first issue of *Fashist* appeared. It proposed, as Lenin's *Iskra* had done, to establish contact with all Russian 'activist' emigrés, to penetrate Russia as the voice of the 'national revolutionary leadership', and to become the nucleus of the new mass fascist movement.

Vonsiatsky, who quickly became the focus of an extraordinary leader cult, introduced the first issue of his paper with an 'open letter' to the principal party body, the 'Russian Fascist Supreme Staff', in which he set down guiding lines for VFO activities. In contrast to Rodzaevsky and the fascists in Manchuria, who made it their first task to draft a programme, Vonsiatsky rejected any kind of political 'programme-mongering', for this would only bring abstract ideas to the consideration of the Russian reality. He devoted his entire attention to the 'tactical struggle for the liberation

[8] This refers to the march of the anti-revolutionary Volunteers in the winter of 1917–18 towards Ekaterinodar (Krasnodar) in fiercely inclement weather. Stökl calls it 'an act of heroic desperation without political significance'; it became for the fascists a symbol of military heroism.

of the Russian people'. He wanted to reach the people who, embittered by hunger, by life in the kolkhoz, and by the coercive measures of the government, were rising again and again in sporadic outbreaks of unrest, to encourage their protest with inflammatory battle-cries. He was convinced, above all, that in an archetypal peasant country like Russia, fascism would have to seek support among the peasants, to co-ordinate their resistance to collectivization and transform it into a 'national popular movement' led by the fascists.

With this in mind, Vonsiatsky put forward three principal slogans for fascist propaganda: protection of private property, distribution of kolkhoz and sovkhoz land among the peasants, and freedom of trade in agricultural products. This programme indicates the high importance which Vonsiatsky attached to tactics. What he added by way of fascist theory to these and similar concrete slogans in the course of time consisted in essentials of borrowings from his like-minded comrades in Manchuria. In an interview given to a Belgrade paper at the end of 1933 he admitted that he and his colleagues had chosen the title 'fascist' primarily because it was popular in the Soviet Union as a synonym for every kind of resistance. Since the Soviet rulers branded everything hostile to them as fascist, they were themselves the best propagandists for fascism among the discontented population.[9]

The first goal of the VFO was to create a 'united fascist front' within the emigration; but the attempt to turn the existing political emigré organizations into fascist bodies, and to bring their leaders together as the general staff of the national revolution, was a failure. Vonsiatsky made a trip to Europe in 1933 to meet the leaders of the various emigré groups, but the only agreement reached was one for close cooperation between the VFO, the Russian National-Socialist Movement (RNSD) in Germany, and the League of Young Russians. For the rest, he had to be content with the setting up of VFO sections in various places in North and South America, Europe, and the Near East. In these circumstances it is easy to understand why Vonsiatsky, 'in the name of 2000 VFO members', welcomed Rodzaevsky's proposal to merge their two parties. Early in 1934 he and his colleague I. D. Kunle were sent by the Supreme Council of the VFO to the Far East to negotiate the agreement.

[9] *Fashist*, 1933, 5, p. 15.

## The All-Russian Fascist Party

On 24 March 1934 the two men arrived in Tokio, where the pleni-potentiaries of the RFP, Rodzaevsky, M.A. Matkovsky, and V. Balykov had come to meet them. The 'White Guard nest in Tokio', as *Pravda* (30 March 1934) called the meeting, reached agreement quickly. Vonsiatsky, who had the clearer conception of what an organization embracing all Russian fascists should be, managed to get his ideas accepted, using as additional enticement the prospect of financial help, of which the RFP was urgently in need. At the first meeting complete 'ideological and psychological' unity was established, in which the theoretical formulations of the RFP leaders found their complement in Vonsiatsky's tactical plans. He proposed the foundation of an All-Russian Fascist Party, whose activities would follow the lines laid down in his 'open letter' of 10 May 1933. The result of the negotiations was set forth in Protokoll No. 1, signed in Yokohama on 3 April 1934. This sealed the amalgamation of the RFP and VFO 'for the purpose of creating a common anti-communist front abroad' whose chief goal it would be to 'take the place of the CPSU'. A central execu-tive committee of eight members was appointed to run the party and its headquarters were for the time being to be Harbin. Vonsiatsky was chairman of the committee and Rodzaevsky general secretary. After a triumphal reception for the '*Vozhd*' in Harbin, culminating on 26 April 1934 in a blackshirt parade and a cere-mony in the Russian club, Vonsiatsky wrote jubilantly to his friends in the United States: 'The tactical unity of Russian fascism has been achieved.'[10]

After these successful negotiations, Vonsiatsky on his return jour-ney visited the fascist sections in Shanghai, Cairo, Alexandria, Paris, Berlin, Sofia, and Belgrade, and these, it appears, like the numerous American groups, gave their support to the new party. In August Rodzaevsky, in agreement with Vonsiatsky, opened a new Higher Party School (apparently the one established in 1932 had been stillborn) where a six-months training course was to be given to fascist agitators and organizers. Shortly thereafter, how-ever, the 'tactical unity of Russian fascism', so recently celebrated, faced a test it could not withstand.

[10] Ibid., 1934, 11, pp. 2, 10, 14.

Apart from any personal rivalries, which no doubt existed, and from the distance separating the Harbin and American centres, which virtually excluded the constant contact essential to a party, difficulties arose from the widely differing conditions in which the two groups had to work. While the Russian fascists in the United States enjoyed the liberties of a tolerant democracy which did not in any way encroach on their independence, the Japanese were not inclined to grant the Russian emigrés a freedom of which the use might work to the disadvantage of Japanese interests. Rodzaevsky had to reach an understanding with them, but this was impossible without concessions to the pro-Japanese Ataman Semenov. Semenov, recognized by part of the Russian emigration as the legitimate successor of the 'Supreme Regent' Admiral Kolchak, had maintained contact with the Japanese from the time of the Civil War when he commanded White troops in Siberia. After the conquest of Manchuria, he again worked closely with them, no doubt with a view to combined intervention in the Soviet Union. He deplored the 'extreme enthusiasm of our young people for fascism and for Hitler's national-socialism' and tried to counteract it, which naturally enough made the Russian fascists in the United States highly indignant.

Using the efforts of the Russian fascists in Manchuria to work together with the Japanese and with the Ataman as his point of departure, Vonsiatsky, in an 'open letter' dated 31 December 1934, condemned Rodzaevsky's 'deviations' from the policy agreed on in Yokohama and Harbin. He objected to the terms on which Rodzaevsky had made his peace with Semenov – that 'in the event of war . . . he would be in command of the Russian forces attached to the Japanese army'. Vonsiatsky was convinced that Semenov would only repeat the mistakes made by the Whites, and that the aims he pursued in Russia were incompatible with those of the Russian fascists, and he took the fascists in Harbin to task for having given their party the reputation of an interventionist party. He could not share Rodzaevsky's optimistic view that 'Japan is the only country interested not in the dismemberment of Russia, but in the creation of a great and powerful Russia which would be Japan's friend'.[11] Although the Russian fascists in the United States regarded themselves as 'defeatists' who, if it were to come to

[11] Ibid., 1935, 15, p. 1; *Natsiya*, 1935, 8, p. 50.

hostilities between the USSR and another power, would wish the Soviet Union to be defeated in order that the war might then turn into Civil war, the cooperation with the Japanese in Manchuria was clearly going too far for them. Vonsiatsky explicitly emphasized that the party's primary goal remained the preparation of the national revolution from within, with the support of the discontented workers and peasants. The national revolutionary struggle, he wrote later, could in no circumstances 'be waged according to the instructions of the government of a foreign power'.[12] He took as his model for the Russian liberation struggle the Spanish Civil War, in which the fascist powers supported Franco without themselves intervening directly or revealing any annexationist intentions.

On the other hand, the *Vozhd* rebuked the general secretary in Harbin for having started 'ferocious anti-semitic propaganda, which could only weaken the national revolutionary struggle against the one chief enemy, Soviet communism'. The argument could hardly have been meant or taken seriously as a pretext for breaking off relations, since Vonsiatsky knew that the RFP leaders, before the amalgamation with the VFO, had waged a vigorous campaign in their paper *Nash Put* against the Jews and Freemasons. This anti-semitism, which in fact harked back to the same phenomenon in pre-revolutionary Russia, but was also influenced by German national-socialism, was one of the most important areas of disagreement between the fascists in the United States and in Manchuria.[13] Vontsiatsky published a pamphlet he had written in 1932, *On Russian Jews*, which opened with the words: 'Among Jews only the red Jew is our enemy. Do not touch the peaceful Jewish inhabitant, his wife and children. We are Christians. We do not shed innocent blood; we do not lament the guilty'[14]

Since peaceful agreement could clearly not be reached, the Russian fascists in the United States set up a new central executive

---

[12] *Fashist*, 1935, 21, p. 2.

[13] The objects of the campaign, waged from 1933 on, were endorsed by the third congress, which demanded the formation of an 'anti-freemason, anti-Jewish, and anti-communist front'. *Natsiya*, 1935, 6, p. 43, 8, p. 51; *Nash Put*, 1935, No. 78. In later issues of *Fashist* the dictatorship of the CPSU was occasionally equated with the rule of 'a Jewish clique'.

[14] *Brat Russkoi Pravdy, O Russkom Evreistve* (1932). The pamphlet was distributed in the United States as giving 'the official attitude of the party on the Jewish question'.

committee of their own early in 1935 and started a vigorous campaign against Rodzaevsky and the Far East fascists in the pages of *Fashist*. Financial help from the United States having ceased, Rodzaevsky accused Vonsiatsky of indulging a 'personality cult', had him expelled from the party, and in his turn set up a new committee. His actions were explicitly approved at the third party congress, held in the summer of 1935 in Harbin, and he was confirmed as leader of the VFP. This completed the breach between the two wings. In the long run his organization, the larger of the two and the one which retained the party name, seems to have proved more attractive to the sections. From the autumn of 1935 Vonsiatsky's group took the name of the All-Russian National Revolutionary Party, and appears to have had little success thereafter.[15] Rodzaevsky, on the other hand, announced on 22 May 1935, the fourth anniversary of the party's foundation, that it numbered all together 20,000 'activists', organized in 597 local groups, 63 districts, and 29 provincial centres. This, he said, concluded the first stage of the fascist movement, 'the preparation and rallying of forces'. To open the second stage, he announced a three-year plan which was to 'liquidate Jewish rule over the Russian land' and to culminate in the accession of the fascists to power on 1 May 1938.[16] It is not without interest, therefore, to examine their ideas as to the nature of the 'third fascist Russia' which they hoped to build after that date.

Almost all the plans for establishing a fascist regime in Russia derive from Rodzaevsky, who presented a fairly full outline in his book *The Russian National State*.[17] The party programme, briefly summarized in Balakshin's book, gives important indications. The general principles on which the regime was to be based can also be deduced from the articles which appeared in *Natsiya* and from the 'short course for fascists' published in the April-May 1935 issue of *Fashist*.

In the opinion of its Russian advocates, fascism was the outcome of a 'search for new roads, of the aspiration for an alternative and

---

[15] Vonsiatsky admitted in 1940: 'We were far from taking full advantage of the opportunities offered by the world situation' (*Fashist*, 1940, 57, p. 2). I know nothing of the subsequent fate of the party.

[16] *Natsiya*, 1935, 6, p. 1.

[17] Balakshin, op. cit., 1, pp. 112, 125.

counter-weight to materialism, to anti-national tendencies, the class struggle, and class rule as exemplified in socialism'. The goal of fascism, which was to replace liberalism and socialism throughout the world, was the 'National Labour State' founded on the religious idea, the national idea, the idea of social justice. The watchword of the third fascist Russia, which would succeed pre-revolutionary and post-revolutionary Russia, was 'God, Nation, Labour'.

In interpreting these three principles, the Russian fascists were concerned to preach the opposite of what the Soviets stood for. The Government in Moscow pursued an atheistic policy, and so the fascists advanced the religious idea, for 'a striking example of the importance of religion and of religious education is given by the situation in the USSR, where an active struggle against religion is being waged. The frightful moral licence, the disintegration of the family, the complete spiritual impoverishment of the Russian people – these are the results of the Soviet regime's anti-religious policy.' In contrast, Russian fascism, which its adherents even called 'Christian fascism', wished to re-establish the authority of religion and morals in personal, social, and political life. Its first task would be 'to restore to the Russian people their religion and their Orthodox Church'. Relations between church and state would be regulated by an alliance ruling out intervention by one side in the affairs of the other, but the state would undertake to give the maximum support to the church and to the religious education of the people. How this was to be reconciled with the full religious freedom also proclaimed in the programme, or with the anti-semitism characteristic of the Russian fascists in the Far East, was not elucidated.

The Communist International, 'which is using Russia as the base from which to deploy the forces of world revolution', was betraying the interests of the Russian people. 'The USSR ... is the state of the Third International, which has settled on the territory of what was once Russia, appropriated the country's wealth, and like a slaveholder rules the Russian people.' Fascism was to combat the communist 'tendency to cosmopolitanism, to national suicide, because Russian fascism like fascism everywhere, is the highest form of nationalism, because it stands for service to the nation, the highest value and the greatest achievement of man'. But if national consciousness, embodied in the slogan 'Russia for the Russians', was to triumph over the international class consciousness propagated by the Soviets, the question arose whether the Great Russians alone were capable of this consciousness, or whether the other nationalities embraced in the state could share it. On this all Russian fascists were at one: since one of the most significant characteristics of a nation was a common historical destiny, it was not only the Great Russians 'but all nations inhabiting the territory of the Russian realm who belong to the Russian nation'.

The VFP itself, Rodzaevsky pointed out, embraced members of all nationalities. The fascist Russian state would in any case guarantee that the rights of the nationalities would not be infringed; these peoples could shape their development according to their own ideas. General P. I. Konovalov suggested that as a result of this exemplary policy practically all the neighbouring small states would wish to unite with Russia, for that would be more advantageous to them than their continued precarious existence as small states. 'In Europe, Finland, Latvia, Estonia, Poland, Lithuania, Galicia, and even Rumania and Bulgaria, and in Asia, Persia, Afghanistan, and Mongolia will voluntarily unite with Russia . . . And Russia will become the leading power in the two continents.'[18]

Russian nationalism, however, was not to prevent the future fascist Russia collaborating with other fascist powers. On the contrary, Rodzaevsky looked forward to an alliance between fascist Russia, Japan, and national-socialist Germany (astonishingly enough completely overlooking Italy, in so many respects his model fascist state). Only such an alliance could 'solve all world problems, establish lasting peace, and break the world domination of the Jews and freemasons'. However, this alliance, or indeed any collaboration with Germany, would be a difficult matter so long as the policy towards Russia outlined in Hitler's *Mein Kampf* was maintained. The attempt to get Hitler to revise these passages obviously failed.[19] When *Fashist* published some relevant excerpts

[18] *Fashist*, 9, p. 9; *Natsiya*, 1934, 5, p. 8; 1935, 6, p. 3; Balakshin, 1, p. 112.

[19] A letter from the head of the Eastern Department of the foreign political office of the NSDAP, Dr Leibbrandt, to Rosenberg, dated 4 September 1936, discusses the possibility of a Russian translation of *Mein Kampf*. The translator made it conditional on 'an introduction by the Führer to the Russian edition withdrawing passages referring to Russia, or explaining that they had now lost

from Hitler's book, the editors in their introduction praised the statesmanlike wisdom of the author in the years since he had written the book, which would no doubt ensure that he would not forfeit the trust of a great potential ally by ill-considered action against the Russian people. In no circumstances would the Russian fascists tolerate conquest of Russian soil. When the Red Army became the Russian Army, 'woe to him who is not with us'.

Finally, fascist Russia would 'reconcile labour and capital' and cut the ground from under socialism by subordinating class to national interests. The corporative state as conceived by the Italian fascists would provide the basis for the solidarity of all classes and groups in the name of the supreme national interest. After its victory, fascism in Russia would organize all the 'creative forces' of the country along occupational lines. These *natsionalnye soyuzy* of employees and employers within a given occupation would form a national corporation, questions in dispute being decided by a court of arbitration presided over by a government representative. Although the state would maintain constant supervision over the entire economy, the national unions would not only represent the professional interests of their members, but also form the basis of the fascist administrative system. Their elected representatives, together with representatives of the fascist party, would act as the local and central governmental bodies. At the summit of the system there would be an All-Russian *Zemski Sobor*, a kind of estates assembly on the model of the sixteenth and seventeenth centuries.

Precisely because these ideas were taken over from Italy, the Russian fascists sought for analogous phenomena in Russian history. Kozmin, president of the RFP, was convinced that 'the activities of the Zemskie Sobory in the sixteenth and seventeenth centuries, representing the organized social groups of those times, were a striking example of the value of the corporative system'. And General A. I. Spiridovich regarded Zubatov as the first Russian fascist and advocate of the idea of the corporative state, employing in 1901–3 the methods later adopted by Mussolini.[20] Both these

their validity. The Führer is said to have expressed willingness to do so. It seems to me desirable to settle this question'. Bundesarchiv Koblenz. NS-Mischbest. 1580 (250-d-18-05/5).

[20] *Natsiya*, 1932, 3, p. 14; 1934, 5, p. 12. In the fascist journals I have been able to consult there is no reference to the 'fascist character' of the pre-revolutionary Russian Right. Cf. H. Rogger, 'Was there a Russian Fascism?' in *Journal of Modern History*, 1964, 4.

men, however, believed that only a strong central power, standing above classes, could ensure the success of the corporative system, and both thought in terms of a monarchy. But it was on this question of the precise state form of the future Russia that the fascist leaders were unwilling to commit themselves. Rodzaevsky would go no further than to say that there was no question of a republic or a democracy, for these would bring with them 'corruption, class struggle, the battle of parties, and the dictatorship of the plutocracy'.[21] What the leaders continually emphasized was that in order to save Russia there would first have to be a dictatorship of the fascist party. That meant, in the final analysis, that the Russian people, having been the object of a communist experiment, would now become the object of a fascist experiment, and in this sense Russian fascism could hardly be considered an alternative, for the dictatorship of a party could scarcely be reconciled with that 'liberation of the Russian people' which it proclaimed as its goal. The choice would be between an existing dictatorship and a new dictatorship whose consequences none could foretell.

## The end of the All-Russian Fascist Party

The aim of seizing power in 1938, and the blueprints for the future fascist Russia, were proclaimed in the middle thirties. This was the high-point of the movement. It is true that in 1937 Rodzaevsky extended the VFP into the Russian Fascist Union (RFS) by establishing relations with one emigré organization in Germany and two in South America; and it is also true that at first collaboration with the Japanese went smoothly. When the latter set up a bureau for Russian emigré affairs in Harbin in 1935 to maintain supervision over their activities, Rodzaevsky and the VFP took a leading part in it. The statement of the chairman of the military department of the VFP, Sergei Dolov at the third party congress in 1935, that his job was to make military cadres out of resolute patriots, was undoubtedly made with Japanese approval. But in the autumn of 1937 difficulties arose, and the Japanese banned the fascist daily *Nash Put*. The party organizations, however, were left undisturbed, and the periodical *Natsiya* became a weekly, published in Harbin.

[21] Because of the strength of the monarchists in the Far East emigration, Rodzaevsky in 1940 declared his readiness to re-establish the monarchy in the event of a fascist victory. The small group which sympathized with Vonsiatsky preferred a fascist dictator. Cf. Bundesarchiv Koblenz, NS-Mischbest. vorl. 1589 (250-d-18-10/3).

With the advance of the German troops in the west in 1940 most of the Russian emigré associations in Europe were dissolved, and Rodzaevsky took the opportunity to declare that now the Russian Fascist Union in Manchukuo was the only independent centre capable of organizing all Russians throughout the world. These hopes were as illusory as those based earlier on the prospect of German-Soviet or Japanese-Soviet hostilities, to which they had for a while clung even after the Soviet-German pact of 1939. In the years 1941–5 the Japanese, with their eye on relations with Russia with whom a non-aggression pact had been concluded in the spring of 1941, steadily reduced the activities of the Russian fascists. The entry of Soviet troops into Manchuria in late summer 1945 brought them to an end. Rodzaevsky at first took refuge in Shanghai, whence he wrote a personal letter to Stalin in which he regretted his past mistakes and expressed the hope of being able to 'spend the rest of his days in enthusiastic work for the fatherland, the party, and the leader' in the Soviet Union.[22] After a long debate with himself whether to heed the enticing promises of the Soviets or the warnings of his friends, he surrendered voluntarily to the Soviet authorities. In Moscow in 1946 he was condemned to death and executed.

It is worthy of note that when the VFP was having its greatest success among the emigrés, in the Soviet Union itself there was a marked turn towards 'Soviet patriotism', although there can scarcely have been any direct connection between the two. But this new Soviet nationalism, which became more and more marked especially during the second world war, nullified the appeal of one of the most important Russian fascist watchwords, the fight against internationalism. Together with the partial rehabilitation of Russian historical traditions and of the Orthodox Church, this Soviet nationalism induced a number of emigrés to return to the USSR after the war. So it was not a wholly opportunistic move on Rodzaevsky's part to write to Stalin in 1945: 'Stalinism is precisely what we mistakenly called Russian fascism, cleansed of all extremes, illusions, and errors.'

[22] Balakshin, 2, pp. 122–35.

# The Hero in the Empty Room
## José Antonio and Spanish Fascism

## Hugh Thomas

'Slowly he returned to his table to start on his task once more in silence. It was seven o'clock in the evening. All Rome, the day's work over, was already in the streets, in the warm night. The Corso was all activity and gossip, like the Alcala (in Madrid) at the same time – people going in and out of cafés and cinemas. One might think that the Duce alone remained at work, next to his reading light, in the corner of an immense empty room, keeping vigil for his people, for Italy, whose breathing he could hear, heaving like an infant daughter. What apparatus of government, what system of checks and balances, councils or assemblies, could replace this picture of the Hero become Father, watching by a nightlight the toil as well as the rest of his people?'

Thus José Antonio Primo de Rivera, recalling the end of an interview with Mussolini, in a prologue to a Spanish translation of the Duce's *Fascism*. Something of the nature of the only real leader of Spanish fascism becomes immediately clear. Not the rather purple, almost advertisement-style prose, for it would obviously be possible to find such bastard romanticism on the lips of many European fascists. But the conception of the Father-Saviour appears specially strong, the longing for a new Solon, who will not only abolish futile democratic striving but do this without even an apparatus of government. No party, no singing gymnasts, no actual mass contact. He is not necessarily a Puritan, indeed he positively likes to hear in the distance the noise of people laughing in the cafés: the breathing is after all of a daughter and one with whom the Solon's relations clearly border on the incestuous. Solon is not a politician, he is an amateur who, because he knows the world (*'intuicismo'*, as José Antonio put it elsewhere), is loved by the people. This romantic personality recurs in the writings and speeches of José Antonio, and though he may have sometimes given the impression that Mussolini expressed that personality for Italy (and perhaps believed so) there is no doubt whom he really had in mind: not himself by any means, but his father, the old general, the dictator of 1923–30.

No doubt in life José Antonio's relations with his father were of an extreme ambiguity. He took no part in politics when his father was in power, though he was of an age to have profited from the relationship – he left the university in 1924. Between the serious, single-minded, poetic son and the easy-going, sensual, gay father there could hardly have been much real contact. His father's sudden downfall, exile, and death evidently troubled José Antonio, and he began his short political life immediately afterwards, with the specific aim of defending the memory of the old dictator. Although temperamentally conservative, he could not understand and therefore could not forgive the action of the conservative parties in deserting the dictatorship. He began to devise some framework which would rationally or even poetically, but at all events intellectually, justify his father's unintellectual approach to government. This intellectual effort led him of course into conflict with genuine intellectuals, for he believed that it was the efforts of university professors which had led to his father's fall. (This antipathy did not, however, include Ortega y Gasset, with his vague notions of a 'creative minority', even though Ortega had been a bitter enemy of the elder Primo de Rivera.)

José Antonio's attempt to recreate his father is the starting point of Spanish fascism, and to a great extent the history of Spain since 1939 has been dominated by that attempt also: the intellectual stuffing of the present regime in Spain, such as there is, no doubt derives via Serrano Suñer distantly from José Antonio, to whom there are monuments everywhere; but the support for Franco derives from the conception of him as a reincarnation of Primo de Rivera *père*, a harsh, bloody-minded, ascetic reincarnation no doubt, but nevertheless the embodiment of the spirit of military order, the man who has abolished political parties, but has nevertheless led the way (ultimately only, it is true) to increased prosperity, the man who inherited political turmoil and afterwards gave peace (in Primo's case the endless street-fighting in Barcelona, in Franco's the civil war), and, for many people perhaps most important, the man who preserved the 'integrity of Spain' – which, both before Franco and before Primo de Rivera, seemed to be splitting into several autonomous entities, to the cost of age-old Castille, the glory of old Spain. Just before the Asturias rising in 1934, José Antonio wrote to Franco a curious letter which, if it did not precisely ask Franco to seize the leadership of the anti-democratic forces in Spain, at least opened the way for a dialogue on the subject: but Franco does not seem to have replied. Significantly, the letter itself chiefly described the likelihood of a socialist revolution resulting in the final separation of Catalonia from Spain: 'I know that, barring a complete catastrophe, the Spanish state could recapture Catalonia by force . . . But Spain would then have before it not simply Catalonia but all that Antiespaña of other European powers.'

The letter shows a little more of the identity of José Antonio's rationalization of his father's politics. Before the general came to power in 1923, Catalonia had been for at least six years in a state of semi-civil war, in which the Spanish state found itself faced by both anarcho-syndicalism and Catalan nationalism. Primo de Rivera solved the problem with a whiff of grapeshot, defending the integrity of Spain by denying Catalonia any hope of autonomy: the consequence being that the Catalan regionalist movement even tried (unsuccessfully, it is true) to establish relations with the communists. In trying to point out to Franco the dangers to Catalonia José Antonio was stressing what would be one of the central points of the Spanish fascist creed, and one which has to a great extent survived till this day: instead of the nazi desire to incorporate all Germans everywhere under the same flag, Spanish fascism presented the limited and more easily realized goal of the permanent and if necessary enforced unification of all Spain within the same centralized state. 'Better a red Spain than a broken Spain', *rojo* better than *roto*, was one of the slogans of the monarchist leader Calvo Sotelo. The letter also further propagated the useful concept of Antiespaña, a block of powerful enemies, not precisely enemies of the Spanish people but of the idea of a united Spain, a block whose membership has often seemed to shift during the years, but which certainly has often been held to mean freemasonry, liberalism, the entire nineteenth century, the Jews, as well as socialism or communism – though antisemitism is necessarily weak.

It would be misleading to think of Spain, of course, as having only two fascist leaders, José Antonio and Franco: indeed, the identification of Franco as a fascist at all begs a good many questions, even though he has been the embodiment for many years of the fascist yearnings of some Spaniards. Indeed, before José Antonio's entry into politics as a candidate for the post of *jefe* (leader) of the various fascist groups in Spain, there were several separate drives towards a 'fascist solution', each helping the formation of a climate of opinion where fascism could be successful. Students of European fascism will note one point of demarcation from other countries: there were also no forces deriving from the disgruntled Left. The Spanish fascists made overtures to both anarchists and to Prieto, but failed: I find two members only of the Falange who were ever members of the communist party – Oscar Perez Solis and Santiago Montero Rios.

First, though not in order of time, were several small groups who genuinely aped the nazi or fascist movements in Germany and Italy. To begin with, these were hardly more offensive than Mosley's New Party in its early days and a good deal less formidable even than that, since they lacked any personality of Mosley's stature. Had it not been for developments beyond these leaders' control, the names of these little groups would merit hardly more than a footnote in the history of Spain; as it is, most of their leaders were engulfed in the catastrophe of the civil war and killed. Of these leaders, Ramiro Ledesma had a certain nazi quality, being a desperately unhappy youth who had run away from the almost inconceivably narrow society of Zamora, where his father was a village schoolmaster, when aged fifteen; after flirtations with German philosophy he founded an explicitly fascist party of ten members, all about 25, all with university backgrounds, just before the collapse of the monarchy, in March 1931. Clearly affected as he was by Hitler (whom he tried to copy physically), Ledesma was also aware that in Spain the only movement which wished to break completely with the past, to reject all bourgeois and democratic ideas, was the anarcho-syndicalist: and he called himself a national syndicalist. Nevertheless, he apparently founded his first political weekly, *La Conquesta del Estado*, with money given to him by the last monarchist government, whose secret service operators supposed Ledesma would create dissension among liberals. There was never any serious interaction between him and the anarchists, who of course were a huge nation-wide movement of perhaps 250,000. The second of the proto-fascists was Onesimo Redondo, who also, like Ledesma, came from Old Castille. Redondo had been to Germany and had admired the nazis' goosesteps. But he was bent on revival as much as renewal – revival of traditional Spanish Catholicism, the spirit of the Inquisition, of medieval intolerance, of medieval asceticism. About the time Ledesma was founding the *Conquista del Estado*, Redondo was working as manager of a sugar-beet growers' union in Valladolid; he did not found this union, but he became its chief personality. He was essentially a defender of the small farmer's union, a kind of Poujade in embryo, protesting not against taxes but against capitalists, the *haute bourgeoisie*, separatists, anti-clericals almost equally. He had some relations with *Accion Catolica*, but that well-meaning middle-class association quite soon seemed to him wholly unsatisfactory, since of course it lacked any appeal to violence. His views were second-hand and frenzied: 'Coeducation . . . is a chapter in the history of Jewish atrocity against free nations.'

Slightly larger in size though more old-fashioned was the party known as nationalists, following Dr Albiñana of Burgos, a doctor nearly fifty and a deputy, who, however, was in no way an innovator. He was interested chiefly in tradition, and only in his followers' attachment to street fighting could he really be regarded as in any way a fascist. In addition there were a number of individuals in Spain about 1930/31 who, like Gimenez Caballero, were attracted by Mussolini or by Hitler but who did not think it necessary to found movements to articulate this – or were incapable of doing so. Some occasionally wrote for Ledesma, others were nominally members of other political movements which perhaps they hoped, a little imprecisely, to sway to their way of thinking.

The second main development leading towards fascism was the far stronger based and far more powerful Carlist or traditionalist movement. This, of course, had its origin in the protests against constitutional liberalism voiced by the first Don Carlos in 1835 and later by his grandson in the 1870s. The movement had been a continuous threat to constitutional monarchy throughout the 80s and 90s, and the fear that a falsely-timed progressive move would upset the orthodox restored dynasty in favour of the Carlists had been a permanently limiting force on Spanish prime ministers at the time of the American War. Later, the movement had rather fallen away among semi-literary disputes between *Mellistas* and *integristas*, between attitudes to Alfonso XIII and towards Primo de Rivera *père*, and indeed it might outwardly have seemed little more than a rather stronger Jacobitism. On the other hand, the failure of the Alfonso line, the coming of the Republic, and the almost immediate threats to the Church actively revived Carlism, particularly in the old stronghold of Navarre; but soon every region had Carlist representatives; its newly elected chief in Spain (representing the ageing candidate to the throne Don Alfonso Carlos), Manuel Fal Conde, was a lawyer from Seville. The whole movement was given new point by the steady rise and growing expectations of the Basque nationalist movement, which hoped to gain, for the four largely Basque-speaking provinces (Navarre included), the same sort of independent privileges as earlier gained by the Catalans. Paradoxically, the Basque nationalist cause owed something to nineteenth-century Carlism, since it had been partly to defend local rights of the Basque province that the Basques had risen in the 1830s with the Carlists; however, twentieth-century Basque nationalism, if strongly Catholic like Carlism, was too bourgeois, democratic, and liberal to be able to establish any relation with the twentieth-century Carlists, who, from being in the nineteenth century advocates of a paternalist, Catholic, absolute monarchy with some degree of regional devolution, became in the twentieth more strident, more authoritarian, less concerned with regional than with state control, provided the state was firmly under the monarch, and having no truck with anti-clerical, liberalizing political parties. Carlism or traditionalism had strong attractions for *señoritos* or sons of good families who might otherwise have been drawn towards more orthodox fascism, but also among some bankers and industrialists (particularly those centred on Bilbao who could not feel enthusiasm for the Basque nationalist cause), for some small farmers in Navarre and Catalonia who felt threatened by anarchist promises of total collectivization of the land, and by many army officers. Among the Carlists, a vague anti-semitism – anti-commerce – was never far from the surface.

The third main force making for fascism in Spain was the army itself. Its long history of political action in the nineteenth century concluded with the long crisis of the Cuban war 1895-8, bringing back a number of angry post-imperial officers, first to a time of inaction and then to another long imperial war in Morocco, lasting from 1909 till 1926. Once again the officers returned, bitter against politicians, more drawn to their Moroccan enemies than to the working classes of their own country, and already having drawn sword against those working classes in strikes or other affrays, such as the great strike of 1917. Some infantry officers had in that year organized themselves in political *juntas*, themselves perhaps influenced by anarcho-syndicalism. By the time of the fall of the monarchy, the Spanish army officers resembled a somewhat exhausted political party, drawn in all directions (some remembering their fathers' Carlist War past, others drawn towards fascism, others still actively liberal, anti-clerical, and republican), most of them with ambiguous attitudes towards both the monarchy and towards Primo de Rivera (whom they had helped get into power and had not sustained in the end); they awaited in fact a new call and a new leader, not initially to give them a new political role but to give them unity. They moved in their majority rather slowly against the Republic, as first Azaña's reforms threatened (though absurdly gently) to castrate their political power and prestige forever, and then as it became clear that with rising hostility from both Left and Right the Republican government could maintain order only with difficulty. To many officers their future role – combat – became clear even in 1931 and 1932.

The fourth element in the making of Spanish fascism was another group of individuals, more respectable intellectually than the real proto-fascists round Ledesma and Redondo, though more literary in their general outlook. Thus a supporter of Ortega y Gasset, Garcia Valdescas, tried to found a central nationalist movement above parties. There was also a great deal of orthodox monarchical plotting even from the beginning of the Republic; though this was carried on chiefly by aristocrats and army officers, there was interaction among the personnel with Carlists and later with followers of José Antonio.

It was out of an eventual amalgamation of all these forces that Spanish fascism was eventually formed. Before the civil war, however, no Spanish fascist movement gathered much strength; it was first necessary that the constitutional groups of the Right should fail, either in government or in opposition, above all the proto-Christian-democratic movement, the CEDA, headed by Gil Robles, whose followers for some time clearly imagined him as a possible fascist-type leader, though probably not with his encouragement: certainly Gil Robles was saluted at his meetings with cries of *Jefe* and demands that he should be given the Ministry of War and 'all the power'. The failure of the CEDA to win the elections in February 1936 did not, however, focus attention on any fascist leader – instead of the outwardly constitutionalist, nominally monarchist, ex-finance minister to Primo de Rivera, Calvo Sotelo. A man of considerable ability and vigour, he had evidently toyed with fascism though, being of an older generation, he had had no following among the young men around Ledesma. He was also personally disliked by José Antonio, chiefly because he was supposed to have deserted his father, like so many others. At the same time, the army was plotting: if General Mola or General Goded could certainly have fitted into a regime presided over by Mussolini, they could also have been monarchists. General Franco's plans were ambivalent.

War brought a solution of a kind. Already in 1931, Ledesma's and Redondo's groups had joined together in a movement they long-windedly called the *Juntas de Ofensiva Nacional Sindicalista* (JONS). In 1934 the JONS merged with the little group which José Antonio had founded, the *Falange Española*, José Antonio sharing the leadership with Ledesma. Still the group was too exclusive to make any headway in Spanish politics, and José Antonio had to make gestures towards the orthodox political Right in order to survive financially. In consequence, Ledesma left the movement altogether in 1935, and went back to the post office. José Antonio put out feelers towards both the younger army plotters (the *Union Militar*) and towards the Carlists – indeed, his shock troops for the street battles against the students and militants of the Left were trained by the same colonel (some Carlists had gone to Italy to be trained also). Still, despite continued financial assistance from the Right he had hardly broadened the basis of his support by the time of the elections of February 1936 when he refused to enter the National Rightist front. Afterwards, his followers persuaded him to countenance increased violence, in what was anyway an increasingly violent atmosphere. Several supporters of the CEDA joined him, and in particular the rather ineffective CEDA youth movement, led by Ramon Serrano Suñer, General Franco's brother-in-law, an ambitious lawyer, also linked up with the Falange just about the time that the socialist youth joined the communists. Meantime, José Antonio himself had at least one meeting with the dissident Rightist generals, including Franco. Arrested in March because of his followers' policy of violence, José Antonio was now himself swept aside by events which he watched as a restless and increasingly powerless spectator from prison in Alicante. Some of his last letters and statements seem to give the impression that he had already given up hope of avoiding a straightforward military-type regime; others suggest that he was still anxious even in June to avoid collaboration with the orthodox Right. With the Carlists his relations were still cordial but on a national level far from close; locally, the Falange representative frequently made common cause with his Carlist *confrère*.

The rising came in July. The conspiracy was of course directed by army officers who, at the top level, hardly communicated with José Antonio's group until the end; they were far more perturbed about the Carlists who were holding out for a firm undertaking to restore the monarchy on Carlist lines. The nominal head of the rising, General Sanjurjo, had strong Carlist affiliations. Only one general, Yague, had actually joined the Falange before the out-break of war, and even his loyalties were far more anchored to the army than to the party. The first months of the war killed most of the first rank of Falange leaders – José Antonio himself, Ledesma, Redondo, Ruiz de Alda – and a number of others were captured and imprisoned. The army had the field to itself. Franco, without as yet any declaration of principles, became Chief of State as well as Head of Government; the Falange were not even consulted. Nor were the Carlists (their leaders were away at their Pretender's funeral). In April 1937 the last act of reunification was finally carried out, after the rump of José Antonio's Falange had tried feebly to assert itself when it was too late: Franco formally de-clared the unification of both Carlists and old Falange as well as other parties which supported the 'Nationalist Movement': the *Falange Española Tradicionalista de las Jons*, signifying all things to all people, to which all functionaries of the regime would belong, a vast mass movement without a political life. Symptomatically, its chief organizer in the early days was Serrano Suñer, who had never even had a membership card of the old Falange of José Antonio's day. It satisfied no one, and does not do so today; but it articulates at one remove the expressed sentiments of José Antonio. The solitary man who even now sits in the Prado keeping vigil for his people; in his own eyes at least he is the Hero become Father.

# Fascism, Right and Left

## Hugh Seton-Watson

Twenty years after the destruction of the Third Reich, the essence of fascism is still elusive. There are at least two governments in existence today, in Spain and Portugal, which can plausibly be described as fascist. The first owed its victory in large measure to the support of Mussolini and Hitler, and in both countries official spokesmen were at one time proud to identify themselves with fascism. Apart from this, communists freely use 'fascist' as a smear-word, designed not so much to identify anything specifically fascist as to discredit persons or groups which appear, for whatever reason, to be hindering communist purposes. The word is also often used as a term of abuse by woolly-minded persons of 'left-wing' views, many of whom are too young personally to have suffered, or to have faced serious danger, as a result of fascism.

Polemical and inexact use of the word has inevitably discouraged scholars. Some may be tempted to argue that it can only usefully be applied to one party and regime which have a limited but important place in the history of one country, Italy. Yet there remains a complex political and social phenomenon of the first half of the twentieth century which historians have the duty to examine. There remains a family relationship between a number of movements which had a part to play in the 1930s and 1940s. One could perhaps describe them by some neutral jargon phrase like 'non-Marxist totalitarianism'. But it seems to me preferable to use the word 'fascism' in full awareness of its subjective and emotional elements. Scientific precision is not at present attainable, and one may doubt whether it ever will be. One can pursue a more modest aim, to throw some light, by the comparative method, on a trend and a period in history of which imprecision, irrationality, and passion are inescapable features.

Let us begin not with a definition but with an attempt to narrow the field of discussion. All fascist movements combine, I suggest, in varying proportions, a reactionary ideology and a modern mass organization. Their leaders, when in opposition, extol traditional values, but they appeal for support to the masses, and exploit any form of mass discontent that is available. In their original ideas they often closely resemble old-fashioned conservatives, but their methods of struggle, indeed their whole notion of political organization, belong not to the idealized past but to the modern age. Their outlook may be nostalgic, and it is certainly elitist, but as a political force they are more democratic than oligarchic. The study of fascism requires an understanding both of nineteenth-century European conservatism and of the social conflicts within both the advanced industrial and the underdeveloped economies which co-existed within Europe between the world wars.

There is a vast literature on European conservatism, covering its ideas, its personalities, and its political action. But comparative study has certainly not yet exhausted its possibilities. A recent publication of great merit in this field is a symposium on *The European Right*, edited by Professors Hans Rogger and Eugen Weber of the University of California in Los Angeles.[1] Though the following arguments are not a summary of its contents, and indeed I do not always agree with the interpretations of its contributors, I must express my appreciation of this book, and recommend it to all readers of this journal.

The word 'reactionary', perhaps even more than the word 'fascist', has become a term of abuse in political propaganda. Yet the word has a perfectly clear and legitimate meaning. A reactionary is one who wishes to resurrect the past, and reactionary ideologies are based on visions of the past, usually more mythical than real, which are intended to inspire political action in the present. A conservative, by contrast, should be one whose aim is not so much to

---

1 *The European Right: a historical analysis*, editors Hans Rogger and Eugen Weber, University of California Press, 1965, pp. 589, $9.50. The book suffers to some extent from the diversity of approach which seems to be inevitable in works by many authors (in this case, ten). The distinction between the traditionalist and the modern 'Rights', between classical conservatism and 'right radicalism', is not always clear. Some contributors concentrate on the ideas of the period before the emergence of fascist movements. Others have given surveys of political history rather than political or social analysis. Outstanding in my view are the three contributions by Professor Weber – a general Introduction and a chapter each on France and on Rumania. I must also mention Mr Deak's chapter on Hungary, which has perhaps less depth than Mr Weber's but is both perceptive and clear.

resurrect the past as to conserve what he believes to be valuable in the traditions and institutions which still exist. In practice the difference between reactionaries and conservatives has been blurred. Reactionaries have usually called themselves conservatives. The Right in most European countries has had a reactionary wing, in some cases forming a distinct faction, in others operating within a larger conservative group.

Those ideas derived from the European Right which have been important in the intellectual formation of the leaders of fascism have been essentially nostalgic and reactionary. They may be briefly examined under the four main headings of religion, the state, the social structure, and the nation.

The identification of the church with reactionary ideas, and the tendency for reactionary spokesmen to take their stand on religion, to denounce their political opponents as enemies of God, and indeed to regard most modern ideas and institutions as works of the devil, can be found to some extent almost everywhere, but is most marked in Catholic and Orthodox countries. In England the official church was respectable and conservative, but hardly reactionary. In Germany the Lutheran church, like the Hohenzollern monarchy, was more reactionary, yet as a political factor too vacillating to be a strong bulwark of reaction. In Spain, France, Austria, and Italy the church was a powerful reactionary force. There were of course variations. In France there was always a strong minority trend towards Catholic democracy, and the task of Catholic reactionaries was complicated by the difficulty of deciding which of the mutually hostile secular reactionary groups they should support. Austrian Catholicism abandoned oligarchic for demagogic procedures with the rise of Karl Lueger's movement, yet can hardly be said to have much modified its reactionary political outlook. Italian Catholicism after 1870 was in a sense the most reactionary of all, since it was committed to hostility to the Italian State as such. In the only Orthodox State with centuries of continuous independence behind it, the Russian Empire, the political attitude of the church was overwhelmingly reactionary. The outstanding spokesman was of course Pobedonostsev. But the role of the church was diminishing, as the secular reactionaries were not only losing their own religious faith but paying less attention to it as an influence on the people. On the other hand there were a few dissident voices, believers who rejected the existing secular social and political order. They were not many, but they included men of the stature of Vladimir Solovyov, Berdyaev, and Struve. In the new Balkan states the Orthodox church by no means always stood for reaction. The reason was that the church had been emotionally committed to the struggle for liberation from the Turks, which was inescapably linked with democratic ideas. This was least true of Rumania, whose liberation was more the result of war and diplomacy by the Great Powers, and less of her people's own efforts, and in which the social structure was more rigid and oligarchical than in Serbia, Bulgaria, or Greece.

Reactionaries aim to restore a past political system as well as to restore religious belief. In this sense there can hardly be said to have been any reactionaries in England. No one aimed to return to the age before Simon de Montfort's parliament, or to restore Stuart despotism, or even to undo the Reform Bills of 1832 or 1867. At most one can quote the dislike of Milner, Chesterton, or Belloc for modern political parties. In France, however, the desire to undo the work of 1789, to bring back the Kings who had made France great, was long a powerful emotion, even if it was held only by a minority. The Carlists in Spain, and the supporters of the Bourbon monarchy in the Italian South, left their mark on the political scene in both countries. In Prussia and Austria the task was rather to conserve privileges and obstruct reform than to restore the good old days of the Holy Roman Empire. In Russia we have the paradox that in the nineteenth century those who held the purest reactionary views about the State were reformers, and those who upheld the autocracy as it was were to some extent modernizers. The early Slavophils wished to return to a mythical past, in which they claimed that the people, represented by its *zemskii sobor*, had enjoyed a happy communion with the Tsar. The germanized bureaucracy created by Peter the Great and his successors must be abolished, the peasants freed from serfdom, and educated men from censorship and police rule. By contrast, the bureaucrats of the Tsars, resolutely opposed to all liberty, viewed with realism the need to bring Russia into the modern world of industry and conscript armies. Only in the last decades of the Empire, after the reforming zeal of the Slavophils had been worn away by decades of official obstruction, and their intellectual descendants had been carried away by russifying nationalism, did a new reactionary synthesis of demagogic autocracy begin to appear.

The reactionary view of the social structure had two main elements, a dislike of the industrial urban economy and a belief in a common interest uniting the old ruling class with the masses against the capitalists. The myth of a golden age of rural harmony in the past was usually an important feature of such doctrines. Their exponents came sometimes from the upper classes but more often from the professions – from writers, academics, soldiers, or government officials, often though not always derived from families of the lesser nobility or provincial gentry. It is worth stressing the strength of traditional anti-capitalist and anti-liberal values, which survived within the educational systems and within the intellectual elites long after industrial capitalism had become dominant in the economy, and even after socialism had arisen and gained strength as a force challenging liberal and capitalist values from the base of the social pyramid and from a post-industrial point of view. The cliché of successive feudal, capitalist, and socialist stages greatly distorts the historical reality. The three stages overlapped. The combination of the two sorts of anti-capitalism, from above and from below, looking to the past and looking to the future, is an essential trend in modern European history, still under-rated by historians, still blurred by the conventional wisdom of Western democracy, and especially important for the origins of fascism. It was important even in England, the classical home of the capitalist ethos and bourgeois values. In the synthesis of capitalist and traditionalist outlooks promoted by the Victorian 'public schools' – whose function was to draw the children of the new rich into the upper class – it is by no means clear which element was the stronger. The idea of the common interest between old elite and common people against money-grubbing materialism is found in 'Young England', in Disraeli, in Milner, and in G. K. Chesterton, to take only a few obvious names. Something similar can even be found in the United States, whether in New England or the Old South. In France and in Prussia anti-capitalism of both kinds was even stronger, but cooperation between them was inhibited by a fiercer hatred between classes. The memories of 1793, 1848, and 1871 in France, and the contempt of the Prussian Junker for the mob, made almost impassable barriers.

It must also be noted that everywhere in western Europe capitalism and industry were defeating the pre-capitalist ruling class. The capitalists became rich, and acquired social and political power.

They were now a large part of the ruling class. But essentially they were conservatives, not reactionaries. They wanted to preserve and secure their own power, not to restore the past. The social programme of the reactionaries was different – to limit or even reverse industrialization, and to build on the solid foundations of the peasant class, allegedly the heir to the best moral and spiritual values. An important distinction should be made here. In the countries of southern and eastern Europe whose economy was still agrarian, and the bulk of whose population lived in villages, the peasant problem was the problem of the masses, and peasant discontent was the main potential force of social revolution. But in the industrial countries the advocacy by intellectuals of the simple virtues of peasant society was reactionary utopianism. It was not of much importance in England, to whose problems it was demonstrably irrelevant, or even in the three western Latin countries, where the cultural tradition was overwhelmingly urban. But it was a factor of great importance in Germany.

The cementing force in reactionary ideologies from the end of the nineteenth century onwards was nationalism. This is of course something of a paradox. The doctrine of nationalism is essentially a product of the Enlightenment and of 1789. To place above all the interests of the nation is to reject traditional concepts of legitimacy, to diminish the claims of God and the King. In the age of Metternich, reactionaries were against nationalism. But in the decades that followed the unification of Italy and Germany they made a bid to take over the national idea for themselves. It no longer made sense to argue that the community, within which elite and people were united against materialist money-grubbers, was simply the community of the King's subjects: the right word was the Nation. The outstanding doctrinaire was Charles Maurras, whose *nationalisme intégral* became a model for nationalist intellectuals in many lands.

It is worth noting some different aspects of nationalism, depending on the situations in which different nations found themselves. It is a paradox that it was in France, whose national identity was centuries old and whose national independence was not threatened, that an intellectual doctrine of nationalism was formulated. The explanation can perhaps be found in the sense of humiliation resulting from the defeat of 1870. In the other country of ancient national identity, England, there has never been any function for a nationalist movement or doctrine to perform, and it can hardly be said that either has existed. In Italy and Germany the sense of national identity was still precarious after 1870, and it is understandable that intellectuals in both countries should have felt obliged to emphasise it. There is a vast difference between the Latin word 'nation', with its background of Roman church and law and modern Enlightenment, and the Germanic word 'folk', with its suggestion of dark emotions, tribal loyalties, and Teutonic forests. But the similarity of the post-1870 status of both nations is important, and was reinforced by the German defeat and Italian disillusion in 1918. Further east in Europe nationalism was a simpler and more straightforwardly revolutionary force. There were nations demanding independence (Poles, Czechs, Slovaks, Croats, Balts, Finns, Ukrainians), or demanding that their incomplete independence should be perfected by union with their unredeemed brothers (Greeks, Serbs, Rumanians, Bulgarians). There were other nations again whose aim was to prevent their multi-national subjects from breaking away, by imposing their own nationality on them. Such were the Hungarians and Russians, and to a lesser extent the Prussians and Austrian Germans.

A special case were nations which had attained, at least for a large part of their number, an independent State, but still felt themselves to be dominated by foreigners. This was especially the case in the agrarian states of eastern Europe, where the growing industries were largely owned either by foreigners or by members of economically more advanced alien minorities in their midst. Greeks in Rumania, Germans in Hungary, formed such minorities, but far more important were the Jews. It is not possible simply to correlate the intensity of anti-semitism with the economic power of the Jewish minority. Maurras denounced Jews and Protestants as alien bodies in France, and the Dreyfus Affair was the greatest anti-semitic event in nineteenth-century Europe. But it cannot seriously be argued that Jews dominated the cultural or economic life of France. This could however certainly be argued of Hungary, yet before 1914 Hungarian Jews had little cause to complain. The rulers of Hungary from 1867 were landed noblemen whose leaders had grown up with liberal ideas. As the years passed their liberalism waned, but they had no motive to deprive the Jews of the liberties they had originally granted them. They wanted Hungary industrialized, but did not themselves want to go into business: the Jews did a necessary job for them. For their part the Hungarian Jews became ardent Hungarian patriots. Hostility to the Jews came from peasants, and from the small but growing number of peasant children entering business or the intellectual professions, especially among the non-Hungarian nationalities. In Vienna, where Jewish influence in business and in the professions, though very great, was still less than in Budapest, anti-semitism was much stronger. The reason is that the German middle classes of Vienna, both business and intellectual, were not only numerous but politically influential, and their interests were in direct conflict with those of the Jewish middle classes. In Germany the proportion of Jews in the population, and their economic and cultural influence, were relatively far less than in Vienna, but were sufficient to provoke hostility from the German upper and middle classes. To nostalgic reactionary intellectuals the Jews were an obvious object of dislike, a symbol of the urban materialist corruption which threatened the idyllic medieval Germanic peasant virtues. But the area of most widespread anti-semitism was the belt of heavy Jewish settlement extending from Lithuania through eastern Poland, western Ukraine, Slovakia, Bukovina, and Moldavia, from the Baltic to the Black Sea. Most of this territory was within the Russian Empire until 1917, part was within Hungary and Rumania. Hungarians and Russians were not much inclined to anti-semitism, but among Poles, Ukrainians, Slovaks, and Rumanians it was very strong.[2] The artificial social structure of the Jewish community, which was excluded from agriculture and government service, and thus confined to business, the intellectual professions, and employment in crafts or factories, deepened the gulf between the Jews and their neighbours. To the peasant, the Jew was the shopkeeper who took his small cash income; to the official, the rootless half-educated fanatic who peddled ideas; to the would-be indigenous small capitalist, his successful established rival who prevented him from getting a footing in business; to the government, the most active element in the discontented urban proletariat. In the eastern belt, despotic governments, reactionary

[2] Russian anti-semitism in fact was concentrated in the Ukraine and Bessarabia, and though its leaders regarded themselves as Russians, they were mostly of Ukrainian, Polish, or Rumanian origin. In the central Muscovite core of Russia anti-semitism had much weaker roots.

ideologues, discontented peasants, and to some extent also industrial workers could unite in hating the Jew, blaming their various fears and sufferings on him, the foreign exploiter and agent of subversion.

Reactionary ideologies and political programmes, varied mixtures of religious intolerance, historical myth, social utopia, nationalism and anti-semitism, were present in most European countries around 1914. But fascism is more than a reactionary ideology: it is a movement, based on substantial mass support. The significant fascist movements all started·in opposition to existing regimes. All had to struggle for power, and some were severely persecuted. All regarded their victories (some of which were of brief duration) as triumphs of a revolutionary idea. None aimed at restoring the past. Their ideologies were essentially reactionary, but they cannot correctly be described as 'counter-revolutionary', for they did not seek to replace something overthrown by a previous revolution. They were essentially revolutionary movements. The fact that their aims and policies were distasteful to me entitles me to call them evil revolutions, but not to deny their revolutionary character.

The 1930s and 1940s were the period of fascist success. Inevitably fascist policies and institutions were aped by others. Obvious examples are Hungary under Gömbös, Yugoslavia under Stojadinovic, and Rumania under King Carol. But in these cases no fascist revolution took place. The existing regimes were only superficially changed, and even the anti-Jewish measures were comparatively mild. The true fascists were not deceived. Arrow Cross, Ustashe, and Iron Guard bided their time, and when it came they showed, in orgies of butchery, that they were men of a different stamp.

There are some marginal cases. The regime of Dollfuss in Austria was copied from the Italian model. But it was introduced from above, without any forcible seizure of power, and it never succeeded in organizing much genuine mass support. It was without doubt reactionary, but it is hard to say whether it was fascist. The Spanish case is also obscure. During the civil war there were revolutionary fascists on Franco's side, but after victory they lost much of their influence. At least by the 1960s Franco's Spain looked less like fascism than like an old-fashioned military dictatorship with bureaucratic and capitalist support. As for Italy itself, it may even be paradoxically argued that it was 'less fascist' than some other regimes. Certainly it never attained the totalitarian perfection which Mussolini proclaimed as his goal.

Of the Nazi regime in Germany, all that need be noted here is that no simple formula will describe it. Hitler got money from German capitalists, but once in power he subjected them to his will, even if he left them good profits. Among his supporters were not only 'petty bourgeois' (whatever that may mean) and peasants but also hundreds of thousands of workers (even if a minority of the working class as a whole). Hitler had no plan for social revolution, but the totalitarian regime which he installed not only exterminated hundreds of thousands of German Jews (as well as millions of Jews outside Germany), but transformed the life of every individual and every class of the German people. To deny the epithet 'revolutionary' to this monstrous process is doctrinaire perversity.

The impact of fascism on the social structure of eastern Europe was different. It became a powerful force in Rumania, Hungary, and Croatia, and a considerable factor in Poland and Slovakia. In these countries in the 1930s the dominant social group was the bureaucracy. In Hungary and Poland large landowners were also powerful. Capitalists were in all five countries becoming more important, and included a large proportion of Jews. The bulk of the population were peasants, mostly very poor. There was a small skilled working class in a few established industrial centres, and a rapidly growing unskilled element flocking into the cities from the overpopulated countryside. The situation was in general similar to that of Russia at the turn of the century. As in Russia, the leadership of political movements challenging the regime came from the intelligentsia, in particular from students, professors, lawyers, and journalists, to a lesser extent from school-teachers. It is misleading to speak of 'the middle class': there were three distinct middle classes, separated by vertical compartments – bureaucrats, business men, and intelligentsia. The first of these formed the hard core of the regime, the second either supported the regime or was politically neutral, and opposition came essentially from the third. The intelligentsia was a definite social group with a distinct political role of its own. It was not part of a bourgeoisie: no culturally homogeneous bourgeoisie, in the West European sense, existed in these countries. The intelligentsia provided the leadership of all radical or revolutionary movements, and mass support came from the peasants and the unskilled workers. The skilled workers, for example the printers, and a section of the intelligentsia, remained loyal to social-democracy in Hungary, and virtually the whole industrial working class in Poland was socialist.[3] The unskilled workers in Hungary and the Balkans were on the whole divided between communists and fascists.

In Hungary and Rumania fascism was a powerful mass movement. In both countries it is arguable that a majority of peasants remained loyal to democratic parties, but certainly a very large minority of Hungarian peasants seeking a distribution of the great landed estates, and of Rumanian peasants demanding relief from the appalling poverty of the Depression years, were attracted by fascism. Both fascist movements also won working-class followers. The coal-mines of the Pecs area were a stronghold of the Arrow Cross, the Malaxa Works in Bucarest of the Iron Guard. The Croatian Ustashe and the Slovak People's Party are rather different: here the driving force was plain nationalism, the social composition broad but the working-class element almost completely lacking. The Ustashe specialized in assassination, and once in power they achieved a record of butchery comparable with that of Hitler himself. They operated in a smaller area, but the proportion of victims to total population was probably surpassed only in occupied Poland and Ukraine. In Poland convinced fascists (as opposed to conservative politicians aping fascist slogans) were numerous in the intellectual youth, but almost completely failed to attract peasant or working-class support.

Rumanian fascism attracted to its leading cadres not only thugs but also young people who were both honourable and intelligent. There was in Rumania a fascist populism which recalls the 'going to the people' in Russia in the 1870s. I saw something of this phenomenon at the end of the 1930s in both Rumania and Yugoslavia. The young Serbian *narodniki* were Marxists, and some were disciplined Communist Party members: the young Rumanian *narodniki* were fascists, and some were disciplined members of the Iron Guard. The social types, and the emotional attitudes, were very similar. The different orientation is not hard to explain. Rumanians feared Russia, and the capitalist enemy in their midst was often a Jew. The Third Reich was against both their

---

[3] There was a minority among the Polish workers who followed the illegal Communist Party, but virtually no Polish workers were fascists.

internal and their external enemy, Hitler appeared their protector, and they swallowed his doctrines. Serbs feared Germany and loved Russia, and there was no Jewish problem in their country. Marxism offered answers to their difficulties, and was backed by the might of the Slav elder brother. The two trends went different ways. All the talents and idealism of the one group were burned out in a series of ignoble crimes and repressions, and ended with their country's defeat. The similar gifts of the young Serbs were used to glorious effect in the War of Liberation, and the survivors have built a new Yugoslavia. It is easy to sneer at the Rumanian dead, or to praise the Yugoslavs for better judgment. But both were to a large extent victims of their environment. A historian should aim at deeper compassion than this, and I at least remember with equal affection my friends in both countries.

An obviously important feature of fascism which often gets left out, and which can perhaps never be well explained, is the charismatic leader. Mussolini, Degrelle, and José Antonio Primo de Rivera were clearly men of outstanding abilities. Szalasi and Codreanu were complex personalities, combining ruthlessness with strange flashes of nobility of character. Hitler still defies analysis. It is true, but not enlightening, that he came from the 'petty bourgeoisie'. More significant is that he came from the morally and culturally uprooted drifting population of the great city. Lacking the discipline of a systematic education or of membership in an organized class, profession, or church, driven by ambition and obsessed by a few crude hatreds, he pursued his aims with relentless logic and tireless effort. Hate propaganda was of course nothing new, but Hitler did not stop at words: he went ahead and exterminated six million Jews, and made preparations to uproot and exterminate many more millions of Poles, Ukrainians, and Russians. This was something new: the crimes of the religious wars and the conquest of the Americas were on a smaller scale, and the massacres of Djengiz Khan lacked the hideous trappings of modern science. These horrors started from an apparently insignificant little unsuccessful painter from Vienna, assisted by other colourless uprooted men, from Himmler down to the concentration camp commandants. It is worth noting that the other great mass exterminator of our age was also a half-educated, classless, uprooted figure. Tiflis and Baku were different from Vienna, and simplified

Marxism was different from a hotch-potch of Austrian reactionary ideology and anti-semitism, but the figures of Hitler and Stalin have many features in common which deserve serious study. One may hope that the like of these two men will never be seen again, but that the uprooted, classless, faceless hordes of the big cities of Europe and America have other monsters in store for us is pretty certain.

We still do not know enough about fascism, indeed we have hardly begun to study it. This is not just a task for academic scholars. The nagging questions remain, 'Has fascism a future?' and less simply, 'What social and political movements of the present or the near future can be better understood by a better knowledge of fascism?'

The Spanish and Portuguese regimes retain undoubted elements of fascism, but both appear to be in decline, and neither offers much inspiration to other countries. The only strong fascist regime to appear since the end of the Third Reich was in Argentina. Peron held power for ten years, enjoyed powerful support from the working class, and progressed a long way from old-fashioned Latin American military dictatorship towards stream-lined modern totalitarianism. In the end the church and the army were too strong for him, but his personal myth and his brand of fascism still enjoy mass support. In the Middle East the Moslem Brotherhood, with its combination of religious fundamentalism, terrorism, and populism, bore some resemblance to the Rumanian Iron Guard in its early days. The Young Officers' group of Nasser were certainly not fascists in their conspiratorial days, but the regime built by Nasser in the last ten years appears to have its similarities with fascist totalitarianism. President Soekarno's constant aping of Mussolini, in his personal style, his slogans, and his formal institutions, can hardly be unconscious. But the reality of fascist organization is missing: the only disciplined forces are the Communist Party and the national army. In Japan there are right-wing movements which may yet revive, in some modified form, the revolutionary terrorism of the 1930s.[4] The new African dictatorships pride themselves on

---

[4] Whether the right-wing terrorists should be called fascists is arguable. See Richard Storry's admirable book *The Double Patriots*. See also *Thought and Behaviour in modern Japanese Politics*, by Masao Maruyama. I must confess to some disappointment with these essays by the outstanding Japanese

being 'socialist'. Yet the fact that they recite Marxist formulas, and seek the friendship of the Soviet Union or China, may prove less important than it at first appears. Revolutionary nationalist regimes, applying techniques of mass mobilization, injecting into their quasi-socialist ideologies strong doses of racialism and of historical mythology, and moving from simple dictatorship ever further to-wards totalitarianism, may end up nearer to the Third Reich than to the Soviet or Chinese model. As for their leaders, the Osagyefo certainly seems to possess more of the hysteria of Hitler and the vanity of Mussolini than of the cold genius of Lenin.

Anti-semitism is not at present a major factor in world politics. But it is worth noting a limited but significant analogy. The Jews were the outstanding case of a community of commercially and intellectually gifted people set in the midst of more numerous and more backward nations. This made them symbols of foreign exploitation or spiritual corruption, and offered them as ideal scape-goats to demagogues. There are other such communities. The Greeks and Armenians of the Arabic-speaking successor states of the Ottoman Empire, the Chinese of South-East Asia, the Indians of Burma and of some surviving British island colonies, the Lebanese of West Africa, are the main examples. But the analogy can even be extended to cover all communities of white-skinned business-men or technicians in Asia and Africa. The doctrine of 'neo-colonialism' deliberately concentrates hatred against these ready-made scapegoats. All that is wrong in new states can be attributed to them by demagogues, as all that was wrong in Hungary and Rumania was once attributed to the Jews. The argu-ment is the more effective because it contains a good deal of truth: European capitalists *do* still largely dominate new states in Asia and Africa, and North American capitalists older states in Central and South America, just as Jewish capitalists, both Rumanian and foreign citizens, largely dominated the Rumanian economy.

In the Western democracies there is not much sign of fascism today. There are of course persons, both Jewish and Gentile, who with a mentality which can only be compared with that of Hitler's race-experts, insist that Germans are by their birth or by their

authority on fascism. Learned and enlightening on the Japanese scene, he seems to lose his bearings when generalising on a wider scale: in particular, though he has clearly studied German sources carefully, he seems to me to have missed the essence of Hitler's national-socialism.

blood inescapably and eternally aggressive, totalitarian, and Jew-hating. Happily the reality of Germany today gives small support to them. In France the danger of a fascist movement based on returned Algerian *colons* and on the submerged remnants of followers of Darnand and his kind seems to have passed. In the United States McCarthyism seems to have been connected with a coincidence of increased social mobility with the dismayed discovery that America was no longer invulnerable. Something rather similar has occurred in Britain – a small but significant increase in social mobility coinciding with the collapse of the British Empire and a steady decline of Britain's status in the world.[5] But this has so far produced nothing more dangerous than 'angry' literature and journalism. Potentially more serious might be some sort of Negro fascism in the northern United States, or a totalitarian trend within Québécois nationalism. The tragic pressures on the white South Africans, who once for all their bitter resentments formed a democratic community, seem to be pushing them towards some form of fascism.

The purpose of these observations was not to offer definitions or to provide final answers, but simply to note a number of aspects of the movements which it is still best to call fascist. Comparative study of fascism is much needed today, not only to fill gaps in historical knowledge but to warn new generations of old dangers before they recur.

---

[5] An increase in social mobility inevitably creates bitterness among those who enter the elite but find no social acceptance. This problem existed in England in the early nineteenth century. However the *parvenus* were soon absorbed in a country which was at the height of its economic and political power. The failure of the post-Second World War elite to absorb a new influx of *parvenus*, and consequent poisoned atmosphere of contemporary British public life, is due to the fact that the influx coincided with a period of rapid decline in Britain's position in the world.

Revised December, 1966

# harper ✚ torchbooks

## HUMANITIES AND SOCIAL SCIENCES

### American Studies: General

THOMAS C. COCHRAN: The Inner Revolution. *Essays on the Social Sciences in History* TB/1140
EDWARD S. CORWIN: American Constitutional History. *Essays edited by Alpheus T. Mason and Gerald Garvey* △ TB/1136
CARL N. DEGLER, Ed.: Pivotal Interpretations of American History TB/1240, TB/1241
A. HUNTER DUPREE: Science in the Federal Government: *A History of Policies and Activities to 1940* TB/573
A. S. EISENSTADT, Ed.: The Craft of American History: *Recent Essays in American Historical Writing*
Vol. I TB/1255; Vol. II TB/1256
CHARLOTTE P. GILMAN: Women and Economics: *A Study of the Economic Relation between Men and Women as a Factor in Social Evolution.* ‡ *Ed. with an Introduction by Carl N. Degler* TB/3073
OSCAR HANDLIN, Ed.: This Was America: *As Recorded by European Travelers in the Eighteenth, Nineteenth and Twentieth Centuries. Illus.* TB/1119
MARCUS LEE HANSEN: The Atlantic Migration: 1607-1860. *Edited by Arthur M. Schlesinger* TB/1052
MARCUS LEE HANSEN: The Immigrant in American History. TB/1120
JOHN HIGHAM, Ed.: The Reconstruction of American History △ TB/1068
ROBERT H. JACKSON: The Supreme Court in the American System of Government TB/1106
JOHN F. KENNEDY: A Nation of Immigrants. △ *Illus.* TB/1118
LEONARD W. LEVY, Ed.: American Constitutional Law: *Historical Essays* TB/1285
RALPH BARTON PERRY: Puritanism and Democracy TB/1138
ARNOLD ROSE: The Negro in America TB/3048
MAURICE R. STEIN: The Eclipse of Community. *An Interpretation of American Studies* TB/1128
W. LLOYD WARNER and Associates: Democracy in Jonesville: *A Study in Quality and Inequality* ¶ TB/1129
W. LLOYD WARNER: Social Class in America: *The Evaluation of Status* TB/1013

### American Studies: Colonial

BERNARD BAILYN, Ed.: Apologia of Robert Keayne: *Self-Portrait of a Puritan Merchant* TB/1201
BERNARD BAILYN: The New England Merchants in the Seventeenth Century TB/1149
JOSEPH CHARLES: The Origins of the American Party System TB/1049

LAWRENCE HENRY GIPSON: The Coming of the Revolution: 1763-1775. † *Illus.* TB/3007
LEONARD W. LEVY: Freedom of Speech and Press in Early American History: *Legacy of Suppression* TB/1109
PERRY MILLER: Errand Into the Wilderness TB/1139
PERRY MILLER & T. H. JOHNSON, Eds.: The Puritans: *A Sourcebook of Their Writings*
Vol. I TB/1093; Vol. II TB/1094
EDMUND S. MORGAN, Ed.: The Diary of Michael Wigglesworth, 1653-1657: *The Conscience of a Puritan* TB/1228
EDMUND S. MORGAN: The Puritan Family: *Religion and Domestic Relations in Seventeenth-Century New England* TB/1227
RICHARD B. MORRIS: Government and Labor in Early America TB/1244
KENNETH B. MURDOCK: Literature and Theology in Colonial New England TB/99
WALLACE NOTESTEIN: The English People on the Eve of Colonization: 1603-1630. † *Illus.* TB/3006
LOUIS B. WRIGHT: The Cultural Life of the American Colonies: 1607-1763. † *Illus.* TB/3005

### American Studies: From the Revolution to 1860

JOHN R. ALDEN: The American Revolution: 1775-1783. † *Illus.* TB/3011
MAX BELOFF, Ed.: The Debate on the American Revolution, 1761-1783: *A Sourcebook* △ TB/1225
RAY A. BILLINGTON: The Far Western Frontier: 1830-1860. † *Illus.* TB/3012
W. R. BROCK: An American Crisis: *Congress and Reconstruction, 1865-67* ○ △ TB/1283
EDMUND BURKE: On the American Revolution: *Selected Speeches and Letters.* ‡ *Edited by Elliott Robert Barkan* TB/3068
WHITNEY R. CROSS: The Burned-Over District: *The Social and Intellectual History of Enthusiastic Religion in Western New York, 1800-1850* △ TB/1242
GEORGE DANGERFIELD: The Awakening of American Nationalism: 1815-1828. † *Illus.* TB/3061
CLEMENT EATON: The Freedom-of-Thought Struggle in the Old South. *Revised and Enlarged. Illus.* TB/1150
CLEMENT EATON: The Growth of Southern Civilization: 1790-1860. † *Illus.* TB/3040
LOUIS FILLER: The Crusade Against Slavery: 1830-1860. † *Illus.* TB/3029
DIXON RYAN FOX: The Decline of Aristocracy in the Politics of New York: 1801-1840. ‡ *Edited by Robert V. Remini* TB/3064
FELIX GILBERT: The Beginnings of American Foreign Policy: *To the Farewell Address* TB/1200
FRANCIS GRIERSON: The Valley of Shadows: *The Coming of the Civil War in Lincoln's Midwest: A Contemporary Account* TB/1246

† The New American Nation Series, edited by Henry Steele Commager and Richard B. Morris.

‡ American Persectives series, edited by Bernard Wishy and William E. Leuchtenburg.

* The Rise of Modern Europe series, edited by William L. Langer.

¶ Researches in the Social, Cultural, and Behavioral Sciences, edited by Benjamin Nelson.

§ The Library of Religion and Culture, edited by Benjamin Nelson.

Σ Harper Modern Science Series, edited by James R. Newman.

○ Not for sale in Canada.

△ Not for sale in the U. K.

FRANCIS J. GRUND: Aristocracy in America: *Social Class in the Formative Years of the New Nation*   TB/1001

ALEXANDER HAMILTON: The Reports of Alexander Hamilton. ‡ *Edited by Jacob E. Cooke*   TB/3060

THOMAS JEFFERSON: Notes on the State of Virginia. ‡ *Edited by Thomas P. Abernethy*   TB/3052

JAMES MADISON: The Forging of American Federalism: *Selected Writings of James Madison. Edited by Saul K. Padover*   TB/1226

BERNARD MAYO: Myths and Men: *Patrick Henry, George Washington, Thomas Jefferson*   TB/1108

JOHN C. MILLER: Alexander Hamilton and the Growth of the New Nation   TB/3057

RICHARD B. MORRIS, Ed.: The Era of the American Revolution   TB/1180

R. B. NYE: The Cultural Life of the New Nation: 1776-1801. † *Illus.*   TB/3026

FRANCIS S. PHILBRICK: The Rise of the West, 1754-1830. † *Illus.*   TB/3067

TIMOTHY L. SMITH: Revivalism and Social Reform: *American Protestantism on the Eve of the Civil War*   TB/1229

FRANK THISTLETHWAITE: America and the Atlantic Community: *Anglo-American Aspects, 1790-1850*   TB/1107

ALBION W. TOURGÉE: A Fool's Errand. ‡ *Ed. by George Fredrickson*   TB/3074

A. F. TYLER: Freedom's Ferment: *Phases of American Social History from the Revolution to the Outbreak of the Civil War. 31 illus.*   TB/1074

GLYNDON G. VAN DEUSEN: The Jacksonian Era: 1828-1848. † *Illus.*   TB/3028

LOUIS B. WRIGHT: Culture on the Moving Frontier   TB/1053

## American Studies: The Civil War to 1900

THOMAS C. COCHRAN & WILLIAM MILLER: The Age of Enterprise: *A Social History of Industrial America*   TB/1054

W. A. DUNNING: Essays on the Civil War and Reconstruction. *Introduction by David Donald*   TB/1181

W. A. DUNNING: Reconstruction, Political and Economic: 1865-1877   TB/1073

HAROLD U. FAULKNER: Politics, Reform and Expansion: 1890-1900. † *Illus.*   TB/3020

HELEN HUNT JACKSON: A Century of Dishonor: *The Early Crusade for Indian Reform. ‡ Edited by Andrew F. Rolle*   TB/3063

ALBERT D. KIRWAN: Revolt of the Rednecks: *Mississippi Politics, 1876-1925*   TB/1199

ROBERT GREEN MCCLOSKEY: American Conservatism in the Age of Enterprise: 1865-1910   TB/1137

ARTHUR MANN: Yankee Reformers in the Urban Age: *Social Reform in Boston, 1880-1900*   TB/1247

WHITELAW REID: After the War: *A Tour of the Southern States, 1865-1866. ‡ Edited by C. Vann Woodward*   TB/3066

CHARLES H. SHINN: Mining Camps: *A Study in American Frontier Government. ‡ Edited by Rodman W. Paul*   TB/3062

VERNON LANE WHARTON: The Negro in Mississippi: 1865-1890   TB/1178

## American Studies: 1900 to the Present

RAY STANNARD BAKER: Following the Color Line: *American Negro Citizenship in Progressive Era. ‡ Edited by Dewey W. Grantham, Jr.*   TB/3053

RANDOLPH S. BOURNE: War and the Intellectuals: *Collected Essays, 1915-1919. ‡ Edited by Carl Resek*   TB/3043

A. RUSSELL BUCHANAN: The United States and World War II. † *Illus.*   Vol. I TB/3044; Vol. II TB/3045

ABRAHAM CAHAN: The Rise of David Levinsky: *a documentary novel of social mobility in early twentieth century America. Intro. by John Higham*   TB/1028

THOMAS C. COCHRAN: The American Business System: *A Historical Perspective, 1900-1955*   TB/1080

FOSTER RHEA DULLES: America's Rise to World Power: 1898-1954. † *Illus.*   TB/3021

JOHN D. HICKS: Republican Ascendancy: 1921-1933. † *Illus.*   TB/3041

SIDNEY HOOK: Reason, Social Myths, and Democracy   TB/1237

ROBERT HUNTER: Poverty: *Social Conscience in the Progressive Era. ‡ Edited by Peter d'A. Jones*   TB/3065

WILLIAM L. LANGER & S. EVERETT GLEASON: The Challenge to Isolation: *The World Crisis of 1937-1940 and American Foreign Policy*   
Vol. I TB/3054; Vol. II TB/3055

WILLIAM E. LEUCHTENBURG: Franklin D. Roosevelt and the New Deal: 1932-1940. † *Illus.*   TB/3025

ARTHUR S. LINK: Woodrow Wilson and the Progressive Era: 1910-1917. † *Illus.*   TB/3023

GEORGE E. MOWRY: The Era of Theodore Roosevelt and the Birth of Modern America: 1900-1912. † *Illus.*   TB/3022

RUSSEL B. NYE: Midwestern Progressive Politics: *A Historical Study of Its Origins and Development, 1870-1958*   TB/1202

WILLIAM PRESTON, JR.: Aliens and Dissenters: *Federal Suppression of Radicals, 1903-1933*   TB/1287

WALTER RAUSCHENBUSCH: Christianity and the Social Crisis. ‡ *Edited by Robert D. Cross*   TB/3059

JACOB RIIS: The Making of an American. ‡ *Edited by Roy Lubove*   TB/3070

PHILIP SELZNICK: TVA and the Grass Roots: *A Study in the Sociology of Formal Organization*   TB/1230

IDA M. TARBELL: The History of the Standard Oil Company: *Briefer Version. ‡ Edited by David M. Chalmers*   TB/3071

GEORGE B. TINDALL, Ed.: A Populist Reader ‡   TB/3069

TWELVE SOUTHERNERS: I'll Take My Stand: *The South and the Agrarian Tradition. Intro. by Louis D. Rubin, Jr., Biographical Essays by Virginia Rock*   TB/1072

WALTER E. WEYL: The New Democracy: *An Essay on Certain Political Tendencies in the United States. ‡ Edited by Charles B. Forcey*   TB/3042

## Anthropology

JACQUES BARZUN: Race: *A Study in Superstition. Revised Edition*   TB/1172

JOSEPH B. CASAGRANDE, Ed.: In the Company of Man: *Twenty Portraits of Anthropological Informants. Illus.*   TB/3047

W. E. LE GROS CLARK: The Antecedents of Man: *Intro. to Evolution of the Primates. ○ △ Illus.*   TB/559

CORA DU BOIS: The People of Alor. *New Preface by the author. Illus.*   Vol. I TB/1042; Vol. II TB/1043

RAYMOND FIRTH, Ed.: Man and Culture: *An Evaluation of the Work of Bronislaw Malinowski ¶ ○ △*   TB/1133

DAVID LANDY: Tropical Childhood: *Cultural Transmission and Learning in a Puerto Rican Village* ¶   TB/1235

L. S. B. LEAKEY: Adam's Ancestors: *The Evolution of Man and His Culture. △ Illus.*   TB/1019

ROBERT H. LOWIE: Primitive Society. *Introduction by Fred Eggan*   TB/1056

EDWARD BURNETT TYLOR: The Origins of Culture. *Part I of "Primitive Culture." § Intro. by Paul Radin*   TB/33

EDWARD BURNETT TYLOR: Religion in Primitive Culture. *Part II of "Primitive Culture." § Intro. by Paul Radin*   TB/34

W. LLOYD WARNER: A Black Civilization: *A Study of an Australian Tribe. ¶ Illus.*   TB/3056

## Art and Art History

WALTER LOWRIE: Art in the Early Church. *Revised Edition. 452 illus.*   TB/124

EMILE MÂLE: The Gothic Image: *Religious Art in France of the Thirteenth Century. § △ 190 illus.*   TB/44

2

E. H. CARR: German-Soviet Relations Between the Two World Wars, 1919-1939    TB/1278

E. H. CARR: International Relations Between the Two World Wars, 1919-1939 ° △    TB/1279

E. H. CARR: The Twenty Years' Crisis, 1919-1939: An Introduction to the Study of International Relations ° △    TB/1122

GORDON A. CRAIG: From Bismarck to Adenauer: Aspects of German Statecraft. Revised Edition    TB/1171

WALTER L. DORN: Competition for Empire, 1740-1763. * Illus.    TB/3032

FRANKLIN L. FORD: Robe and Sword: The Regrouping of the French Aristocracy after Louis XIV    TB/1217

CARL J. FRIEDRICH: The Age of the Baroque, 1610-1660. * Illus.    TB/3004

RENÉ FUELOEP-MILLER: The Mind and Face of Bolshevism: An Examination of Cultural Life in Soviet Russia. New Epilogue by the Author    TB/1188

M. DOROTHY GEORGE: London Life in the Eighteenth Century △    TB/1182

LEO GERSHOY: From Despotism to Revolution, 1763-1789. * Illus.    TB/3017

C. C. GILLISPIE: Genesis and Geology: The Decades before Darwin §    TB/51

ALBERT GOODWIN: The French Revolution △    TB/1064

ALBERT GUÉRARD: France in the Classical Age: The Life and Death of an Ideal △    TB/1183

CARLTON J. H. HAYES: A Generation of Materialism, 1871-1900. * Illus.    TB/3039

J. H. HEXTER: Reappraisals in History: New Views on History and Society in Early Modern Europe △    TB/1100

STANLEY HOFFMANN et al.: In Search of France: The Economy, Society and Political System in the Twentieth Century    TB/1219

A. R. HUMPHREYS: The Augustan World: Society, Thought, & Letters in 18th Century England ° △    TB/1105

DAN N. JACOBS, Ed.: The New Communist Manifesto and Related Documents. Third edition, revised    TB/1078

HANS KOHN: The Mind of Germany: The Education of a Nation △    TB/1204

HANS KOHN, Ed.: The Mind of Modern Russia: Historical and Political Thought of Russia's Great Age    TB/1065

WALTER LAQUEUR & GEORGE L. MOSSE, Eds.: International Fascism, 1920-1945. ° △ Volume I of Journal of Contemporary History    TB/1276

WALTER LAQUEUR & GEORGE L. MOSSE, Eds.: The Left-Wing Intelligentsia between the Two World Wars. ° △ Volume II of Journal of Contemporary History    TB/1286

FRANK E. MANUEL: The Prophets of Paris: Turgot, Condorcet, Saint-Simon, Fourier, and Comte    TB/1218

KINGSLEY MARTIN: French Liberal Thought in the Eighteenth Century: A Study of Political Ideas from Bayle to Condorcet    TB/1114

L. B. NAMIER: Facing East: Essays on Germany, the Balkans, and Russia in the 20th Century △    TB/1280

L. B. NAMIER: Personalities and Powers: Selected Essays △    TB/1186

L. B. NAMIER: Vanished Supremacies: Essays on European History, 1812-1918 °    TB/1088

JOHN U. NEF: Western Civilization Since the Renaissance: Peace, War, Industry, and the Arts    TB/1113

FRANZ NEUMANN: Behemoth: The Structure and Practice of National Socialism, 1933-1944    TB/1289

FREDERICK L. NUSSBAUM: The Triumph of Science and Reason, 1660-1685. * Illus.    TB/3009

DAVID OGG: Europe of the Ancien Régime, 1715-1783 ° △    TB/1271

JOHN PLAMENATZ: German Marxism and Russian Communism. ° △ New Preface by the Author    TB/1189

RAYMOND W. POSTGATE, Ed.: Revolution from 1789 to 1906: Selected Documents    TB/1063

PENFIELD ROBERTS: The Quest for Security, 1715-1740. * Illus.    TB/3016

PRISCILLA ROBERTSON: Revolutions of 1848: A Social History    TB/1025

GEORGE RUDÉ: Revolutionary Europe, 1783-1815 ° △    TB/1272

LOUIS, DUC DE SAINT-SIMON: Versailles, The Court, and Louis XIV. ° △ Introductory Note by Peter Gay    TB/1250

ALBERT SOREL: Europe Under the Old Regime. Translated by Francis H. Herrick    TB/1121

N. N. SUKHANOV: The Russian Revolution, 1917: Eyewitness Account. △ Edited by Joel Carmichael
Vol. I TB/1066; Vol. II TB/1067

A. J. P. TAYLOR: From Napoleon to Lenin: Historical Essays ° △    TB/1268

A. J. P. TAYLOR: The Habsburg Monarchy, 1809-1918: A History of the Austrian Empire and Austria-Hungary ° △    TB/1187

G. M. TREVELYAN: British History in the Nineteenth Century and After: 1782-1919. ° △ Second Edition    TB/1251

H. R. TREVOR-ROPER: Historical Essays ° △    TB/1269

ELIZABETH WISKEMANN: Europe of the Dictators, 1919-1945 ° △    TB/1273

JOHN B. WOLF: The Emergence of the Great Powers, 1685-1715. * Illus.    TB/3010

JOHN B. WOLF: France: 1814-1919: The Rise of a Liberal-Democratic Society    TB/3019

## Intellectual History & History of Ideas

HERSCHEL BAKER: The Image of Man: A Study of the Idea of Human Dignity in Classical Antiquity, the Middle Ages, and the Renaissance    TB/1047

R. R. BOLGAR: The Classical Heritage and Its Beneficiaries: From the Carolingian Age to the End of the Renaissance △    TB/1125

RANDOLPH S. BOURNE: War and the Intellectuals: Collected Essays, 1915-1919. △ ‡ Edited by Carl Resek    TB/3043

J. BRONOWSKI & BRUCE MAZLISH: The Western Intellectual Tradition: From Leonardo to Hegel △    TB/3001

ERNST CASSIRER: The Individual and the Cosmos in Renaissance Philosophy. △ Translated with an Introduction by Mario Domandi    TB/1097

NORMAN COHN: The Pursuit of the Millennium: Revolutionary Messianism in Medieval and Reformation Europe △    TB/1037

C. C. GILLISPIE: Genesis and Geology: The Decades before Darwin §    TB/51

G. RACHEL LEVY: Religious Conceptions of the Stone Age and Their Influence upon European Thought. △ Illus. Introduction by Henri Frankfort    TB/106

ARTHUR O. LOVEJOY: The Great Chain of Being: A Study of the History of an Idea §    TB/1009

FRANK E. MANUEL: The Prophets of Paris: Turgot, Condorcet, Saint-Simon, Fourier, and Comte △    TB/1218

PERRY MILLER & T. H. JOHNSON, Editors: The Puritans: A Sourcebook of Their Writings
Vol. I TB/1093; Vol. II TB/1094

MILTON C. NAHM: Genius and Creativity: An Essay in the History of Ideas    TB/1196

ROBERT PAYNE: Hubris: A Study of Pride. Foreword by Sir Herbert Read    TB/1031

RALPH BARTON PERRY: The Thought and Character of William James: Briefer Version    TB/1156

GEORG SIMMEL et al.: Essays on Sociology, Philosophy, and Aesthetics. ¶ Edited by Kurt H. Wolff    TB/1234

BRUNO SNELL: The Discovery of the Mind: The Greek Origins of European Thought △    TB/1018

PAGET TOYNBEE: Dante Alighieri: His Life and Works. Edited with Intro. by Charles S. Singleton △    TB/1206

ERNEST LEE TUVESON: Millennium and Utopia: A Study in the Background of the Idea of Progress. ¶ New Preface by the Author    TB/1134

PAUL VALÉRY: The Outlook for Intelligence △    TB/2016

PHILIP P. WIENER: Evolution and the Founders of Pragmatism. △ *Foreword by John Dewey*  TB/1212
BASIL WILLEY: Nineteenth Century Studies: *Coleridge to Matthew Arnold* ○ △  TB/1261
BASIL WILLEY: More Nineteenth Century Studies: *A Group of Honest Doubters* ○ △  TB/1262

## Literature, Poetry, The Novel & Criticism

JAMES BAIRD: Ishmael: *The Art of Melville in the Contexts of International Primitivism*  TB/1023
JACQUES BARZUN: The House of Intellect △  TB/1051
W. J. BATE: From Classic to Romantic: *Premises of Taste in Eighteenth Century England*  TB/1036
RACHEL BESPALOFF: On the Iliad  TB/2006
R. P. BLACKMUR et al.: Lectures in Criticism. *Introduction by Huntington Cairns*  TB/2003
JAMES BOSWELL: The Life of Dr. Johnson & The Journal of a Tour to the Hebrides with Samuel Johnson LL.D.: *Selections*. ○ △ *Edited by F. V. Morley. Illus. by Ernest Shepard*  TB/1254
ABRAHAM CAHAN: The Rise of David Levinsky: *a documentary novel of social mobility in early twentieth century America. Intro. by John Higham*  TB/1028
ERNST R. CURTIUS: European Literature and the Latin Middle Ages △  TB/2015
GEORGE ELIOT: Daniel Deronda: *a novel. Introduction by F. R. Leavis*  TB/1039
ADOLF ERMAN, Ed.: The Ancient Egyptians: *A Sourcebook of Their Writings. New Material and Introduction by William Kelly Simpson*  TB/1233
ÉTIENNE GILSON: Dante and Philosophy  TB/1089
ALFRED HARBAGE: As They Liked It: *A Study of Shakespeare's Moral Artistry*  TB/1035
STANLEY R. HOPPER, Ed: Spiritual Problems in Contemporary Literature §  TB/21
A. R. HUMPHREYS: The Augustan World: *Society, Thought and Letters in 18th Century England* ○ △  TB/1105
ALDOUS HUXLEY: Antic Hay & The Giaconda Smile. ○ △ *Introduction by Martin Green*  TB/3503
ALDOUS HUXLEY: Brave New World & Brave New World Revisited. ○ △ *Introduction by Martin Green*  TB/3501
HENRY JAMES: The Tragic Muse: *a novel. Introduction by Leon Edel*  TB/1017
ARNOLD KETTLE: An Introduction to the English Novel. △ Volume I: *Defoe to George Eliot*  TB/1011
Volume II: *Henry James to the Present*  TB/1012
RICHMOND LATTIMORE: The Poetry of Greek Tragedy △  TB/1257
J. B. LEISHMAN: The Monarch of Wit: *An Analytical and Comparative Study of the Poetry of John Donne* ○ △  TB/1258
J. B. LEISHMAN: Themes and Variations in Shakespeare's Sonnets ○ △  TB/1259
ROGER SHERMAN LOOMIS: The Development of Arthurian Romance △  TB/1167
JOHN STUART MILL: On Bentham and Coleridge. △ *Introduction by F. R. Leavis*  TB/1070
KENNETH B. MURDOCK: Literature and Theology in Colonial New England  TB/99
SAMUEL PEPYS: The Diary of Samuel Pepys. ○ *Edited by O. F. Morshead. Illus. by Ernest Shepard*  TB/1007
ST.-JOHN PERSE: Seamarks  TB/2002
V. DE S. PINTO: Crisis in English Poetry, 1880-1940 ○  TB/1260
GEORGE SANTAYANA: Interpretations of Poetry and Religion §  TB/9
C. K. STEAD: The New Poetic: *Yeats to Eliot* △  TB/1263
HEINRICH STRAUMANN: American Literature in the Twentieth Century. △ *Third Edition, Revised*  TB/1168
PAGET TOYNBEE: Dante Alighieri: *His Life and Works. Edited with Intro. by Charles S. Singleton*  TB/1206
DOROTHY VAN GHENT: The English Novel: *Form and Function*  TB/1050
E. B. WHITE: One Man's Meat. *Introduction by Walter Blair*  TB/3505

BASIL WILLEY: Nineteenth Century Studies: *Coleridge to Matthew Arnold* △  TB/1261
BASIL WILLEY: More Nineteenth Century Studies: *A Group of Honest Doubters* ○ △  TB/1262
RAYMOND WILLIAMS: Culture and Society, 1780-1950 ○ △  TB/1252
RAYMOND WILLIAMS: The Long Revolution. ○ △ *Revised Edition*  TB/1253
MORTON DAUWEN ZABEL, Editor: Literary Opinion in America  Vol. I TB/3013; Vol. II TB/3014

## Myth, Symbol & Folklore

JOSEPH CAMPBELL, Editor: Pagan and Christian Mysteries *Illus.*  TB/2013
MIRCEA ELIADE: Cosmos and History: *The Myth of the Eternal Return* § △  TB/2050
MIRCEA ELIADE: Rites and Symbols of Initiation: *The Mysteries of Birth and Rebirth* § △  TB/1236
THEODOR H. GASTER: Thespis: *Ritual, Myth and Drama in the Ancient Near East* △  TB/1281
C. G. JUNG & C. KERÉNYI: Essays on a Science of Mythology: *The Myths of the Divine Child and the Divine Maiden*  TB/2014
DORA & ERWIN PANOFSKY : Pandora's Box: *The Changing Aspects of a Mythical Symbol. △ Revised edition. Illus.*  TB/2021
ERWIN PANOFSKY: Studies in Iconology: *Humanistic Themes in the Art of the Renaissance. △ 180 illustrations*  TB/1077
JEAN SEZNEC: The Survival of the Pagan Gods: *The Mythological Tradition and its Place in Renaissance Humanism and Art. △ 108 illustrations*  TB/2004
HELLMUT WILHELM: Change: *Eight Lectures on the I Ching* △  TB/2019
HEINRICH ZIMMER: Myths and Symbols in Indian Art and Civilization. △ *70 illustrations*  TB/2005

## Philosophy

G. E. M. ANSCOMBE: An Introduction to Wittgenstein's Tractatus. ○ △ *Second Edition, Revised*  TB/1210
HENRI BERGSON: Time and Free Will: *An Essay on the Immediate Data of Consciousness* ○ △  TB/1021
H. J. BLACKHAM: Six Existentialist Thinkers: *Kierkegaard, Nietzsche, Jaspers, Marcel, Heidegger, Sartre* ○ △  TB/1002
CRANE BRINTON: Nietzsche. *New Preface, Bibliography and Epilogue by the Author*  TB/1197
MARTIN BUBER: The Knowledge of Man. △ *Ed. with an Intro. by Maurice Friedman. Trans. by Maurice Friedman and Ronald Gregor Smith*  TB/135
ERNST CASSIRER: The Individual and the Cosmos in Renaissance Philosophy. △ *Translated with an Introduction by Mario Domandi*  TB/1097
ERNST CASSIRER: Rousseau, Kant and Goethe. *Introduction by Peter Gay*  TB/1092
FREDERICK COPLESTON: Medieval Philosophy ○ △  TB/376
F. M. CORNFORD: Principium Sapientiae: *A Study of the Origins of Greek Philosophical Thought. Edited by W. K. C. Guthrie*  TB/1213
F. M. CORNFORD: From Religion to Philosophy: *A Study in the Origins of Western Speculation* §  TB/20
WILFRID DESAN: The Tragic Finale: *An Essay on the Philosophy of Jean-Paul Sartre*  TB/1030
A. P. D'ENTRÈVES: Natural Law: *An Historical Survey* △  TB/1223
MARVIN FARBER: The Aims of Phenomenology: *The Motives, Methods, and Impact of Husserl's Thought*  TB/1291
HERBERT FINGARETTE: The Self in Transformation: *Psychoanalysis, Philosophy and the Life of the Spirit* ¶  TB/1177
PAUL FRIEDLÄNDER: Plato: *An Introduction* △  TB/2017
ÉTIENNE GILSON: Dante and Philosophy  TB/1089
WILLIAM CHASE GREENE: Moira: *Fate, Good, and Evil in Greek Thought*  TB/1104

6